Politics of the Visible

Politics of the Visible

Writing Women, Culture, and Fascism

Robin Pickering-Iazzi

 University of Minnesota Press
Minneapolis
London

Copyright 1997 by the Regents of the University of Minnesota

Published by the University of Minnesota Press
111 Third Avenue South, Suite 290
Minneapolis, MN 55401-2520

Printed in the United States of America on acid-free paper

Library of Congress Cataloging-in-Publication Data

Pickering-Iazzi, Robin Wynette.
    Politics of the visible : writing women, culture, and fascism /
Robin Pickering-Iazzi.
        p.   cm.
    Includes bibliographical references and index.
    ISBN 0-8166-2922-6 (hc : alk. paper). — ISBN 0-8166-2923-4 (pb : alk. paper)
    1. Italian literature—Women authors—History and criticism.
    2. Italian literature—20th century—History and criticism.
    3. Fascism and culture—Italy.   4. Fascism and women—Italy.
    5. Women—Italy—Social conditions.   6. Women in literature.
    I. Title.
    PQ4055.W6P53   1997
    850.9′9287′09041—dc21   96-6589

The University of Minnesota is an equal-opportunity educator and employer.

To Paolo and Andrè Iazzi

Contents

Acknowledgments

The ideas "delivered" here have been enhanced, sometimes occasioned, by memorable encounters of different sorts. Since I embarked on the project, Panivong Norindr and Marina Perez de Mendiola have given uncompromising readings of the individual studies in a bold fashion of enduring friendship. An earlier version of chapter 1 benefited from suggestions offered by Lynn Worsham. The critical comments generously offered by Keala Jewell helped me reshape the ideas in the chapter on poetry. I am indebted to Barbara Spackman for her insightful analysis of the arguments proposed in the essays and their implications for the project overall. Her suggestions, especially regarding "opposition" and matrilinearity, enabled me to view the materials from a new angle in the final stage of the book. I also want to extend my deep appreciation to Carole C. Gallucci, Ellen Nerenberg, and Jacqueline Reich for their observations and encouragement, as well as their contributions to this changing area of study. I give my warm thanks to Fiovo Bitti, who worked miracles in Italian archives and supplied key texts.

I have received various forms of institutional support at the University of Wisconsin-Milwaukee as the book evolved. First of all, I extend my gratitude to Marshall Goodman, Dean of Letters and Sciences, and Jessica Wirth, Associate Dean of Letters and Sciences, for the crucial support they gave to this research. The persevering assistance provided by the staff in the interlibrary loan department facilitated my research on interwar writings. In 1989, my fellowship in the stimulating space created at the Center for Twentieth Century Studies, under the direction of Kathleen Woodward, afforded the time for reading and discussion that shaped the first chapter, "Unseduced Mothers," an important point of departure for the project. A sabbatical leave in 1994 made it possible to write the chapters on the romance novel and realism. A University of Wisconsin-Milwaukee Graduate School Research Award (1993) funded the initial archival research in Italy on women's interwar poetry. The International Studies and Programs Faculty Travel Award (1995) and an award from the Consiglio Nazionale Delle Ricerche (1995) were invaluable for bringing the final chapter to completion. Members of the staff in the Department of French and Italian also made appreciated contributions. Sally Gendron conducted bibliographic research on women's writings published during Fascism. Darlene Hagopian applied her technical computer knowledge to make production of the manuscript possible. Renée Kuban invested long hours printing different versions of the chapters. John Bowden painstakingly prepared the electronic version of the manuscript for submission.

I am also grateful for the pleasurable working relation the University of Minnesota Press has cultivated throughout the phases of this project. Biodun Iginla and Elizabeth Knoll Stomberg generously gave their time to discuss the manuscript and initiate the review process. The book has benefited in several ways from the editorial expertise and talents that Lisa Freeman demonstrated as she saw the manuscript through the revision stage. I have especially appreciated her free exchange of ideas coupled with vigorous support and assistance. Robin Moir gave key assistance as the book went into production. I owe many thanks to Louisa Castner, whose queries and suggestions showed the exceptional thoughtfulness and skills she brought to the book as copy editor.

My life and work have been graced by my family and friends. I want to thank my parents, Wayne L. Pickering and Norma C. Pickering, for their loving patience and inspiration. Andrè Iazzi's wry sense of humor and intrepid spirit have prompted lively detours along the way. I owe special thanks to Paolo Iazzi for his passion for debate, day-to-day sustenance, and willingness to become an itinerant traveler.

Some sections of this book were previously published in somewhat different form. Chapter 1 originally appeared in the collection *Feminine Feminists: Cultural Practices in Italy*, edited by Giovanna Miceli Jeffries

(Minneapolis and London: University of Minnesota Press, 1994), and chapter 2 was published in *Italica* 71.2 (summer 1994) as "The Politics of Gender and Genre in Italian Women's Autobiography of the Interwar Years." Grateful acknowledgment is also extended to the following publisher for permission to include English translations of poetry selections, reprinted from Antonia Pozzi, "The Closing Door," *The Defiant Muse: Italian Feminist Poems from the Middle Ages to the Present,* edited by Beverly Allen, Muriel Kittel, and Keala Jane Jewell (New York: Feminist Press, 1986), 57. Copyright 1986 by Beverly Allen, Muriel Kittel, and Keala Jane Jewell. All rights reserved.

Introduction

Visualizing F/fascism Today: Signs and Meanings

JUDD ROSE [voice-over]: . . . Mussolini was the Saddam Hussein of his time, a tyrant who used poison gas to kill hundreds of thousands of Ethiopians and sent thousands of Italian Jews to their deaths at Auschwitz. But Alessandra dismisses all that.

MS. MUSSOLINI: He did a lot for Italy. Maybe you don't know that because you're American. He did a lot for Italy. And so I think I've had enough of this.

ROSE: How can you ignore those things? They're—

MS. MUSSOLINI: I don't know! It's just . . . it's just the past, just history.

ROSE: You just wipe it away?

MS. MUSSOLINI: No, not wipe it away! It's a part of history. It's a part of . . .

PrimeTime Live (1992)[1]

As both a product and production of the intensifying fascination with what the North American mass media have termed the *fashionable face* of fascism in Italy these days, a wave of exposés has appeared on television and in publications ranging from the *New York Times* to *Elle*. In the course of this "coverage" Alessandra Mussolini—currently a member of the Italian Parliament for the National Alliance Party—has become the symbol of neofascism; she *is* the fashionable face. In contrast, fellow party member Gianfranco Fini represents the brains.[2] Yet in order to explain what Alessandra Mussolini ostensibly stands for, reporters trace her genealogy to her grandfather Benito Mussolini. Telescoping the period of Fascist rule, which spanned some two decades (1922–1943), the

1

media tend to focus on relatively few moments: the years just after the movement's founding in 1919, when blackshirt squads put violence on public display; and the latter stage of the dictatorship that saw Mussolini launch Fascist Italy in the theater of world politics as an aggressor in colonial expansion and, finally, an ally of Nazi Germany in World War II.[3] This strategy serves to make Fascism easily readable among contemporary audiences, while safely situating both the historical regime and neofascism as the Other in the social imaginary. In a certain sense, the ties of filiation and affiliation that the media present to trace the lineage of fascism create an ironic twist, as the "tyrannical," "brutish," and hyper-virile traits that brought infamy on Mussolini and Fascism are now invoked through the ultrafeminine and, by many standards, glamorous face of Alessandra Mussolini. On the other hand, this logic rings familiar for the way in which it underwrites man as producer of meaning and woman as symbol and thus reproduces a system worthy of Mussolini and Fascist ideologues.

For those of us in the United States who might view Alessandra Mussolini and the National Alliance Party—indeed, Italian politics in general—with the momentary curiosity of detached spectators distanced by oceanic spaces, history, culture, and so on, Umberto Eco offers a cautionary message in his essay "Ur-Fascism" (1995).[4] Eco's discussion is especially important because he reassesses contending properties exhibited by the Fascist regime in light of current political trends, questions, claims, and promises debated in Italian homes and voting booths today. These concern revisionist positions on the "measurable" achievements and value of the Resistance movement; the perceived national "need" for reconciliation between the ranks of Fascists and anti-Fascists who fought in the War of Liberation; and calls to bury the past. Although Eco assures readers that it is virtually impossible for Italian Fascism, German Nazism, and other totalitarian regimes active in the 1930s and 1940s to reappear now, cloaked in the same shapes and signs, his formulation of "Ur-Fascism" (or "Eternal Fascism") gives us pause for thought. Attempting first to bring into clearer focus the fuzzy picture of Fascism, which derives, Eco says, from the contradictions of its weakly formulated philosophy, he then proposes fourteen features associated with Ur-Fascism. In fluid configurations, Ur-Fascism commonly presents, for instance, the cult of tradition, the obsession with taking action for action's sake alone, racism, nationalism, and the transference of the will to power onto the field of sexual relations, manifested in "machismo." The linguistic practices that Eco identifies with Ur-Fascists merit special attention, for they conform to a brand of Orwellian Newspeak, characterized by "impoverished vocabulary" and "elementary syntax," a malleable form of language that may even appear on television talk shows. If, on the one hand, the features that Eco identifies with the Ur-Fascist category are too broad to account for necessary distinctions, on the other hand, he shows that Fascism needs to be taken seriously and therefore encourages a salutary critical awareness. As he argues, "Ur-Fascism is still around us, sometimes in plainclothes. . . . Ur-Fascism can come back under the most innocent of disguises" (15).

It is apropos here to return briefly to the interview from which the epigraph is drawn and look at the visual logic organizing the television representation of Alessandra Mussolini. For the most part calm and collected, the commentary provided by Judd Rose, the interviewer, gives a unified, totalizing narrative form to the variety of materials incorporated in the exposé, featuring slices of documentary footage of Benito Mussolini, coverage of Alessandra at campaign rallies along with clips from her B-rated movies and scenes from the interview. At a certain point, however, words seem to fail both Rose and Mussolini in their attempts to define "those things" that took place during Fascism and what they are "a part of." Clearly frustrated and angry, the politician calls Rose a "fascist" and then storms away, the camera's eye only able to follow her offstage. This Italian woman ("ill-tempered," in Rose's words) breaks the etiquette of the interview. More significant, she creates a rupture in the dominant vision structuring the hegemonic relations between North American and Italian politics, which the voice-overs and concluding remarks cannot fully repair, though Sam Donaldson, coanchor on the program, reminds viewers that in Italy "governments come and go," not unlike fashion trends, one might add. Certainly, we should not minimize the serious implications of Alessandra Mussolini's own deployment of her name and the variety of meanings it evokes, or the manner in which she and members of the National Alliance Party jockey the issue of their relation to the ideology and practices of the Fascist dictatorship. Yet the way in which she exposes elements of her public identity and also withdraws her bodily presence, refusing to legitimate the meanings that Rose claims she bears as a symbol of fascism, offers a provocative enactment of the politics of the visible, a notion that operates in several ways in this book.

Politics of the Visible puts into question current mass-mediated images of Italian Fascism of the 1920s and 1930s served up for American consumption as well as formative notions entrenched in scholarly studies in history and literature, by reviewing the discourses that women produced in so-called high and mass culture and how these literary texts figured in the broader spheres of life and society during the dictatorship. I propose new ways of looking at writings by women authors who, although now virtually absent from literary histories and anthologies (the works that in panoramic fashion direct the reader's attention toward selected sights and structure her or his perception), achieved a high profile in the public eye by virtue of the fiction, prose, and poetry they wrote throughout the interwar years. During this period unprecedented numbers of women successfully pursued the vocation of writer as such new talents as Alba De Céspedes, author of the internationally best-selling novel *Nessuno torna indietro* (1938; *There's No Turning Back,* 1941), the avant-garde poet and theorist Maria Goretti, the acclaimed novelist and short story writer Gianna Manzini, and romance author Liala, who launched her career with the blockbuster *Signorsì!* (Yes, sir!) in 1931, joined well-established literary figures.[5] Among the authors who had already achieved notoriety with general audiences and critics alike were, for instance, Sibilla Aleramo, Grazia Deledda (recipient of the Nobel Prize for literature in 1926), Paola Drigo, and Ada Negri. Of particular importance is the variety of sites that these artists, among many others, fashioned to address diversified reading communities. In addition to publishing novels, autobiographies, and poetry collections, critically recognized and popular writers contributed short fiction and poems to literary journals, magazines, and the flourishing women's press, as well as to the highly esteemed cultural page of nationally distributed newspapers.

While capturing the attention of the emergent mass readership, the thematic and aesthetic innovations designed by women writing in diverse genres and modes earned the attention of eminent intellectuals of their time. The critical assessments written by Benedetto Croce, Giuseppe Antonio Borgese, and Giuseppe Ravegnani, among others, cast doubt on the notion that female authors were resigned or passive objects of repression and ideological seduction during Fascism, who either withdrew from the public arena of literary production or, if they continued to write, merely reproduced the traditional models of femininity promoted by some Fascist circles. On the contrary, hardly retiring, women authors loomed on the literary field as a formidable presence, challenging male authority, as the critic G. Titta Rosa colorfully suggests. In his article "Scrittori e sirene" (Writers and sirens), written on the occasion of the 1931 Viareggio Literary Prize ceremony, Titta Rosa surveys the battlefield as contending men and women vie for victory:

> And yet again, women are the ones who have shown the greatest enthusiasm for battle, and an Amazonian strength worthy of celebration; I'm speaking about the women candidates, our beloved and proud women writers who are now following hot on the men's heels in the literary race, not even a neck or a hair's distance behind them. Strengthened by smaller competitions, their hair streaming back in the wind . . . and their eyes ablaze with the love of glory, they goad their fellow male writers on, not even letting them catch their breath. (8)

Tinged with irony, Titta Rosa's representation gives an ambivalent cast to this field of contenders yet inscribes changing power relations in the republic of letters.

Moreover, the reviews, essays, and books dedicated to the fiction and poetry written by women suggest that their works constituted part of the interwar canon and made significant contributions to genre formation. If such texts as the autobiography *Stella mattutina* (Morning star, 1921) by Negri, the neorealist novel *Maria Zef* (1936) by Drigo, and the poetry by such futurists as Goretti and Mina della Pergola have paled from view in canonical histories, this does not mean that the literary value or significance of the works has waned. Rather, the process of postwar editings of the canon has failed to maintain the material, critical apparatuses initially generated by women's writing, which, as Michel Foucault (1972a, 123) tells us, are necessary to preserve discourses "in the field of memory." Foucault's theorization of discursive *rémanence* invites speculation that women's literary production was repressed not by Fascist cultural management, but by the gaps in visual memory created by the literary establishment after the "liberation."[6]

The Politics of Reading: Critical Positionings, Terms, and Questions

The overarching aim of this examination is thus to retrain critical focus on writing women and the speaking positions that they crafted in the hegemonic field of cultural and political discourses operating during Fascism, subjects of inquiry set forth in the title of this book. At the same time, the terms and issues posed by the title *Politics of the Visible: Writing Women, Culture, and Fascism* are meant to convey the dynamics of the critical positions and approaches that I adopt. Specifically, amid the variety of possible texts and interpretations, my choice of women's literary works, archival materials, and theoretical models brought into the study's purview represents a particularized process of "writing women," as well as Fascism and culture. Indeed, as the first book-length study dedicated to the literature authored by women during the Fascist regime, this work is conceived as an exploratory investigation. It does not attempt to fill in the lacuna in women's literature of the interwar years, or to provide a comprehensive literary history. Nor do I claim to document a more accurate or authentic appraisal of the writings discussed and the meanings attached to them in the 1920s and 1930s. With the exception of the studies on the short story genre and poetry, the readings focus on a few selected works, chosen for what I see as their significance in the respective genres and in cultural formations of the time. I am also interested in the ways they lend themselves to speculating about broader critical issues concerning Fascism, sexual difference, mass culture, and the politics of aesthetics, a point I will take up shortly. Although admittedly partial, the revisionary interpretations that I advance insist on foregrounding history and therefore build on recent historiographic works on women and Italian Fascism. This approach, which I problematize in the opening chapter, is designed to examine the performative value of women's literary discourses within the specific sociocultural conditions that bear on the writing and reading of texts as historically contingent practices of signification. The individual studies chart the shifting positionalities inscribed as female authors negotiate dominant codes and signs produced by the regime's writers, as well as intellectuals and artists working within and beyond the orbit of official Fascist culture, thereby enabling us to theorize the politics of women's forms of textuality.

Given the sometimes difficult translation of critical discourses across disciplinary borders, the coupling of politics and literature, though useful to many readers, to others may present a problematic blurring of two discrete spheres. Therefore, at this juncture it is necessary to explain how and why I employ the political as an interpretative category for reading women's literary culture of the Fascist period. Although analyses of Italian Fascism that work within established parameters defining the formal political sphere—encompassing policies, institutions, and associations—have enhanced our understanding of authoritarian states, such works as *How Fascism Ruled Women* by Victoria De Grazia (1992), *Rethinking Italian Fascism,* edited by David Forgacs (1986), and *Fascism in Popular Memory* by Luisa Passerini (1987) have also identified the limits of such an approach. These scholars, among others, recast this field of study by insisting on the importance of the micropolitical as the terrain where the multiple determinants of gender, class, generation, and location bear on social subjects as they negotiate relations of power and authority in daily life. Likewise, critical theories of culture proposed by, for example, Raymond Williams, Edward Said, and Gayatri Spivak, which expand on many of Antonio Gramsci's insights, amply illustrate the central function of culture in politics, as it fabricates myriad sites where power arrangements are staged, generated, played out, and refashioned. Edward Said's (1983) discussion of the way in which Gramsci formulates "elaboration" as a productive cultural practice shows it would be erroneous to bifurcate the domains of politics and culture:

> To elaborate [advances] the proposition that culture itself or thought or art is a highly complex and quasi-autonomous extension of political reality and, given the extraordinary importance attached by Gramsci to intellectuals, culture, and philosophy, it has a density, complexity, and historical-semantic value that is so strong as to make politics possible. Elaboration is the ensemble of patterns making it feasible for society to maintain itself. (170–71)

Thus, by examining a fuller range of thought and creative invention articulated in activities of elaboration, we gain a sharper understanding of the different constituencies forming Italian society during the interwar years and the configurations of politics as they emerge.

The positions and ventures that the Fascist state devised for high and mass culture also suggest that we cannot easily separate the political and cultural dimensions of life. Envisioning the creation of Fascist national culture as a means for cultivating Fascist social subjects, the regime generated sustained discussions about the political functions and meanings of art. This linkage is clearly articulated in such writings as "Artists and the Corporate State," "Art and the Regime," and "Outlines of a Politics of Art" by Giuseppe Bottai, a journalist and powerful figure in the elaboration of Fascist cultural programs.[7] The regime's colonization and development of sites for the production of culture, ranging from the foundation of the prestigious Academy of Italy to mass leisure-time organizations, should hardly surprise us. However, the state sponsorship of a plurality of competing aesthetic projects proposed by some of Italy's most talented artists and intellectuals as models for a new, Fascist art to revolutionize society makes the artistic field of verbal and visual discourses much more equivocal than might be assumed. Of special interest here is the way that the image of Mussolini circulates, invoked in writings as well as on posters and exhibition materials, to authorize, and perhaps reconcile, conflicting movements—from futurism and *novecentismo* to neorealism—as expressions of Fascist culture.[8] The issues and questions arising from the contradictions posed within cultural theories and practices elaborated under the auspices of Fascism have begun to receive warranted attention, as illustrated by the issue of the *Stanford Italian Review* (1990) titled "Fascism and Culture"; *Fascist Modernism* by Andrew Hewitt (1993); *Bodily Regimes* by Karen Pinkus (1995); and *Fascist Virilities* by Barbara Spackman (1996). In general, however, the ways in which women's literary representations and practices might refute, alter, or support the terms of current debates about the politics of culture during Fascism remain to be seen.[9]

As the essays in *Politics of the Visible* suggest, the tendency to overlook the political significance of women's literary texts in the years of the regime confirms what Fredric Jameson (1981) sees as suspect criteria of classification, which uncritically perpetuate the notion of politics and culture as separate spheres. He cautions us, stating that "the *convenient* working distinction between cultural texts that are social and political and those that are not becomes something worse than an error: namely, a symptom and a reinforcement of the reification and privatization of contemporary life" (20, emphasis added). Within the specific context of postwar editings of the interwar literary canon, the differentiation between political and nonpolitical works arguably affects writings by both men and women, but with a difference. For example, critics have consistently represented hermeticism as the key movement informing lyrical production of the thirties and, not inconsequentially, attached anti-Fascist meanings to its intimist, crepuscular poetics. Yet this does not dictate the exclusion from anthologies of male poets, perhaps minor, working in other modes. In contrast, the names of such award-winning women poets as Ada Negri and Sibilla Aleramo rarely appear in contemporary histories profiling poetry written between the wars, or in studies on the politics of poetics during Fascism. Scholars thus miss the opportunity to examine the diversity of poetic discourse, and literature in general, as they contribute to the heterogeneity of artistic forms, which, in Gramsci's view, constitutes the very strength of culture.

Although literary criticism, as well as historical scholarship on women during Fascism, tends to evacuate the political significance of women's fiction and poetry, the Fascist regime conceived of female culture as a concern of national magnitude. The theories of woman, organizations for girls and women of different classes, and representations of feminine models in social commentaries clearly attest to the political meanings ascribed to a vast array of female cultural practices, which encompassed everything from the literary enterprises of internationally recognized authors to such leisure activities as reading romance fiction and going to the cinema, as well as fashion trends. Less clear, however, is the trajectory of the regime's sexual politics. This indeterminacy derives largely from the internal diversification of Fascism's ideological designs and their articulation in power relations that shape the changing configurations of the cultural hegemony from the 1920s to the 1940s. The variety of representations of woman—her "essence," familial roles, social duties, and position in the Fascist nation—incorporates both acknowledgments of and solicitations to behaviors we would likely consider emancipated, along with summons to assume the demeanors and responsibilities invoked by the traditional figure of the woman-mother. Such initiatives as the demographic campaign (a series of policies developed to increase the birthrate), ceilings on the numbers of women employed in state positions, and higher tuition rates for female university students exemplify the unmistakably repressive interventions legislated by the state to address socioeconomic problems and reinstitute male authority in the Italian family and society, topics discussed in chapter 1. As De Grazia (1992, 2) reminds us, however,

> Fascism stood just as visibly for the camaraderie of volunteer organizations and for recognizing rights and duties for women in a strong national state. Not the least of all, the dictatorship was identified with the physical freedom and more emancipated behaviors associated with the spaces and occasions of modern leisure pastimes.[10]

Putting such diverse female images as the glamorous actress, the prolific countrywoman, the protean athlete, the factory worker, and the literary woman on exhibition, the verbal and visual registers furnished by Fascist thinkers both contest and constitute new female subject positions.

The mobile, conflictual features manifested in associations that the authoritarian state attempts to make between women and the culture of art and everyday life raise a series of problems for theorizing the locations and performative functions of women's literary production during the regime. First of all, the agonistic, competing interpellations of women subtending the grandiose, totalizing optics of Fascist national culture resist global schematization. Therefore, what kind of approaches can be formulated to create a framework for resituating women's ideas and representational practices in the discursive field? Similarly, in the process of constructing a critical context, which strategies might attenuate the unavoidable risk of stabilizing dynamic, mutable signs and the diverse meanings that they make possible? Moreover, if the discourse of Fascism, and the sexual politics it authorizes, works as Barbara Spackman (1995, 103) maintains, by binding "together ideologically incompatible elements, both progressive and the reactionary," then how do we ascertain which terms, if any, achieve dominance and thereby provide a key for charting Fascist positions on the cultural terrain?[11] Similarly, which signs might function as a measure of comparison for assessing the relations between Fascist ideology and the speaking positions and sub-jectivities generated in women's texts? As a means of exploring these interrelated issues, each of the studies gathered here elaborates differ-ent forms of microdiscursive analysis. Intended to be read against each other, the discussions focus on the strains of discourse—the threads and tensions—produced by Fascist thinkers and writing women as they en-gage with selected nodal figures and constructs that bear on the forma-tion of social identities. Among other models, these include the woman-mother, the lesbian subject, the intellectual woman, the femme fatale, and the urban working-class woman, as well as diversified conceptions of technology, consumerism, collectivity, the country and the city, and the nation. The essays thus attempt to consider the encodings of plural terms of identity construction where sex and gender intersect with class, generational differences, and geographic location. Each of these compo-nents suggests a range of dispositions toward language, social conven-tions and beliefs, and forms of affiliation or difference.

The contradictory currents of Fascist ideology, simultaneously claim-ing social revolution for the future and the conservative, patriarchal order of the past, obviously complicate interpretation of the regime's cultural politics. I find Homi K. Bhabha's formulation of "temporal ne-gotiation" particularly helpful for approaching this problem, which is not exclusive to Fascism. In general, as Bhabha (1994) explains, "Political positions are not simply identifiable as progressive or reactionary, bour-geois or radical, prior to the act of critique engagé, or outside the terms and conditions of their discursive address" (22). Adapting this insight, I resituate the ideas, images, and symbols of women's invention in relation to writings by Fascist ideologues and artists, and by critics representing the literary establishment, along with materials appearing in the mass media, and everyday practices of living. For example, my reading of the romance novel *Signorsì* locates Liala's encoding of aviation as an unlim-ited horizon for the articulation of female desire in such diverse contexts as futurist aeropoetics, medical writings, the press, and Fascist state-ments, which dedicated notable space to record-breaking Italian women pilots and female "flying fever." By re-collecting (not recapturing) vari-ous imbricating frames of reference, the study highlights ways that women's notions of self-fashioning engage with prevalent social codes and, in the process, engender potentially new meanings among communities of readers.

The sites, social models, symbols, and concepts of exchange form the ground for assessing how women's discourses relate to dominant structures of thought and representation during Fascism—the focal concern of this project. However, the analytical positions and use of evaluative terms vary from one essay to the next because of changes in both my critical perception and interests, and in the field at large. Therefore, although each study more or less considers the points where women's discourses may intersect, reinvent, or contend with those authored by Fascist writers, the analyses, which appear in the order they were written, increasingly inflect the terms of these relations toward the process of negotiation rather than negation. This point needs explanation because it shows how, overall, the review of women's literary production and reception forces questions about the conceptualization of power arrangements generated by the Fascist regime and about such terms as *repression, opposition,* and *subversion.*

The differences between the first and last chapters best illustrate this shift in emphasis. Written some seven years ago, the opening chapter was designed to construct a critical paradigm for theorizing women as speaking subjects in literature and society during the authoritarian Fascist regime. It developed in response to what I, as a literary critic in Italian studies, saw as a tendency to uncritically accept the notion that the years of the dictatorship represented a gap in the history of women's literature. This position derived from a persistent reliance on historiographic studies of the 1970s, which focused on "consent," figuring women as the objects of ideological seduction. Drawing on more recent archival and theoretical works in history, sociology, and anthropology, my examination then maps the trajectories of women's "oppositional" practices (in the Foucauldian sense) and the ways in which their cultural productions contend with the ideology of the woman-mother constructed in Fascist discourses. However, by focusing primarily on the ways that models of female subjectivity transgress the figure of the woman-mother, the essay overly reduces the heterogeneity of Fascist ideology and conceives the positionalities adopted by women writers only in terms of negativity, or opposition, a point I will expand momentarily. Although readers will find new materials highlighting the microspacial politics of the cultural page framing the short fiction discussed, I have chosen not to adapt the essay to my current perspective for two reasons. First, the arguments illustrated critical possibilities as well as problems therein and may be germane for current debates. Second, it is not my intention to offer a unified/unifying train of thought on the relations between Fascism and writing women, a critical stance that would be implicated in the totalitarian. Rather, I see working through one set of problems to raise new ones as integral to this project, a process that especially shapes the final chapter, on women's production of poetry. While exploring the differentiated positionalities crafted by female poets working in the avant-garde futurist movement and outside it, the readings spotlight the moments of exchange, the "transit" and transformation of meanings where the productivity of relations between women artists and male-dominated, even misogynist, movements may be visible. This approach attempts to address both the inhibiting and productive components of the cultural hegemony during Fascism.

Such a proposition does not mean abandoning the critique of dominative power and its distribution in the social and symbolic spheres. In theoretical and cultural writings important figures in the Fascist hierarchy attempted to remap the nation's cultural geography, redrawing the borders between the male and female sites of production. Although the state never defined strict parameters for women's culture, or men's, it brought degrees of pressure on certain individual writers. The testimony provided by Alba De Céspedes, an anti-Fascist who later joined the Resistance movement, conveys the material repression levied by the dictatorship:

> I had a lot of trouble during the Fascist period. Everything of mine was prohibited. The same thing that happened to other writers, too, for that matter, to [Alberto] Moravia, for example. . . . I was constantly summoned to the Ministry of Popular Culture. The last time Minister Mezzasoma, who was, however, a good person, called me and said, "It's as if you're dead. You can't write for any newspapers." (I was a regular contributor to the *Messaggero* then.)[12]

Thus, we clearly must keep in consideration forms of oppression instituted in the Fascist dictatorship. However, we cannot forget the key Gramscian insight that power, even as it applies limits, is also productive.

Indeed, the growing ranks of women authors during the twenties and thirties and the broad diffusion of their works in fiction and poetry, in general widely read and reviewed, beg questions concerning how inter-war modernization and Fascism may have enabled precisely the modern, transgressive practices of literature and life that the dictatorship ostensibly also sought to contain. Giuseppe Petronio and Luciana Martinelli (1975) identify several sociocultural changes during Fascism that unquestionably expanded the publishing market and the possibilities it offered women. Among these, they explain, are

> the development . . . of a technological civilization, the broad increase in literacy, the initial formation of a publishing industry, the birth of mass society, the emancipation of women along American models, the formation of a wide range of professions entrusted to women and requiring a certain level of culture. (359)

Likewise, if previously the fame and success achieved by such familiar literary figures as Grazia Deledda, Ada Negri, and Sibilla Aleramo fostered the dream of becoming a woman writer, during the interwar period the expansion of the women's press and the short story market in daily newspapers made literary and journalistic writing feasible occupations for women. Furthermore, though it raises the issue of complicity, the network fostered by the regime for women's organizations (the National Fascist Association of Women Artists and Degree Holders, 1929), for instance, clubs, leisure activities, exhibitions, and awards, politicized and publicized female cultural enterprises.

Yet it is perhaps the productivity of Fascist discourse—sustaining contradictory images, unstable categories, and modern as well as traditional interpellations of female social subjects—that raises the most complex, troubling dilemmas concerning the politics of women's literary culture. The novels *Maria Zef* by Paola Drigo (1936) and *Nessuno torna indietro* (1938), translated as *There's No Turning Back*, by De Céspedes exemplify this problem. As I argue, Drigo quite openly critiques poverty, incest, and disease in a young girl's fight for survival in a mountain area of the north, whereas De Céspedes problematizes the sexual politics of space in Rome as they bear on the multiple terms negotiated in women's fashionings of social identity. The visages they create of women in the countryside and city collide with and contradict the myths of the country, Rome, and the Fascist nation promoted in the ruralization and demographic campaigns. Yet these novels were published. Numerous reviews appeared in newspapers and journals. Drigo's book was even represented in a 1939 anthology featuring the works of great contemporary Italian authors, intended for foreign readers. And, although the regime blacklisted *There's No Turning Back*, the novel soon became a best-seller. Thus, we must reasonably ask how "subversive" these works, among others examined, might be. Does the status of women's literary works necessitate the rethinking of "opposition" and "counterdiscourse" as formulated in relation to Fascism?

The critical approaches to deep saturating hegemonic systems developed by Raymond Williams (1977) and Edward W. Said (1983, 1994) offer fruitful directions for pursuing this direction of inquiry and contribute to the structure of thought underlying much of this study. If, as both critics argue, the struggle between dominant and marginal practices operates in an ongoing fashion, manifesting dynamic relations where power is exerted, resisted, transformed, and challenged, then images of the rebel woman in *Cosima* by Deledda, the eroticized mother poet crafted by Aleramo, or the lesbian subject narrativized by De Céspedes may represent emergent oppositional terms of identity. Furthermore, as Said (1983) contends, "In human history there is always something beyond the reach of dominating systems, no matter how deeply they saturate society, and this is obviously what makes change possible" (246–47). And we must not forget that dominative authority may selectively intervene, repress, appropriate, or ignore elements alien to itself. At the same time, it is essential, I think, to problematize the interrelations between the images and ideology invented in Fascist texts and those in women's writings, an issue beyond the primary scope of my study that warrants further attention. Indeed, engagements with prevailing intellectual and representational models, even if declaredly oppositional, also imply some meaningful exchange. Moreover, as Bhabha (1994) cautions, the critical notion of a purely "oppositional" stance fails to acknowledge "the historical connectedness between the subject and object of critique" (26) and, as it reduces the heterogeneous terms of political and social identities, slips into the paradigm of a naturalized "unitary object."

In order to locate the points of tension and agonism within the discursive field during Fascism, the readings examine responses elicited among critics and Fascist commentators by women's representations of the social and symbolic female body. This approach conceives of writing—its metaphors, symbols, and rhetoric—as an aesthetic system, and a modality of power as well. The discursive analysis insists on the connectedness between the symbolic and material conditions in literature as a signifying system where authors invent meanings that can mediate perceptions of the relations between self and society.[13] Indeed, the samples of cultural criticism suggest that it would be unwise to minimize the potential functions performed among reading publics by forms of social critique and female subjectivization created in women's writings. The regime's ideologues appear preoccupied by the visages that modern women expose to public view and by the locations that they appropriate for the staging of female self-fashioning. Read as signs foreboding dire political and moral consequences, women's cultural practices register the disarray of desired gender arrangements in the regime; they transgress the conservative model of the woman-mother, angelic caretaker of family and home, and the modern model of the Fascist woman, called into public review as a symbol of the female collective in national life. Within the visual regime surveyed, women's encodings of feminine subjectivities call into doubt the authority of the rural and urban faces of Fascism, and the epic myths distinguishing their features.

The drifts I chart in literary criticism appraising the themes, practices, and aesthetics elaborated in women's fiction and poetry exhibit a similar concern over what the authors make visible and how they challenge the dominant construction of femininity as a literary and social ideal. The critic Giuseppe Ravegnani represents this general tendency as he charges women authors with deploying traditionally "masculine" markers in their representations of female concerns, behaviors, and desires. More specifically, such figures as Camillo Pellizzi and Benedetto Croce decry the excessive self-exhibitionism in literary works by Aleramo, Negri, and Amalia Guglielminetti, who, they claim, represent this typically "female" vice. While betraying certain assumptions and biases shaping the sexual politics of literary assessment, these documents are invaluable for the way that they inscribe the points of contiguity and divergence between the aesthetics elaborated in different genres by female authors and by their male counterparts. Furthermore, they tell us much about the gendered symbolic meanings invested in specific genres, an issue of major concern in this study.

This book also works through genre as an essential interpretative frame, examining women's writings in the short story, autobiography, the romance novel, poetry, and the realist novel. As some feminist scholars have argued, genre theory and the paradigms it has fostered tend to perpetuate men's texts as the normative model, casting women's writings on the margins, if not entirely ghettoizing them in a separate sphere.[14] Thus, the method I elaborate, anchored by critical appraisals of the interwar years that constituted women's literary texts as part of the canon, scrutinizes the construction of now-prevailing representations of genre formation. Each chapter offers a brief overview of current notions defining the genre in question and the model texts from which they are extrapolated. The subsequent analysis of sample writings by acclaimed and popular women authors endeavors to speculate about their contributions to genre formation by exploring how certain features might intersect or differ from conventions considered dominant today. I am also interested in the ways that the authors may play on more or less established generic forms and expectations to derive new meanings of their own making. Genre functions, as Rita Felski (1989) proposes, "as the organizational framework which mediates between the text and context; the text becomes meaningful only insofar as it is read in relation to existing expectations governing the reception of forms of textual communication" and "provides the cultural matrix against which the significance of the individual text can be measured" (82–83). The meanings that members of the literary elite associated with such genres as autobiography, poetry, and the novel bear out this formulation and furnish a measurement of the disruptive power wielded by female authors in the cultural hegemony. Literary debates about poetry exemplify this point, as the articulation of the Crocean aesthetic of pure poetry worked to erase the sexual politics maintaining the authority of the universal (read male) poetic subject. Although ready to concede the novel as a female-gendered space presumably tailored to women's intellectual and artistic aptitudes, male critics and artists show a pronounced effort to stave off women's incursions into poetry, territorialized as a preserve for the expression of male subjectivity. While constructing a different vantage point for viewing the field of interwar literary discourses, an embattled arena dramatizing the struggle over signs and expressive possibilities for the production of meaning, *Politics of the Visible* implicitly calls for further study of the antagonisms and cross-textual relations between forms of textuality crafted by women and men.

In addition to investigating issues associated with the genres discussed, each study works through a theoretical problem. As explained above, the opening chapter proposes a paradigm for examining women as the subjects of discourse in literature and daily living during Fascism. It focuses on the systems of address and representation in the short stories contributed by women authors to the coveted cultural page of Italian newspapers. These texts are particularly well suited to speculating about how the representations of alternative female aspirations, interests, socioeconomic problems, and desires might have engaged women among the reading public, since this form of fiction reached a much larger audience than books, still costly for the lower classes. Expanding on the model of women as the subjects of discourse, chapter 2 poses questions regarding autobiography and sexual difference within both the specific context of interwar Italian models and in current theories of the genre. I pursue these concerns with readings of *Stella mattutina* (1921) by Ada Negri, a rich example of female working-class autobiography that went through three Italian editions from 1927 to 1932 and appeared in English translation in 1930, and *Cosima* (1937) by Grazia Deledda, which tells the story of this Nobel Prize laureate's childhood and formative development as a self-styled woman author in the southern, rural community of Nuoro, in Sardinia. These life writings enable us to see the multiple components of subjectivity, such as gender, class, and geographic location, creating terms of difference in the process of reinventing female literary identities during the class warfare of the Red Years and the latter stage of the dictatorship, respectively.

While engaging in broader, transnational debates about F/fascism, modernism, the avant-garde futurists, realism, and mass culture, chapters 3 through 5 also exemplify reasons for adopting the kind of microdiscursive analysis I conduct, which situates specific texts against the threads of Fascist ideology and cultural politics knotting together conservative and progressive trends. The study on the romance novel raises two related problems: the general linkage made between Fascism and mass culture as apparatuses that constitute passive consumers, a proposition articulated by Theodor Adorno, among other theorists; and the tendency in Italian studies to read the heroines, heros, and plots devised in the interwar years as evidence of the fascistization of female fantasy. I test these positions by situating Liala's novel *Signorsì* in the field of discourses on technology, sexology, beauty canons, and consumer culture, and by interrogating the profound contradictions cast by the sociocultural changes of modernity accompanying Fascism, which the heroine and reader must negotiate.

The chapters on the realist novel and poetry are companion pieces in the sense that they explore two ports of entry into the intriguing problems concerning the performative political and symbolic value of realist, modernist, and avant-garde aesthetics, and the ways in which they might respectively subvert, affirm, or lend themselves to appropriation by authoritarian ideological structures. While considering the entrenched assertion that Fascism is antithetical to realism, as elaborated by Georg Lukács (1934) and echoed by Susan Sontag (1974), the first part of the essay on realism examines the paradigms for neorealist projects elaborated in theory and literature by leftist Fascists as well as anti-Fascist male authors. Within this highly equivocal aesthetic system, I attempt to theorize the locations of "oppositional" feminist discourses of realism, a mode generally assumed to reinscribe the patriarchal structures that it seeks to displace. With readings of two widely acclaimed novels published in the late thirties, *Maria Zef* by Drigo and *There's No Turning Back* by De Céspedes, the analyses focus on the sexual politics of the "migrational" country and city, and how the emergent terms of female identities and affiliation posited relate to Fascist visions of Rome, country life, and the nation.

The final chapter engages with the controversy of the politics of aesthetics by exploring the variety of speaking positions that female poets constructed as they wrought avant-garde and more or less mimetic modes of signification. Although this study, like the preceding ones, endeavors to chart the shifting coordinates of women's locations in the complex discursive hegemony, comprised in this case by futurism, "pure poetry," and hermeticism, the scope and the order of problems differ. First, I chart the subject positions forged by such artists as Benedetta, Fulvia Giuliani, and Maria Goretti in the futurist movement, posing questions about the productive aspects of women's engagements with the male avant-garde. I then inflect the critical emphasis toward the differences between women poets, with readings of works by Goretti, Negri, Aleramo, and Antonia Pozzi. Focusing on the poets' notions of the figure of the *generatrice*—the mother poet—as a referential sign of comparison, my analysis looks at the differentiated ideas, symbols, and experimental and readerly practices they fabricate to put the female-sexed body into poetry as a site for multiple forms of generation, encompassing the creation of self, life, and art.

The critical positions and textual readings posited here establish different critical visualizations in order to investigate the diverse registers of women's writings as formative sites for the production of art and meaning during Fascism and, therefore, will perhaps promote the archival research and analysis that this field clearly merits. Likewise, by reading women's works of fiction and poetry in dialogic relation to the prevailing currents of thought in the arts, life, and society, this study endeavors to suggest new directions for canon revision and for thinking about fields of inquiry distinguishing the topography of Italian studies. Written from the perspective of an Italianist, however, this study is also intended to cast a different light on debates about mass culture, the historical avant-garde, and fascism as framed in recent Anglo-American critical thought.[15]

As my discussions of realism and poetry illustrate, with few exceptions Italy occupies a liminal position in controversies over modernism, the politics of aesthetics, and fascism. Indeed, speaking about the "marginal" value of Italian products in the global cultural economy, Renate Holub (1994) offers an important analysis: "Italian cultural goods in general have not been distributed in a fashion in any way comparable to the heavy imports from France and Germany" (239). As Holub points out, a complex variety of factors has contributed to this marginality— affording both strategic advantages and disadvantages. And it owes as much to a colonial status imposed from without as to attitudes and practices adopted within Italian studies. The materials and approaches made available by the essays collected here thus speak to both camps. Ironically, some of the primary texts I examine appeared in English translation soon after their original publication, including *Stella mattutina,* published under the title *Morning Star* in 1930, and *Nessuno torna indietro,* which came out under the title *There's No Turning Back* in 1941. More recently, Drigo's novel *Maria Zef,* Deledda's autobiography *Cosima,* and short stories written during Fascism have become available in English translation. Yet the tendency to overlook such texts has resulted in the oversimplification of the discursive field operating during Fascism, and the ideologies and practices constituting it. By so doing, critical commentary has in some cases constructed the kind of repressive models it ostensibly seeks to critique. For example, the nearly exclusive attention accorded Filippo Tommaso Marinetti as the emblem of the historical avant-garde's misogynism actually forestalls analysis of the vanguardist interventions that futurist women executed to revolutionize art and society prior to and during Fascism. Moreover, as I attempt to show, by examining the shifting, open sets of coordinates orienting Fascist theories and practices of art and the functions they are called on to perform, we see that the need for new, more critical approaches to the politics of aesthetics operating in the regime becomes obvious. And if Fascist cultural politics worked across boundaries between realist, modernist, and avant-garde models and the meanings attached to them, then a fuller understanding of the theories and practices produced by Fascism may have far-reaching implications for how we think about the "oppositional" role that aesthetics and critical theories endeavor to construct in the aftermath of Italian Fascism, German Nazism, the Holocaust, and World War II.

ONE

Unseduced Mothers: Female Subjectivities and the Transgression of Fascistized Femininity

Critical Approaches to Female Subjects and Fascism

> A given socio-historical moment is never homogeneous; on the contrary, it is rich in contradictions. It acquires a "personality" and is a "moment" of development in that a certain fundamental activity of life prevails over others and represents a historical "peak": but this presupposes a hierarchy, a contrast, a struggle. The person who represents this prevailing activity, this historical "peak," should represent the given moment; but how should one who represents the other activities and elements be judged? Are not these also representative?
>
> ANTONIO GRAMSCI, *Selections from Cultural Writings*

Recent historiographic studies on the forms of culture and society in the Fascist state have broadened the parameters of debate beyond the terms of *consent* and *resistance* and produced new paradigms that promote the formulation of more complex notions of gendered social subjects and their relations to discourse. Such works as *Fascism in Popular Memory* (1987) by Luisa Passerini, *Rethinking Italian Fascism* (1986), edited by David Forgacs, *La nuova italiana* (The new Italian woman, 1987) by Elisabetta Mondello, and *How Fascism Ruled Women* (1992) by Victoria De Grazia have contributed to this direction in critical thought and enabled more diversified analyses of subjectivities and discursive mechanisms designed to construct the sites and means of their engagement in society during Fascism. With few exceptions, however, literary scholarship, particularly when speaking of women's writing produced in the years of Fascism, has tended to rely on traditional cultural studies that worked through "consent" as the primary interpretative category.[1] Thus, conventional representations of this period within the tradition of Italian women's literature generally conceive of women as objects of repression (forced into resigned silence) or as objects of ideological seduction (coerced into reproducing the patriarchal ideology of femininity emblematized by the image of the woman-mother). I propose that this notion derives more from the interpretative framework than from women's discourses and how they may have figured in the broader dynamic of culture and society. My concern in the opening section of this essay is therefore to work through some of the problems posed by a critical model developed to interrogate female consent by examining women as speaking subjects in the Fascist regime. At the same time, I posit methods of inquiry that enable us to see different discourses on femininity by mapping the interchanges and contradictions between women's cultural production in life and literature and Fascist discourses intended to reconstruct female self-concept in the image of the supreme wife and mother. Certainly, recent scholarship on Fascist ideology has shown that the female models produced by the regime, along with the functions they were designed to sustain in political life, encompass a full array of competing modern and conventional images, some of which I explore in the following chapters. However, this essay focuses on the visage of the woman-mother because it appears particularly embedded in representations proffered in interwar discourses and in postwar literary criticism. By delineating the configurations of a different female subject, transgressing the dominant ideology of femininity, I intend to make possible more articulated readings of the modes of self-representation, narrative practices, and systems of address that women writers elaborated during Fascism, and how they may have engaged women among the reading public.

Though literary critics in the United States and abroad have made significant progress in the reconstruction of the tradition of Italian women's writing, thereby inviting revisionary readings, relatively few studies have endeavored to examine women in the Fascist regime as writing and reading subjects. Recent years have seen growing interest in Italian romance literature, which experienced a boom among women readers in the twenties and thirties, but the broad range of women's literary achievements during this period in poetry, the novel, and the short story has yet to receive the sustained critical analysis it warrants. Reasons why this subject has been marginalized in literary commentary concern complex problems—periodization, canon formation, and unfamiliarity with both the rich variety of women's literature produced during the dictatorship and its modes of publication. Not the least of these is an ongoing reliance on historical accounts that concentrate on issues of female consent in the regime. This trend has forestalled a consideration of women as producers of social meaning through their practices of writing and reading. Maria Antonietta Macciocchi's study *La donna "nera":* *"Consenso" femminile e fascismo* (The woman in "black": Female "consent" and Fascism) represents the most authoritative historical analysis of women elaborated on the critical model of consent. And though published in 1976, Macciocchi's work continues to exert substantial influence on how literary commentators think about women writing during the dictatorship and their relation to the ideology of femininity disseminated by the Fascist regime.[2] Macciocchi's analysis merits attention for what it reveals about the construction of woman in Fascist ideology and the systems of address utilized in attempts to modernize the vestiges of the traditionally defined female role and, in effect, to reinstitute patriarchal gender arrangements. I wish to argue, however, that the method of examination used in *La donna "nera"* prevents us from seeing the different, if not oppositional, discourses articulated by women in Italian culture and society during Fascism.

Macciocchi's project is admittedly ambitious: "I finally relocate women in collective society," she states, "making them revolutionary agent subjects whom everyone, the right and left complicitous, has ended up negating. Only by starting from the negation and by studying it, I negate the negation of the negation and arrive at the dialectic: *women are the ones who make history*" (22). However, the intent of this undertaking and the interpretative model stand at cross-purposes; Macciocchi proposes to make Italian women subjects in the history of the dictatorship by examining discursive and material mechanisms through which Mussolini "seduced" women into investing their desire in Fascism.[3] This manner of articulating the problem, in tandem with a method of analysis executed by means of a psychoanalytic model that relies on Sigmund Freud's notion of the death impulse, locks women into a symbolic system of meaning in which they are representable only in relation to man as object of desire.

Though never fully theorized by Freud, the notion of the death impulse, along with the related themes of sexual repression, self-sacrifice, passivity, and masochism—components frequently identified with culturally constructed femininity—provides the vocabulary with which Macciocchi intends to clarify how Fascism was ostensibly able to deflate female opposition, and to coerce women into submission:

> From its inception, Fascism aimed at an acceptance, which I have defined masochistic, on the part of women: an acceptance of every "torture," and of a kind of "death impulse" (Freud) celebrated with the everlasting rite of those killed in battle and widows exalting their chastity-sacrifice. . . . From this renunciation of life is born woman's self-negating joy: it is the "joy" of the relation between woman and power: renunciation, subordination, domestic slavery, in exchange for the abstract, verbose, demagogic love of the Leader, the Duce, the greatly virile Fascist clown. (38)

As accurate as Macciocchi's reading of the process designed to fascistize femininity may be, it does not elucidate how this ideology may have been transformed through female subjects, who had achieved increasing degrees of socioeconomic mobility, into daily practices and behaviors. Rather, the author's essentialist theorization of a mass female psychology, aligned with the work of Helene Deutsch and Marie Bonaparte, reproduces the notion that masochistic tendencies constitute a determinant element structuring the female relation to self, sexuality, and social interaction, an idea that had lost currency in psychoanalytic thought by the late sixties. Anticipating female masochism as a means to solicit the female subject, Fascist discourses addressing a female audience operated, Macciocchi tells us, according to the formula "power-joy-sacrifice = joy in sacrifice" and shaped women's relation to power in the state. Thus, she concludes, Mussolini's appeals for female self-sacrifice elicited women's voluntary surrender, performed with "masochistic joy," enabling the duce to "'enchant,' 'mystify' and 'possess' millions of women," seducing them into the prescribed role of Wife and Mother (34). Within this phallic economy, the compensation for female self-effacement consisted of the symbolic love conferred by Mussolini, "the Male par excellence, the Husband of all women, or the lover of each woman," as well as the Father of the children they would give for their country (41).

Yet I question whether this is an account of female subjectivity or an instance of the Fascist body politic's self-representation. One could hardly dispute the claim that Mussolini displayed himself as the model for all Italian males, virile in love and war. Yet Fascist discourses circulated such contrasting female figures as the young woman in uniform, marching in public review; the woman artist, authorized in state-sponsored organizations and exhibitions; and the "socially" committed professional woman working in welfare organizations to assist the disadvantaged. In this semiotic field, it is also true that mass-mediated images disseminated by the regime on posters and in newspaper photos and articles politicized and publicized the maternal woman, encoding this figure as the model female citizen of the Fascist nation. This component of the regime's communications apparatuses can be read as a highly self-conscious "technology of gender" whose business was to reconstitute gender roles along the patriarchal model, in order to strengthen a sex-gender system undermined by the sociocultural and economic changes of modernity. Equating femininity with motherhood, the figure of the woman-mother dominates prescriptive discourses as a trope meant to align women with a politics of demographics, claiming for the maternal institution the fulfillment of female desire, nature, and social mission. But it would be unwise to assume that the image of woman in such writings describes the aspirations, pursuits, and notion of self of historical women in the Fascist state.

Here what concerns me about Macciocchi's study, and others that work through the category of consent, is the tendency to give insufficient attention to the complex processes of discursive address and reception, and thus the other responses that idealized images of woman may have elicited in modern Italian women representing a broad spectrum of class, ideological, and geographic differences. In other words, she collapses the distinction between discursive mechanisms that seek to engineer conformity with the woman-mother ideal and articulations of female subjectivity. In her essay "Semiotics and Experience" (1984b), Teresa de Lauretis elaborates a conceptual framework for examining the potential functions of externally produced representations and experience in the construction of subjectivity, demonstrating how this ongoing process is

> the effect of that interaction—which I call experience; and thus is produced not by external ideas, values, or material causes, but by one's personal, subjective, engagement in the practices, discourses, and institutions that lend significance (value, meaning, and affect) to the events of the world. (1984b, 159)

Privileging the power of language over experience in the process of constituting subjectivity, Macciocchi excludes from her examination the components of experience, which de Lauretis elsewhere (1987) defines as a "complex of meaning, effects, habits, dispositions, associations, and perceptions resulting from the semiotic interaction of self and outer world" (1987, 18). Thus, if we are to examine the positions that women assumed in relation to the models of femininity publicized by the regime, as well as to other cultural images of the feminine, it is necessary to expand the field of inquiry to the practices and discourses that engaged female-gendered subjects.

I do not intend to diminish the ongoing importance of questions regarding why women, or other marginalized social groups, may accommodate, tacitly or otherwise, political powers that operate against their interests. However, because historical accounts interrogating consent to Fascism in Italy generally focus on dominant sociopolitical systems of address and representation while construing social subjects as passively constructed consumers, they have produced limitations in our perception of the discursive field and how women figured in it as not only the objects, but also the subjects of discourse. This critical approach tells much about repressive official structures, but it tells little about how women themselves perceived, thought, or spoke during Fascism. As argued by Michel de Certeau (1988), such "elucidation of the apparatus by itself has the disadvantage of *not seeing* practices which are heterogeneous to it and which it represses or thinks it represses" (41). The theoretical framework developed by de Certeau to examine the sites and means of oppositional activities that normative forces seek to suppress or to redirect toward their own interests has promising applications for examining the subject of women's authorship of the twenties and thirties in its complexity. Three premises elaborated by de Certeau have particular pertinence for the present study, enabling the reconstruction of a different female subject, resisting the fascistization of femininity in Italian life and culture of the twenties and thirties. First, de Certeau restores the fundamental distinction between the originary production/dissemination of representations (performed by institutions of power) and "secondary" or "consumer production" (consisting of the ways "cultural users" utilize those representations in daily life). Second, he conceives of social subjects as agents whose everyday practices (of work, study, reading, and self-presentation in Italy of the twenties and thirties, for instance) constitute means of social activity and cultural production. Finally, de Certeau valorizes instances of popular cultural production as potential sites of resistance to dominant ideas, values, or ideals. The resultant critical paradigm has significant implications for examining women as producers of social meaning during Fascism, when official political structures and discourses denied them as such. Broadening the area of investigation to encompass the different imbricating spheres of cultural production (official, high, and popular) enables us to consider how women may have appropriated their femininity through practices, behaviors, and attitudes marked masculine in the Fascist division of culture and society, thus articulating different forms of female subjectivity. Such a project makes possible the formulation of a more complex notion of the shifting locations of female-gendered subjects within the discursive field. It provides as well an overdue critical framework for reassessing the context and terms of female address, self-representation, and identification in women's literary production of the twenties and thirties.

By way of foregrounding the arguments I advance in the following sections of this essay, I would like to refer briefly to Elisabetta Mondello's work *La nuova italiana* (1987), a history of the women's press during Fascism that offers a suggestive profile of practices of reading and writing in this area of cultural production. Mondello analyzes women's publications, which, as part of media institutions, would come under the scrutiny of government authorities "regulating" cultural production, and thus would be expected to reproduce the staples of Fascist propaganda promoting such "female" virtues as motherhood, self-sacrifice, and obedience. The scope of this project consists primarily of documenting contradictions between the official model of woman prescribed in Fascist discourses and different social and cultural female models delineated in the women's press. Yet the critical importance of this work for literary studies should not be underestimated. For one thing, Mondello's archival research disputes the notion of women as passive consumers reproducing the dominant ideology of femininity and thus creates a space for a different perspective. Assessing the significance of her study for the process of reconstituting women in the regime as historical subjects, Mondello maintains:

> In years like those of the Fascist Regime when the socialization of the private, elevated as the keystone for the construction of the Fascist state, represented the most powerful instrument used in addressing women, mapping a gap between cultural models supported by women's periodicals and the Fascist stereotype of the "exemplary wife and mother," must dispel the most commonly held vision of the role women actually filled in that period. (9)

Even more important, as Patrice Petro has persuasively argued in *Joyless Streets* (1989), the women's press, through its explicit solicitation of female readers, comprises a discursive system that lends itself to the critical examination of the terms of female address, identity, and sexuality. Indeed, what Mondello finds is a multichromatic female mass culture rich with ideological autonomy, innovation, and alternative models valorizing women's intellectual, social, and creative production.

For the purpose of theorizing women as reading subjects, the prefatory statements in women's publications, which delineate the audiences they address and their intent, form a noteworthy reference. They testify to different terms of female identity—evinced by women's practices, concerns, interests, and tastes—which conventional postwar commentary has repressed by concentrating on prescriptive representations of femininity in Fascist discourses. Thus, in 1922 the magazine *Almanacco della donna* (Women's almanac, published in Florence) stated that it would address progressive-minded housewives, professionals, and "women who have neither the time nor means to dedicate themselves to their homes" (cited in Mondello 1987, 58). Its express purpose was to inform and educate its readers about women's organizations, cultural, social, and political achievements, as well as specific professional pursuits of women journalists, writers, playwrights, painters, and sculptors.

Sharing many similar topical concerns was *Rassegna femminile italiana* (Women's Italian review, Rome), directed by Elisa Majer Rizzioli, a recognized supporter of Mussolini. Though *Rassegna femminile italiana* was originally founded as a publication for members of the Fascist women's organization, it represents a means of women's cultural production whose self-management (the staff was almost exclusively made up of female editors, journalists, critics, and contributors) stands in striking contrast to the image of female identity manufactured by the regime. This may have contributed to Mussolini's decision to suspend production of the magazine, which later resumed, albeit with a more subdued tone. The weekly *Il giornale della donna* (The woman's magazine, Rome) addressed women working in small industry. Though this publication became an organ of the *Fasci femminili* in 1929, it publicized a suggestive program in 1930—which was reconfirmed in 1934 and 1935—promising its readers

> very interesting columns on professional schools and schools for home economics, on small industry and handcrafted goods production, articles on literature and the arts, on the home, work, and fashion. It treats all issues that concern women and their work, social services, child welfare, women's spiritual and cultural elevation. (cited in Mondello 1987, 209 n.9)

Finally, the changing publishing policies of the Catholic magazine *Fiamma viva* (The bright flame) merit attention for what they say about the tastes of women readers and their power to direct dominant channels of discourse to their own interests. This magazine maintained a long-standing opposition to romance literature (a position shared by Fascist exponents) on the premise that such fiction instilled a hedonistic notion of love divested of maternal ideals. Such literature thus provided visions of female sexuality and desire suppressed by the Fascist model of femininity. Yet *Fiamma viva* changed its policy and began publishing stories of love and adventure in response to the requests of Catholic women readers. As stated in a letter that one woman wrote to the magazine in 1921, "The greatest error we Catholics and our publications make is to be afraid of speaking about love. . . . Why, for example, couldn't a periodical be published with the title '*Love*'?" (cited in Mondello 1987, 123).[4]

Mondello's historical account of the women's press reveals much about different forms of female subjectivity in Italian culture and society, raising complex issues concerning the extent to which women belonging to the middle classes and social elite, generally assumed to be supportive of Fascist endeavors, responded to the attempted institutionalization of female thought, emotion, and action. Where gender identity is concerned, female practices of reading would suggest a sustained engagement in representations of modernity that address women's social, economic, and cultural issues. In response to the female readership's tastes and interests, women's magazines dedicated substantial space to women's literary production; they published bibliographical information, book reviews, and fiction by such writers as Grazia Deledda, winner of the Nobel Prize for literature in 1926, Ada Negri, Gianna Manzini, Maria Luisa Astaldi, and Clarice Tartufari, regardless of their political orientation. A survey conducted in 1923 by *Almanacco della donna*, asking readers to choose the ten most illustrious Italian women of their times, gives an indication of the immense popularity and admiration generated by women writers (Mondello 1987, 180). Despite scant reader participation (perhaps the reluctance to respond to surveys is not culture bound), the results, reflecting answers submitted by some two hundred of the magazine's seventeen thousand readers, are significant for the kinds of women who were chosen and the order in which they were ranked: Ada Negri, Grazia Deledda, Eleonora Duse, Matilde Serao, Annie Vivanti, Queen Elena, Térésah, the Dutchess Elena of Aosta, Francesca Bertini, and Teresa Labriola. Barring members of the royal family, these female figures (as well as others who did not make the final listing, for example, the lawyer Lydia Pöet and Sibilla Aleramo, author of the internationally acclaimed feminist autobiography *A Woman*, published in 1906) were recognized as much for their progressive emancipated thinking as for their cultural achievements. The parameters of Mondello's study do not include an extensive analysis of the fiction contributed by renowned and popular women writers to the women's press. Yet as I intend to demonstrate in the final section of this essay, the thematics and textual practices elaborated in women's fiction, which generated unprecedented popularity

among readers of the twenties and thirties, solicit a different female subject by creating new terms of identification in their representations of
nontraditional gender roles.

Cultural Productions of Woman in Fascist Discourses and Practices of Daily Living

> Let's not digress into a discussion of whether woman is perhaps supe-
> rior or inferior; let's affirm that she is different.
>
> BENITO MUSSOLINI

In order to avoid reproducing the binary opposition between female and
male culture, which certain Fascist ideologues wished to impose on Italian cultural production during the dictatorship, this section of my essay
maps contradictions between women's practices in everyday life and the
prescriptive and descriptive drifts in hegemonic discourses of the twenties and thirties. These contradictions articulate the configurations of a
female subject whose difference has been repressed. First, however, I
would like to make a different but related point that establishes a new
perspective from which to assess the function of gender politics during
the dictatorship. It must be stressed that in Italy the institutionalization
of gender difference in anthropology, sociology, and medicine does not
represent an innovation attributable exclusively to Fascist ideologues,
though its politicization in mass media possibly does. As demonstrated
by Piero Meldini in *Sposa e madre esemplare* (The exemplary wife and
mother, 1975), the notion of femininity in Fascist ideology owes a profound debt to the positivist anthropology of the 1800s, whose formulation of a "scientific" justification for female oppression roughly coincides with the participation of increasing numbers of women in the
economic, social, political, and cultural dimensions of Italian life.[5] In
such texts as *La donna delinquente, la prostituta, e la donna normale* (The
criminal woman, the prostitute, and the normal woman, 1893) by Cesare
Lombroso and Guglielmo Ferrero, biologistic theory, structuring discourses on the female organism in the sciences, privileges reproductive
organs as *the* determining component of the female, which compro-
mises woman's development, as demonstrated by her inferiority: intellectual, moral, emotional, physical, psychological, and sexual (because

nonphallic). Postulating a causal relationship between female biology and development, Enrico Ferri, an expert in criminal sociology, states:

> I have Darwinistically explained that [inferior sexual sensitivity] in woman is due to the great, miraculous maternal function which, in order to sustain the life of the species, depletes so much of woman's strength, and condemns her to a lower level of biological evolution, between that of a young boy and an adult with regard to physiognomy, voice, and muscular strength, as in psychology. (in Meldini 1975, 30)

Extending the scientific definition of woman, inclusive of "natural" and thus normative behaviors, to the sociocultural scene, turn-of-the-century social commentators in Italy supported a politics of gender designed to contain female desires exceeding the boundaries established to maintain patriarchal relations of power.

At the same time, however, women's practices in Italian life and culture suggest ways in which women appropriated their femininity. In her article "Aridità sentimentale" (Emotional aridity), published in the Turin daily *La stampa* (11 July 1911), Amalia Guglielminetti strongly critiques the scientific method for the assumption that it can articulate female subjectivity simply by analyzing her material body: "Gynecologists and psychiatrists who have dissected women's bodies, listened to their heartbeats, and measured their craniums cannot reveal their intimate essence." Rather, she argues, women, particularly writing women, have the right and responsibility to strip away any falsity, male-designed trappings of femininity, and to write their experience of femaleness in the first person, producing "a document of extraordinary truth." Correspondingly, at the level of everyday life, women deflected the restraints on their socioeconomic activity advanced by the culturally constructed notion of woman as only mother. Numbers of women from impoverished rural areas moved to find work in rice or tobacco fields, and in machine, woolen, and cotton factories, and the expanding clothing industry, as Lucia Birnbaum (1986) notes, provided many forms of employment for women. Middle-class women occupied positions in the business sectors as bookkeepers, typists, and secretaries. Women of different classes increasingly broke into the fields of teaching, journalism, and literary production, as shown by the cases of Negri and Deledda, among others.

Within the broader Italian socioeconomic context, demographic shifts, as well as the intensifying militancy among proletarian, lower middle-class and intellectual working women changed the dynamics of sexual relations, undermining male authority in the interrelated domestic and social spheres.

Not surprisingly, political discourses produced prior to Mussolini's establishment of the regime indicate the different ways that women and men experienced this process of change (accelerated by World War I), the overriding male response being discontent with the ambiguity of gender identities. The writings of Filippo Tommaso Marinetti, founder of the Italian futurist movement, help to explicate the complex inter-section of cultural, economic, political, psychological, and gender issues. As Cinzia Blum (1990) contends in her rereading of Marinetti's writings, profound contradictions mark his representations of woman.[6] Although he ostensibly calls for a cultural revolution that would radically change the institutions of marriage and family, gaps in his discourse inscribe deepening anxiety over already destabilized gender identities. In Marinetti's piece "Contro il matrimonio" (Against marriage, 1919) the ideological and psychological drifts of his argument collide while creating a vivid picture of female social mobility and male identity in crisis. The extensive participation of women in the work market, according to Marinetti, has created a "matrimonial grotesque":

> Due to her job, the wife necessarily leads a life that has little to do with running the household, whereas the husband, since he's out of a job, devotes all of his energies to an absurd preoccupation with keeping the house in order.
>
> A complete family reversal in which the husband has become a useless woman with overbearing male manners and the wife has doubled her human and social value.
>
> An inevitable clash between two partners, conflict, and male defeat. (368)

This passage highlights the connection between a male position marked by a jealous defense of traditional gender roles and the presence of a different female subject who transgresses these roles and thus threatens male control. Hence the predominance of the woman-mother image in hegemonic discourses of the twenties and thirties, implemented to reestablish gender boundaries in the Fascist state, may be ascribed, at the psychological level, not to female masochistic tendencies but to male anxiety manifested in the absence of the object of desire. The persistent adoption in the male discourse on woman of such terms as re-institute, re-construct, re-establish, re-animate, re-instate, and re-valorize can reasonably be considered a response to the experience of loss and/or unfulfilled desire and the anxiety generated by this experience: only in discourse can the male subject conjure the reappearance of the woman-mother.

Meldini's collection of articles published primarily in Fascist journals, to which I referred at the beginning of this section, demonstrates that throughout the years of the dictatorship the representations of the female constructed in sociology, medicine, history, theology, and economics equate the feminine with motherhood. In this context it is important to emphasize that the term *motherhood* refers to biological reproduction (giving birth to a child, preferably a son) as well as to the symbolic mothering of husbands, sons, fathers, and brothers. In an uncanny way, the Fascist discourse on the woman-mother thus coincides with Freud's story of femininity, in which "a marriage is not made secure until the wife has succeeded in making her husband her child as well and in acting as a mother to him" ("Femininity," 112–35). While these male-authored discourses tell the contemporary reader much about male desire, they also inscribe the presence of a female subject whose resistance to the ideal of the woman-mother generates male anxiety. The correlation between male desire and anxiety is exemplified in the 1930 article "Donne e culle" (Women and cradles) by the Fascist writer and social critic Manlio Pompei. Mapping the trajectory of male desire, Pompei claims:

> Nothing bonds us men more and nothing pleases us more than the woman-mother, the woman statuesquely personifying that need for intimacy, attentiveness, and peace that is the inevitable object of our every battle and our every labor, she who in her acting goodness reminds us of our mother's face, she who thus makes an inseparable union of our past and future, where memories of yesterday and hopes for tomorrow meet, uniting in the warmth of a single devoted caress.[7]

But the desired object is lost. As Pompei apprehensively observes, this kind of woman, a deeply religious woman, has disappeared, thereby disrupting his vision of historical continuity. In contrast, the modern woman

> is in a hurry to live and therefore heedlessly guards the treasures of her femininity; she makes man fearful of taking the step to unite himself with her for the rest of his life . . . and because of her extraordinary needs she constitutes an element of disorder and disorientation in families. (in 1975, 182–83)

Though Pompei's article, among others written for journals and newspapers by such diverse Fascist ideologues as Ferdinando Loffredo, Giuseppe Bottai, and Giuseppe De Libero, has the intent of reconstructing the female gender model along traditional lines, it registers modern women's opposition to the male ideal of "absolute femininity," which woman may achieve, according to Julius Evola (1934), only by "giving herself entirely to another . . . whether he is the man she loves or her child . . . thereby finding the meaning of her own life, her joy, her reason for being" (231). As hegemonic discourses inscribe the contradictory relation of Italian women to woman, in an endeavor to redirect women to their "natural" function, so they paradoxically circulate representations of a new culturally articulated femininity, creating different possibilities for female identification with practices that mechanisms of control seek to repress.

Among the most frequently censured expressions of modern female identity that transgress the Fascist ideology of the feminine are women's pursuit of education, employment, and such leisure activities as movie going, reading romance novels, and dancing, as well as their tastes in fashion. The author of the 1933 article "Compiti della donna" (Woman's duties), while arguing that the Fascist woman must undergo a spiritual evolution to develop a sense of self-sacrifice in order to fulfill her social and political mission as mother, supports his position with an account describing the importance of education in modern women's aspirations:

> In the space of little more than thirty years, women have invaded middle schools, then high schools and universities, and today they form a clear majority in some majors; they have a monopoly in some programs of professional study; correspondingly, they are working, the majority of them obtain employment, and they practice a profession. (214)

It is true that females outnumbered males in elementary and middle schools; however, only limited numbers of women had gained access to higher education. In fact, women accounted for only 13 percent of university students in the 1926–27 academic year, and 15 percent in that of 1935–36.[8] By 1942, however, female enrollments in Italian universities had undergone a notable increase, reaching 29.9 percent, according to Alexander De Grand (1976) in "Women under Italian Fascism" (960).

Perhaps more important are women's own ways of speaking about their educational ambitions. In a 1930 article published in the *Giornale della donna*, a female student counters the argument that feminism was responsible for Italy's declining birthrate:

> According to us feminism does not even enter into the desire of women to educate themselves, to better themselves, to act independently. If possibly it is a consequence, it is not a cause of such desires. It is born when the necessity arises to defend and further women's work which has been discouraged and denigrated only because it is done by women. (cited in De Grand 1976, 963)

Testimonies from female adolescents raise further doubts regarding the effectiveness of Fascist discourses and programs intended to reconstruct women's self-concept on the patriarchal model of femininity. Professor Spolverini, the director of an Italian pediatric clinic, reported in 1938 that the foremost desire of young girls, as expressed to their doctors, was not to have a husband and children. On the contrary, their goal was to get an education and practice an intellectual profession (teaching at a high school, college, or university), or to have a well-paying position, so that "they can be self-sufficient . . . and lead an intellectually and economically independent life" (cited in Meldini 1975, 263). Similarly, the attitudes expressed by one thousand Roman schoolgirls between the ages of sixteen and eighteen in interviews conducted by Maria Gasca Diez in 1938 tell us that young women in urban areas may have aspired to something other than being the guardian angel of hearth and family. Though these adolescents had grown up during Fascism, only 10 percent had any interest in domestic tasks and responsibilities, while 27 percent hated them; very few wanted a large family, the clear preference being to have one child, or two at the most. Finally, the majority of young women expressed the wish to command rather than obey. In an article prompted by this survey, published in the woman's magazine *Almanacco della donna italiana* (1938), Luigi Gozzini concludes his findings by urgently advocating a new educational program that would guide woman back "to her natural function in social and national life, a work of education that would reconstruct *ab imis fundamentis* the pillars of family conscience" (cited in Meldini 1975, 263–64).

The majority of articles arguing against women's presence in institutions of learning and the workplace are couched in the politics of demographics conferring sociopolitical legitimacy solely on the female reproductive function. "Have children, have children," Mussolini would declare, "there is power in numbers!" But beneath the facile exterior typical of Mussolini's slogans, complex economic, political, psychological, and gender issues compete; male authority, levied by economic means, is truly at stake. Pompei, in his 1933 analysis of the crisis of family, the smallest unit reflecting the condition of the Fascist state, creates a thought-provoking description of the changing significance that employment outside the home has for women, as well as its "dangerous" implications for men. Though supporting themselves was once an economic necessity for some women, the desire to join the workforce eventually became a trend. Modern women, however, conceive of employment as a right, guaranteeing their autonomy, which strips the title *paterfamilias* of meaning.[9] De Libero, a clerical Fascist, confirms this observation in 1938, though he attributes women's desire for economic independence to the feminist movement, stating that "woman no longer wants to be economically dependent on man in order to form the most perfect of societies, the family; rather, she wants to break away and support herself" (in Meldini 1975, 249). In 1933, Mario Palazzi perceives a more tragic scenario:

> Since the contribution of earnings is what potentially and concretely determines man's supremacy in the family, and since woman is escaping this supremacy to the detriment of other men, producing obvious tension, and a progressive loosening of family bonds and male authority in the bosom of the family, at the rate things are going there will be a matriarchy. (in Meldini 1975, 209)

Echoing the apprehensive tonality of Marinetti's matrimonial grotesque, the voices of Palazzi, Pompei, and Evola speak not of female submission in the late 1930s. They articulate male defeat in their representations of sexual relations where the male sex, who was supposed to win the war between the sexes, "has been ignominiously defeated by masses of strong-willed masculine women" (in Meldini 1975, 211). Instead of keeping their women in line, men have become "entirely dominated," feminized "puppets" (116).

One could hardly argue that Italian society was on the verge of matriarchy in the late thirties, or that male-authored representations of different female desires constitute merely specters of male anxiety. A growing body of historical material, however, documents women's pursuits of their desire and aspirations for economic and intellectual autonomy in Italian society during Fascism. A complex variety of factors—such as age, sexual orientation, class, and geographic location—clearly influenced women's choices regarding education, employment, and childbearing. Yet the oral testimonies examined by Luisa Passerini (1987), for instance, materialize female perceptions of self among the Turin working class as active social subjects whose decisions to be employed in the factories and to have fewer children represent (in the social, political, and symbolic dimensions) the progress they had achieved in relation to their mothers' generation. Employment figures more prominently as a central component of identity formation in oral self-representations provided by women of the middle classes working as typists, secretaries, and teachers. For these women, Passerini maintains, "work seemed to offer not only material independence but also the primary basis for a psychological and social identity, despite relative indifference, especially among clerical workers, toward the content of the job" (50). This different model of female subjectivity, inscribed in women's practices and in social commentary, forces us to reconsider the traditional notion of the ideological system and the discourses, institutions, and practices that constitute it.

Within a broader framework of ideology, which encompasses the quotidian as a site for the production of social meaning, we can also read modern women's employment of their bodies in public self-presentation, carriage, gestures, and dress as appropriations of femininity and as an attack on male authority in what Iain Chambers—adopting Umberto Eco's term—refers to as "sign warfare." Postulating a concept of the social subject as one who, through choices and tastes, constructs a "public identity" interacting with the larger system of signs where ideology is "inscribed in our clothes, our homes, hair styles, reading and viewing habits[,] in our gestures, our sexuality, our selves," Chambers reformulates the notion of resistance, as well as its means and significance in daily living. Objects of fashion, for instance, may be employed to assert oneself in public spaces, threatening identities imposed by dominant institutions, if not creating new ones (Chambers 1986, 212, 54).[10] In an interesting way, Chambers's argument here echoes Paolo Araldi, a clerical exponent of Fascism, who draws a similar conclusion in 1929. He clearly perceives the ways in which women's fashion may disrupt social conventions, though he does not take into account the female consumer's agency or tastes: "As soon as fashion headquarters give the order to take yet another veil off the shrine of her modesty, woman obeys without examining the importance that fashion exerts on customs, which is incommensurable" (in Meldini 1975, 161).

A comparison of the ways in which male social critics write the maternal body and read the modern female body, styled along models provided by favorite movie stars and public figures, explicates the psychic relation between male psychopolitical *desire,* with the woman-mother as its object, and male *anxiety,* attached to a female social subject unseduced by the maternal ideal. The maternal body personifies robust shapeliness, physical and sexual health, and solidity. "Woman," Pompei reminds his readers in 1930, is "home," which is to say, the woman-mother houses, protects, and nourishes all but herself. Instead, the new female body accommodates only herself. Modern women's bodies are "flat, skinny . . . perpetually adolescent" (in Meldini 1975, 182). The new feminine body insinuates itself onto the dominant ideological system as a sign challenging fascistized femininity; this gender indeterminacy marks, for some Fascist readers, the absence of the object of male desire and signals the failure of the regime's demographic politics. Though Mussolini's pronatalist campaign aimed to double the declining birthrate, the number of births per thousand obstinately fell from 23.4 to 22.2 between 1934 and 1936; social analysts reported "frightening numbers" of abortions, estimated to be "as high as 30 per cent of all conceptions" in 1929 (Mack Smith 1983, 160). It would be unwise to read the fluctuations in population growth solely as a manifestation of women's oppositional consciousness.[11] Yet working-class women in Turin speak of how their self-management of reproductive activity signified personal and social agency. And in some cases women do conceive of their decision to limit family size in terms of political resistance to the demographic campaign, as we see from what Fiora has to say:

INTERVIEWER: How many children did you have?
 FIORA: I had three.
INTERVIEWER: Are they alive?
 FIORA: Yes, yes. They're all alive. I would have had more, but you didn't
  to spite Mussolini, you see.
(in Passerini 1987, 150)

Though Fiora's testimony does not provide the basis for a general assessment of how women received Fascist discourses prescribing motherhood as a sociopolitical value, it is suggestive just the same.

Unable to conceive of forms of female identity other than mother, in a defensive gesture, male critics label women's practices of work, education, leisure, and self-fashioning as symptoms of aberrant masculinized sexuality, or bisexuality, the Freudian theory most feared by cultural commentators in the Fascist party. In 1938, well after Fascist authorities had disbanded women's organizations with an oppositional political agenda, De Libero writes that the "feminist movement" or "movement of masculinization" would like "to make a man out of woman, and since their sex prevents this, they do it through expressions, fashion, and gestures in life" (in Meldini, 1975, 249). I would propose that the ways in which women appropriated social practices, spaces, fashions, and attitudes marked "masculine" in Fascist ideology articulate different configurations of female subjectivity. By so doing, they provide a new perspective on women as reading subjects and on the sites and means of their engagement in literary discourses produced by women writers during Fascism.

Reading between the Margins: Women's Stories and the Cultural Page

> No one has ever known anything about us women.
> ADA NEGRI, "Woman with a Little Girl"
> (Signora con bambina)

A correlative to the male distress articulated in samples of Fascist commentary on women's changing social identities can be found in the anxi-

ety inscribed in essays by male critics of literature who appear preoccupied by the claims to authority made by Italian writing women in the
arena of literary production. However, an important distinction is necessary here. The notions of ideal femininity constructed by men of the
literary elite resonate with those advanced by Fascist thinkers, and both,
we could say, participate in the same sociocultural formation claiming
male power and authority in the cultural regime of the masculine and
the feminine. But this does not mean that key male figures in the literary
hierarchy were necessarily Fascist. On the contrary, the interwar cultural
hegemony accommodated a plurality of shifting ideological and artistic
positions. It featured, for instance, such supporters of Fascism as Luigi
Pirandello, recipient of the 1934 Nobel Prize for Literature; the Sicilian
philosopher Giovanni Gentile, who in the process of directing the *Enci-
clopedia Italiana* included entries from authors representing a broad political spectrum, even anti-Fascists; and the journalist and critic Giuseppe
Bottai, who founded the journal *Critica fascista* (1923) and spearheaded
several cultural initiatives. Such authors as Massimo Bontempelli and
Elio Vittorini initially crafted positions as leftist Fascists, committed to
the kind of socioeconomic change the revolutionary face of Fascism
promised yet failed to produce, prompting these figures, among others,
to shift their stance in the 1930s. Although the philosopher and critic
Benedetto Croce clearly opposed Fascism and authored the "Manifesto
of Anti-fascist Intellectuals," in many cases the relations between artists
and Fascist cultural politics appear ambivalent or, as in the case of F. T.
Marinetti, rife with contradictions.[12]

Such heterogeneity raises vexing problems concerning the points
where the sexual politics of literary assessment and Fascist notions of cultural production may overlap. It is possible to say, however, that the Fascist model of the woman-mother, employed as an ideal and a measure to
assess modern women's practices of daily life, generally carries politically
laden markers, casting such values as motherhood, self-sacrifice, and
obedience to male authority as national imperatives for citizenship. In
some cases, literary critics, such as Luigi Tonelli and Stanis Ruinas (1930),
may employ the conservative Fascist paradigm of woman's role in society
to critique the figure of the female author and trends in women's literature. But more typical are the terms of assessment proposed by the

prominent scholar Giuseppe Ravegnani, who reflected at length on the issues posed by women's fiction and poetry in his book *Contemporanei* (Contemporary authors, 1930). The following passage is particularly important for the way that Ravegnani represents trends in women's literature of the twenties and its relationship to the male canon. Likewise, his construction of the "ideal male reader" merits special attention:

> Is there, in Italy, a female literature in the traditional sense, that is to say, something lively, well-nourished, spontaneous, that has definite and clear ties with our own literate climates? Or is there at least an exceptional temperament, an intellectual shrew, a woman-monster? Now there are some women writers, five or six excellent at that: but we do not believe there is a real and well-defined female literature. What such literature there is, by and large, lives and nourishes itself on the margins of another greater, greatly more sober and conclusive literature. It seems to us . . . that female literature, particularly the recent one, has the habit of putting on trousers, and has the mania of putting on its face an unprejudiced and even cynic mask. . . . As for us, we would like a woman, especially if overflowing with ink, to be old-fashioned, maybe romantic, homey, and a little exhausted by housework. (55–66)[13]

In this provocative discussion we see how Ravegnani's notion of the feminine—"romantic," "homey," and admittedly worn-out—structures the male reader's expectations about what a "female literature" would be. Working within these criteria, he attempts to demonstrate that a tradition of female writing does not exist—a topic of heated debate during the twenties and thirties. In the process, however, Ravegnani outlines the different terms of women's literary discourses. Despite his wish to displace women's literature onto the fringes of the Italian literary tradition, the vampirish image he creates of such writing, nourishing itself on the margins of the "greater," that is, male, literature, conveys the potential danger it poses by eating away the boundaries between masculine and feminine, a kind of textual "cross-dressing," to modify Elaine Showalter's term (1983). Since women's literary production of the twenties does not embody Ravegnani's ideal of femininity, he can perceive their claim to the authority of authorship only in terms of masquerade. This critical perspective is symptomatic of Luce Irigaray's notion of the "blind spot" (1985) binding the parameters of the male visual field to an Oedipal trajectory that prevents male vision from seeing forms of female identity, sexuality, and desire differing from features shaping the woman-mother.

Yet in the 1920s and 1930s women's writing in various genres enjoyed an unprecedented boom, heightened, I would speculate, by the short fiction that such critically acclaimed and popular authors as Grazia Deledda, Ada Negri, Gianna Manzini, Maria Luisa Astaldi, and Clarice Tartufari contributed to the cultural page (*la terza pagina* or the third page) of Italian newspapers. This venue of publication has inestimable value for critical issues concerning gender and genre, modes of textual production, circulation, reception, and the intersections of high and mass culture. In order to assess the significance of the visible space that women made for themselves on the cultural page, and the functions their literary writings may have performed among reading publics, a brief overview of this institution, which remains unique to Italian journalism, is necessary.

In 1901, Alberto Bergamini, the editor of the Roman daily *Il giornale d'Italia,* founded the *terza pagina* as a tool to disseminate the ideas of preeminent historians, scientists, philosophers, authors, and critics among the general audience. Creating a kind of public piazza where intellectuals and readers could mingle minds, the cultural page showcased a broad variety of selections on the arts, politics, and social issues and featured serialized novels, short fiction, and poetry as well. The cultural page of *Il giornale d'Italia* soon became a prototype for newspapers throughout Italy, furnishing the topics of conversation in cafés, at tram stops, at work, and at home. In the midtwenties when Mussolini applied stringent controls on the press, the content of the third page began to favor short stories and articles on the arts. Several factors account for this shift in focus, economic considerations not the least among them. Editors published more short stories by authors of both critical and popular repute to increase newspaper circulation. Among the internationally acclaimed writers who regularly contributed short fiction to the cultural page prior to and during Fascism were Deledda, Luigi Pirandello, Aldo Palazzeschi, Negri, Dino Buzzati, and Alberto Moravia, who, however, was then banned from doing so in the late 1930s. In most cases, their short stories were later published in collections, attesting to the quality of this literary form, as well as its contribution to the short story genre. In fact, Luigi Barzini (1970) credits the short stories published on the cultural page with reviving the genre after what critics see as a decline in its fortunes at the turn of the century, prompted by the avant-garde futurists and the Vociani, who challenged the conventions of traditional generic forms. Like Barzini, Enrico Falqui, author of the most authoritative study on the cultural page, *Nostra "terza pagina"* (1965), underscores this institution's remarkable role in the imbricating cultural spheres of literature, journalism, and daily living, providing a useful critical context for theorizing the relations between gender and this genre, and the performative value of the short fiction signed by women and published on the coveted third page during Fascism.

Beginning in the midtwenties, the cultural page undergoes a feminization as increasing numbers of short stories written by women are showcased, although the individual authors contribute selections with varying frequency. For example, Negri and Deledda regularly contributed short stories to the Milanese daily *Corriere della sera*, while respectively publishing poetry and novels. Negri published some eighty short narratives between 1926 and 1942, whereas Deledda contributed more than one hundred short stories from 1923 until 1936, the year of her death. Although the *Corriere della sera* appears to have attracted primarily seasoned authors, *Il giornale d'Italia* published fiction by popular women writers along with works by such critically acclaimed figures as Guglielminetti, Tartufari, and Manzini. Perhaps offering more variety, from 1924 to 1939 this Roman daily featured short stories by more than twenty women authors, including, for instance, Maria Luisa Astaldi, Maddalena Crispolti, Marinella Lodi, and Pia Rimini. In the 1920s and 1930s, readers of the Turin daily *La stampa* could anticipate three to four selections per month by the prizewinning novelist Carola Prosperi, as well as fiction by Rimini and Guglielminetti, among others.

The importance for women of publishing short fiction on the *terza pagina* should not be underestimated. First of all, the economic benefits likely provided some women with the opportunity to become professional writers. It may also have functioned as a sign of independence, and certainly success, in view of the authority conferred on the institution of the cultural page, signified also by its prestigious Elzevir type. The personal meanings that Alba De Céspedes attached to publishing fiction on the cultural page illustrate these points. In an interview with

Sandra Petrignani (1984), De Céspedes shares her early experiences as an aspiring writer in Rome:

> Every day I used to go past the *Giornale d'Italia*'s printing office. I enormously liked the smell of ink emanating from the rooms on the first floor. I'd get right up to the bars on the windows so I could smell it better. My father had let me live on my own with my son (I was already separated) for a period of two years, during which he would send me a monthly check. When this time was up, if I wasn't able to support myself, he would have gradually reduced the amount of money until I would have had to go back and live with my family. I was stubborn and determined to make it. I sent my first short stories to the *Giornale d'Italia* precisely because I'd become attached to its printing office. They were published. And I was paid! Soon I was hired as a contributor. (39)

In addition to providing economic benefits and the opportunity to launch a writing career, publishing on the cultural page enabled authors to perform a direct intervention in the formation of ideas among a mass popular audience for whom the price of books was still prohibitive.[14] For instance, by 1943 Sibilla Aleramo's internationally acclaimed novel *A Woman* (1906) had sold fifty thousand copies. Yet by the midthirties fiction published in the *Corriere della sera* reached more than six hundred thousand readers per day.[15] Antonio Gramsci, a key figure in European Marxist theory who gives concentrated attention to literary production and its relation to the broader historical and social process, has underscored the formative influence that fiction published in the daily press may have on subjectivity by articulating the desires, emotions, aesthetic needs, and aspirations of people in everyday walks of life.

More important, while examining the problematic of an Italian "national-popular" literature, Gramsci details the tastes, interests, and reading habits of women among the mass newspaper readership, a subject that literary commentary has overlooked. Gramsci maintains that in decisions regarding which newspaper to buy "women have a large say in the choice and insist on the 'nice interesting novel.' (This does not mean that the men do not read the novel too, but it is the women who are particularly interested in it and in items of local news.)" Taking generational and economic differences into account, Gramsci goes on to note that political papers were bought by young "men and women, without too many family worries, who were keenly interested in the fortunes of their political opinions" (1985, 207). One may reasonably speculate that these factors continued to bear on reading choices in the twenties and thirties when the cultural page of such major newspapers as the *Corriere della sera, Il giornale d'Italia,* and *La stampa* showcased primarily self-contained short stories rather than serialized novels. Newspaper advertisements for foods, clothing, and vitamins addressed apparently to female consumers testify to sufficiently large numbers of women readers to make such campaigns profitable. Furthermore, as demonstrated by the comprehensive publicity campaign launched in a May 1931 issue of *La stampa* by *Proton* (a product claiming to remedy that "run-down feeling" in everyone from pre-adolescents to menopausal women), the marketplace solicited women through representations of modern female practices—studying, working in offices, doing sports—that convey different terms of modern female identity. The 1929 ads for the Fiat convertible, though not necessarily addressed solely to women, emblematize female mobility at the material and symbolic levels in particularly powerful terms. These images picture the fashionable modern woman, now able to go wherever she desires, sitting alone at the wheel of her convertible, which looms large as it is superimposed on a map of the Italian peninsula.

To be sure, the availability, minimal cost, and length of short fiction published in the Italian daily press likely contributed to its popularity among diverse reading communities who may have had neither the time nor financial means to dedicate to novels. What interests me here, however, are the ways in which women's systems of address, narrative forms, and figurations of modern femininity may have solicited female readers across the class spectrum. I am also concerned with the relations of power between the stories women tell and the media practices developed by the state. For indeed, in some cases the subjects and forms of women's storytelling appear to subvert the very mechanisms of Fascist power authorizing them, which raises intriguing questions about the press as a site of state control over the production of ideology, as well as strategies of resistance that authorities ignore or appropriate. For example, we know that the dictatorship restricted the reporting of crime and prohibited such topics as suicide or sexual "deviance." More generally, as noted earlier, in the course of the intersecting demographic and ruralization campaigns, Fascist discourse exhalted the model of the woman-mother, censuring the modern "crisis woman," in De Grazia's words, "cosmopolitan, urbane, skinny, hysterical, decadent, and sterile" (1992, 73). Thus, how do we explain the publication of such stories as "Man and Death" by Marinella Lodi (1925) and "Echi nella notte" (Echoes in the night) by Pia Rimini (1929), which offer, respectively, sensitive portrayals of female characters who are victims of incest and material conditions leading to prostitution? Similarly, in the construction of social identities, what symbolic functions might have been performed by the highly diversified representations of emancipated female occupations and behaviors?

In order to explore these directions of inquiry it is useful to take a brief look at the microspatial politics of the cultural page, which differ somewhat from those applied to the newspaper sections surrounding it. Francesco Flora's book *Note di servizio* (Press orders, 1945), a broad sampling of the directives issued by the government, provides invaluable information about the endeavors to fascistize Italian newspapers, a process initiated in 1923 with the passage of legislation that limited the freedom of the press. As we would expect, many of the orders given by the Government Press Office, which was incorporated in the Ministry of Popular Culture (Miniculpop) in 1937, concern the topics to be reported or suppressed, and the manner of coverage, as well as indicating photographs to accompany the articles. More surprising is the attention given to such minutiae as the shade of black to be used for headlines and the typesize, which, along with orders regarding the visual images, clearly show the regime's understanding of the power exerted by graphic signs. For the most part, such directives address articles appearing in the national news, foreign affairs, and variety sections and are obviously designed to represent Mussolini and life in Fascist Italy in the most flattering light.[16]

In contrast to the other newspaper sections, the *terza pagina* and, in particular, the short fiction it featured were targeted by relatively few press orders. However, several interventions warrant attention because they highlight the hegemonic relations constituting the cultural page as a site for struggles over expressive power. For example, in the final years of the dictatorship, the Ministry of Popular Culture attempted to regulate contributors with this 1940 directive: "It is prohibited to publish signed works by Italians with non-Italian first names (Marisa, John, Willy, etc.)" (Flora 1945, 97). Likely conceived as a means to promote Italianicity, this order also registers the importance that the state attached to the public exposure afforded by the cultural page. Miniculpop also blacklisted authors at newspapers. As we know, Alba De Céspedes was banned from contributing stories to the press in July 1943, ironically, just one month before Mussolini was ousted by the Fascist Grand Council. But the overall success of such measures is questionable. As a member of the prestigious *Resto del Carlino* newspaper explains: "Now and then Miniculpop . . . would report the names of 'prohibited' authors, which, however, the editors sometimes ignored. At the *Carlino*, for example, Luigi Salvatorelli, whose writing was banned in theory, even contributed during the war (1940–1943)."[17]

Two additional press orders, regarding the campaigns against the formal *Lei* form of address and regional dialects, are especially important. They illustrate the state's attempts to employ the third page for articulating programs designed to refashion the Italian language as an expression of national Fascist identity and, thus for the purposes of this study, provide a critical context for interpreting women's narrative practices. The first directive, issued in 1938, refers specifically to literary selections published on the cultural page, stating, "Do not use the *lei* in the captions of comics, in short stories, and wherever writings in dialogue form appear. Remember to check carefully so that the *tu* and the *voi* always replace the foreign, servile *lei*" (Flora 1945, 100). Attaching multiple associations to the *lei* form, Mussolini and exponents of the anti*lei* campaign claimed that it was "feminine, ungrammatical, foreign, born two centuries or so ago in the time of slavery" (Flora 1945, 101). This form of address thus harked back to the period before Italy's unification, when Austria, France, and Spain ruled territories on the peninsula and islands. Similarly, as part of the initiatives undertaken to create the image of a unified collectivity, in the 1930s directives instructed newspapers to disregard works in theater, poetry, and fiction written in dialect. As late as 1943, one press order states, "Don't treat writings in dialects and the dialects in Italy, surviving elements of the past that the moral and political doctrine of Fascism aims decidedly to surpass" (Flora 1945, 82). Read against such a clear declaration, the continued use of words and expressions from regional dialects, a common feature in the short stories by Grazia Deledda and Lina Pietravalle, could be interpreted as oppositional linguistic practice. But this feature dates back to the earliest novels written by Deledda in the late 1800s. Moreover, exponents of Fascism reached no consensus on this issue, voicing highly contradictory positions. In fact, as a corrective to the depopulation of the countryside, in 1930 G. Cocchiara proposed that regional literature should be the staple of rural education to instill pride in "local life" among the peasants, which would armor them against the lures of the city. Nonetheless, it is reasonable to say that by incorporating forms of expression drawn from dialects and, likewise, the foods, manners of dress, customs, and traditions distinguishing regional communities, the short stories on the cultural page offer a rich variety of social codes that compete with the image of the national Fascist collective.

It is equally difficult to assess how the linguistic innovations crafted in women's forms of storytelling during the 1920s and 1930s relate to what Passerini (1987) terms the "totalitarian" language of Fascism. The discursive systems produced in women's fiction on the third page generally draw on linguistic constructions and vocabulary typical of everyday conversation.[18] The topical nature of the issues thematized, the quotidian settings and events described, and the address to a mass readership likely determine many of the lexical choices. The stories by female contributors give notable space to the subjects, locations, activities, and language of women's sociability, which, along with several distinct textual practices, may solicit women in particular as reading subjects. These include direct address to the female reader, first-person female narrators, and representations of women's private thoughts and conversations, as in "Sensitivity" by Amalia Guglielminetti (1936), "A Life Story" by Clarice Tartufari (1925), and "Dialogue on the Beach" by Elisa Zanella Sismondo (1935).[19] Although written for a mass audience, the fiction displays a strong use of metaphor enriching the texts' polysemic value. In "Portrait of a Country Woman" (1926) and "Baptisms" (1926) by Deledda, such metaphors as the river, the journey, and the initiation ritual invite different readings of the women's lives portrayed, whereas other stories craft the particular signs of modern society—airplanes, the radio, the cinema, fashion—as symbols of changing female subjectivities. Several stories develop the female imagery of makeup as both mask and a form of on-going self-fashioning.

Within the field of interwar discourses, the narrative tendencies exhibited by women's short stories stand in contrast to the high Italian literary style, which Gramsci critiques as an exclusionary address to the social elite. In this sense, women's writing practices create a space on the cultural page for opposition to the patriarchal control of language, a position shared by contemporary Italian feminist writers, among them, Dacia Maraini, Patrizia Cavalli, and Jolanda Insana.[20] But can we extend this theoretical proposition to the field of a "uniformed" Fascist model of language? As Passerini (1987) notes, the growth of the mass media during interwar industrial modernization occasioned state policies on the standardization of Italian. Yet as I stated earlier, the regime proposed internally differentiated, sometimes contradictory positions. Among the statements on literary language offered by Fascist critics, the observations advanced by Eligio Possenti suggest a direction for approaching this dilemma. In his article "Volontà costruttiva e realtà nazionale nella letteratura fascista dell'anno XIII" (Constructive will and national reality in the Fascist literature of 1935), published in the *Corriere della sera,* Possenti outlines the positive attributes characterizing literature produced in the "new" cultural period, including even such anti-Fascist authors as Alberto Moravia and Marino Moretti. He applauds the young authors,

> the majority of whom avoids the temptation of ornament in order to adhere to the truth of facts and men. Their language is lively, fast, with an air of the spoken language of the people; it comes from the piazza and becomes pure with taste and sensitivity. Their aim is to build. (1935, 3)

In this light, literary adaptions of colloquial, conversational forms in women's discourses apparently contribute to a broader phenomenon. If, however, in Fascist art such a language serves to construct a particular vision of reality, creating what Possenti claims is "faith in life itself, the conscience of today, and the belief in tomorrow" (3), then the terms of women's short fiction differ substantially. Moreover, Possenti, among other critics representing Fascist cultural enterprises, privileges the novel and longer literary forms. Giuseppe Bottai actually singles out the prose fragment and reflective prose poems as forms that are not Fascist art. Thus, we could say that the short story genre, a locus for ideological production, representing fragmented and fragmenting moments, is, at the very least, hostile to the epic, unifying modes of Fascist taste and discourse.

The numbers of short stories contributed over two decades by authors as diverse as Manzini and Deledda create a kaleidoscopic, mobile form of visuality putting common and unimaginable events from the most disparate parts of Italy before the readers' eyes. However, women authors pay substantial attention to social critique, bringing into public view such problems as poverty among rural and urban working women, runaway children, adultery and uxoricide, incest, single motherhood, and the crisis of the family. Hardly instilling faith in the socioeconomic or familial spheres of modern life, these sometimes graphic depictions raise questions and uncertainty. Likewise, the many stories about changing relationships between the sexes, picturing images of the modern woman—that distracting, disturbing presence we encountered in cultural writings by Fascist exponents—persistently put pressure to bear on notions of masculinity and femininity. Indeed, a recurrent component of women's forms of storytelling is the recontextualization, through secondary usage, of the idealized model of the woman-mother, achieved by reproducing traditional traits of femininity in opposition to alternative representations of female social identity, sexuality, and desire. This strategy, a form of what Tania Modleski (1986a) terms "mimicry," writes possibilities for diverse gendered negotiations of meaning into the text, for as she argues, the narrative appears to conform with the oppressor's ideas yet provides "a dissenting and empowering view for those in the know" (129).

This practice may account for the widespread popularity of women's fiction among female and male readers and, moreover, may elucidate how fiction of dissent could elude censorship in the media industry. The writers' gender perhaps helped their chances of attracting little attention among censors. Similarly, such innocuous titles as "Woman with a Little Girl" by Negri (1926), "A Boy" by Pia Rimini (1933), or "Portrait of a Country Woman" by Deledda (1926) would hardly imply sociopolitical dissent. Yet these narratives set different visions of female identity against the official cultural image of traditional femininity, in much the same way that women's practices of daily living challenged the ideology of the woman-mother. They thus create different possibilities for female identification. I would speculate that in some cases the author's choice of title manipulates the dominant political discursive code for her own interests. For instance, as the regime attempted to deploy a totalitarian rhetoric of virility, the title "Man and Death" (1925) might suggest a thematic of virility, honor, and war when, in fact, Marinella Lodi tells a story of female adolescence, attempted sexual abuse, and the girl's successful rebellion against patriarchal power in an act of self-assertion. The title "Sensitivity" (1936) could easily lead the reader to expect a story glorifying a female character for her embodiment of this quality. However, Guglielminetti attributes this capacity to respond emotionally, traditionally associated with the feminine, to a male character as well, figuring male sensitivity, not virility, as the quality eliciting female desire.

Nowhere is the circumvention of repressive apparatuses designed to neutralize, if not erase, a different female subject more apparent than in the ways in which women writers decenter the image of the woman-mother in fiction published on the cultural page. They do so, in part, by representing ways other than mothering for women to know themselves, as well as their relation to mechanisms of material and psychological oppression. As in Lodi's "Man and Death," which valorizes autonomy as a productive component of female self-concept, in "The Captain" (1931) Ada Negri elaborates the notion of "a dominating femininity and an intelligent, rash energy" in the figure of a young female girl. Though these particularizing traits of female difference are ultimately repressed by socialization in Negri's piece, Guglielminetti's retelling of the Ariadne myth in "Sensitivity" offers a scathing critique of the objectification of woman in patriarchy while creating a revisionary image of femininity. In fact, much of the narrative concerns problems of male vision and the representation of female desire. Thus, Arianna, whose notion of self is constituted by her intelligence, spiritual qualities, and intellectual curiosity, breaks three marital engagements to men whose vision is bound to her physical beauty—"a varnish destined to decompose and disappear with time." Though Arianna's different desire is fulfilled, her subversive power is not contained within the narrative economy. Rather, Guglielminetti's sardonic closing line, which reveals that Arianna's husband is blind, censures the normative male vision and representation of woman. Also interesting is the representation of a female student of the lower middle class created by Maria Luisa Astaldi in "La biblioteca" (The library, 1935). Here a young woman studies precisely so that she can secure a teaching position and "a small room all for herself, some better clothes, and the movies on Sundays." In an uncanny way, these desires for personal and financial independence resonate with the ideas on education and work voiced in the survey of Roman schoolgirls I examined earlier.

The critical rewriting of motherhood as institution and potential experience constitutes another primary strategy displacing the woman-mother as a desirable ideal for women or society. Far from glorifying the culturally constructed image of the mother, the many visions of motherhood authored by women throughout the twenties and thirties articulate a resisting consciousness to the essentialist ideology of the maternal as they refashion the terms and context of mothering. In view of the importance assumed by the traditional nuclear family in Fascist ideology, a preponderant number of short stories explore the conditions of women's mothering in a nontraditional family nucleus. Abandoned lovers and wives, surrogate mothers, prostitutes, and widows occupy the narratives with no reference to the fathers, dramatizing the subjective and social experience of motherhood, and the changing material realities of the nuclear family. Within this context, such writers as Deledda, Rimini, Crispolti, and Astaldi give particular authorial attention to the ties that bind mothers in a nonproductive scheme of relationship operating on the societal value of maternal self-sacrifice. As these writers transform domestic space, furnishings, and clothing into symbols of confinement and social marginalization, they narrate intimate dramas of entrapment wherein attributes of women's difference have been repressed, and desire figures as a wish for autonomy.

The problems concerning the unrepresentability of mothers as sexual subjects in life, society, and culture constitute the thematic and representational concerns in Maddalena Crispolti's "A Drama in Silence" (1934). Crispolti recontextualizes the dominant notion of motherhood as the sole function of femininity by dramatizing how this cultural ideal merely blinds men to female sexuality. Though women's critical rewritings of

motherhood form a predominantly dismal composite, some short stories evidence a different ethic of mothering. "The Pomegranate" (1936)
by Gianna Manzini, for instance, posits autonomy as a property of productive nurturing. With the image of a pomegranate, symbolizing the
"reconciliation of the multiple and diverse within apparent unity" (Cirlot 1971, 261), the author creates a suggestive metaphor for a new relation
between mother and child that makes both autonomy and connectedness possible. This ideal challenges the patriarchal values of dominance
and control, espoused by the elder members of the mother's family.

This sampling of fiction by women storytellers only hints at the inventive array of women's designs. It thus constructs a starting point for
fuller, more nuanced examinations, while, I hope, demonstrating the
value of pursuing them. By beginning to chart the locations where
women's notions of social identity strain against, or resist, the model of
the woman-mother, we can better question the possible investments of
female-gendered subjects in models intended to fascistize femininity
and in competing literary representations that depict alternative ways for
women to think, act, know, and imagine themselves. Indeed, women's
fiction on the cultural page exposed readers to multiple, constantly
changing possibilities of female self-fashioning, as exemplified in the following passage from "Risveglio" (Reawakening) by Ada Negri (1926):

> In this vital weight of turbid complexity I recognize myself, even physi-
> cally, with the many faces I've had, up to the one I know I have now, since
> every day our face changes; it might be just a line, a shade of color, a barely
> visible wrinkle by our lips or on our forehead. The strange thing is, yes,
> I'm me, but I'm also another woman. Behind closed eyelids, I think about
> myself with an introspective lucidity I certainly won't have when I get up,
> alert, agile, and again become a slave to the discipline I believe outside
> forces impose on me, but that, in fact, I have imposed on myself. (3)

This description beautifully evokes the complexity of the mutable
female visages crafted by women as speaking subjects. Yet the narrator's
reflections on her visions of self also assume an ambivalent cast, raising
further questions, some of which I explore in the following studies. The
present inquiry reads the terms and symbols of modern female subjectivities authored by women *against* the conservative construction of the
maternal woman, focusing on the moments of transgression. But how

do women's discourses relate to other, more progressive figures of the new Italian woman invented in Fascist representations? What positions on masculinity, technology, or the nation are inscribed in women's writings? And how do women authors negotiate the prevailing signs and codes constituting social identities in the moments of exchange, where meanings may be not only resisted, but confirmed or reconfigured? Last, in what ways might a more comprehensive appraisal of the contributions that literary women made to various genres during Fascism alter our perspective on the interwar canon and later neorealist, experimental, and impressionistic modes crafted by such award-winning postwar writers as Anna Maria Ortese, Clara Sereni, and Susanna Tomaro, along with their male counterparts?

TWO

Pathologies of Autobiography and
Outlaw Discourses

The germ of autobiography is even more dangerous and endemic
among women writers than among men who devote themselves to
this same sad craft. The assumption that every acute experience in
our life is, without a doubt, spontaneous material for art is much
more deep-rooted in women. Instinct, however, nearer to the surface
of their spirit, sometimes makes them effective, lively interpreters of
the dark, almost carnal motivations of the soul.

CAMILLO PELLIZZI, *Le lettere italiane del nostro secolo*

In the 1920s and 1930s the poetics formulated by such authors as Sibilla
Aleramo and Amalia Guglielminetti, which called for fellow women
artists to write their lives from their own particular experiences in new
expressive forms in order to create a richer, more nuanced, and perhaps
more veracious range of cultural images of femininity, became so widespread that critics of their time invariably read women's prose and poetry through the interpretative category of autobiography, in its broadest
sense.[1] Furthermore, in formal autobiographies and memoirs published
between the wars, critically renowned women authors claimed the illustrious space of autobiography to tell their stories about how they fashioned unconventional yet successful lives as women of literary culture.
Among these notable works are *Una giovinezza del secolo XIX* (A childhood in the nineteenth century, 1919) by Neera, which was edited by her
daughter and published posthumously; *Stella mattutina* (Morning star,
1921) by Ada Negri; *Il gomitolo d'oro* (The golden clew, 1924) by Clarice

Tartufari; *Fine d'anno* (Year's end, 1936) by Paola Drigo; *Cosima* (1936) by the Nobel prizewinner Grazia Deledda; and *La donna e il futurismo* (Woman and futurism), an experimental text by the avant-garde author Maria Goretti. This last work, published in 1941 during World War II, is a particularly provocative text for the way the author includes auto-biographical passages that performatively enact her rebirth as a futurist subject, as well as poetry and theory.

The critical commentary generated by women's autobiographical writings indicates that such works, in general widely read and reviewed, were constituted as part of the canon during the interwar years. Since the 1950s, however, as critics in Italy and elsewhere have construed auto-biography as a legitimate genre worthy of critical inquiry by virtue of its own merits (and not as a subcategory of biography), autobiographies by women writers have been deleted from the history of how the genre developed in Italy during the 1900s.[2] In contrast, Piero Jahier's *Ragazzo* (A boy, 1919) and Gabriele D'Annunzio's epic, boasting a title few editors would let pass today, *Cento e cento e cento pagine del libro segreto di Gabriele D'Annunzio tentato di morire* (One hundred and one hundred and one hundred pages of the secret book of Gabriele D'Annunzio tempted to die, 1935), have been constructed as model texts. They thereby determine what we think of as "representative" generic norms. Such an editing of the autobiographical canon in Italian studies thus supports Domna Stanton's claim that current trends in generic studies are suspect, structured by the contradiction between the "age-old perva-sive decoding of all female writing as autobiographical" and the omis-sion of women's life writing from the canon (1984, 6).

Here I would like to return to the intriguing, and by no means anomolous, assessment of women's autobiography provided by Pellizzi, which opens this essay. It raises a series of questions that I intend to interrogate through a reading of *Stella mattutina* and *Cosima*. Creating a pathology of autobiography, Pellizzi invokes the term *bacillo* from medical discourse, designating either an agent of disease or transforma-tion, and claims that this "germ" is more dangerous and endemic among women writers. He supports this position with the theory that instinct is closer to the spirit in the female, thus enabling women to effectively interpret the dark, carnal things driving the soul. Pellizzi's use of the disease metaphor and an essentialist description of female instinct creates a gendered ideology of autobiography, alluding to both the danger and pleasure created in women's texts. Although he does not delve into any details, this critic implies that the textual body unfolding in women's discursive practices deviates from organic norms and proprieties and, as a pathogen (to extend his metaphor), perhaps produces changes in other organisms. The figuration of women's autobiography as an agent of disorder that disrupts assumptions and beliefs maintaining sociosexual borderlines in the republic of letters invites investigation of the specific concepts of identity formation, motifs, and narrative properties exhibited in life stories produced by female writers between the wars. Indeed, in the twenties and thirties, male commentary demonstrates a fear of and fascination with the subject of women's autobiography. Which specific elements of women's forms of self-representation captured the attention of critics, provoking such passionate reactions? Given the high profile of women's autobiographies in the interwar years, why have postwar studies on the genre's development and conventions suppressed Italian women's elaborations of autobiography? I am using the term *autobiography* in Philippe Lejeune's manner to indicate an account of the author's life, or significant phases of it, where the writer is both narrator and protagonist, and the term *autobiographism* for the tendency of an author to write about herself or himself in any genre.[3] And last, how might women's life writings challenge the current canon of autobiography constructed in literary histories and genre theory, and the perspectives underwriting it?

I want to develop the proposition that Pellizzi's defensive response to women's autobiographical discourses is symptomatic of the anxiety produced among the critical establishment by the different forms of female self-construction envisioned, which threatened the authority of male discourses on femininity as well as on masculinity. I suggest that Negri and Deledda write both within and against the conventions of formal autobiography—a genre that traditionally safeguards patriarchal relations of power by retelling the stories of manhood—and thus make an especially strong claim to the authority of female self-authorship. The ways in which these autobiographers develop matrilineal structures, recast female models, and constitute themselves as rebel women forging their identities against traditional gender and class roles, customs, and beliefs articulate an "outlaw discourse" to masculinist cultural politics. My notion of this term draws on Jacques Derrida's paradigm of institutionalized generic laws and the territories they rule:

> As soon as the word "genre" is sounded, as soon as it is heard, as soon as one attempts to conceive it, a limit is drawn. And when a limit is established, norms and interdictions are not far behind: "Do," "Do not" says "genre," the word "genre," the figure, the voice, or the law of genre. . . . Thus, as soon as genre announces itself, one must respect a norm, one must not cross a line of demarcation, one must not risk impurity, anomaly or monstrosity. (1980, 203–4)

Expanding on Derrida's line of thought, I am interested in the generic and social laws that Deledda and Negri may cross, the prohibitions that they may break as they reinvent their literary identities. These autobiographical works furnish invaluable testimonies about female social subjects in the twenties and thirties, which have been overlooked by historical studies on the interwar period and Fascism perhaps because Negri and Deledda tell the stories of their childhoods and early formation as writers in the late 1800s. Such neglect likely derives from a misunderstanding of the relationship between the writing self and the recollected self, for as Sidonie Smith (1987) tells us, "the shape [that] . . . the autobiographer's narrative and dramatic strategies take, reveals more about the autobiographer's present experience of 'self' than about her past" (47). Therefore, the materials that Negri and Deledda select for representation, invention, and amplification, and especially the meanings attributed to them, inscribe the configurations of gendered subjectivity as the authors re-create the self in the years between the wars. By examining the symbolic importance of their rebellious female self-images within the context of the changing sociopolitical dynamics, as the Fascist movement gains popularity and Mussolini establishes his conservative dictatorship, we can theorize how the writers' politics of autobiography may have functioned as "agents" of social change among the modern reading public.

The practice of testing new theories of autobiography against writings by both male and female authors, in order to study the genre through the interpretative category of sexual difference, would expand the directions of inquiry outlined in studies of the 1980s. Theorists of formal autobiography in Italy have increasingly focused on this genre's relation to different forms of autobiographical writing and to other genres in order to gain a better understanding of its complex codes and functions. Andrea Battistini (1986) articulates this project of mapping the "autobiographical universe," which charts the genre's "possible diffractions, multiplying their combinative variants situated at their intersections with related genres" (24). Among others who emphasize the malleability of autobiography, Paolo Briganti (1986) maintains that this narrative form constitutes an "ultragenre," which insinuates itself onto other experimental and traditional genres. He amply illustrates this claim with a compendium of strikingly different forms of autobiographical narratives written by such male authors as Gabriele D'Annunzio, Italo Svevo, Benedetto Croce, and Elio Vittorini. Though this particular approach in literary theory ostensibly embraces differences among autobiographical narratives while questioning rigid genre boundaries, it too often ignores the most obvious difference of all—sexual difference—and thus reinforces canonized gender boundaries.

Likewise, methods of representing the thematic and formal vicissitudes of autobiography in generic studies have facilitated the omission of women's autobiographical practices. The following summary admittedly runs the risk of perpetuating some assumptions about literary production between the wars that are now being questioned with the help of new critical theories. However, it highlights relations between male subjectivity and contemporary models of genre formation underpinning the canon and critical studies that represent autobiography as a male-identified enterprise. Scholars typically trace autobiography's "invasion" of the contemporary literary terrain back to the early 1900s and the avant-garde Vociani, attributing its irresistible appeal to the crisis of the novel, as perceived by such figures as Scipio Slataper, Giovanni Papini, Giovanni Boine, and Ardengo Soffici.[4] For these writers, among others, the conceptualization and practice of an autobiographical, self-reflective yet spontaneous, and, above all, lyrical art created possibilities for "authentic" expression of their own experiences of being, which, they disparaged, the novel's structure and codes had exhausted, a perspective I examine more closely in chapter 4. Not coincidentally, in critical and literary texts proponents of this aesthetic claimed autobiographical writing as a privileged site for giving poetic form to modern male subjectivity. The many diversified narratives of self produced by the Vociani, which challenged conventional distinctions between autobiography and autobiographism, strengthened a trend of male self-display in Italian culture, along with its attendant emphasis on personal mythos, individuality, and notions of masculine selfhood.[5] We can also read this textual reproduction of masculinity as a compensatory reaction to the breach of traditional gender boundaries performed by women's own projects of autobiography/autobiographism elaborated, for example, in Sibilla Aleramo's *Una donna* (A woman, 1906), Amalia Guglielminetti's poems in *Le seduzioni* (Seductions, 1909) and her article "Aridità sentimentale" (Emotional aridity, 1911), and Negri's *Le solitarie* (Solitary women, 1917), a collection of short stories inspired largely by women whom the author had known or encountered in her life's travels.

The tendency for literary histories and criticism to privilege the *prosa d'arte* as the most representative autobiographical form of the interwar years has also contributed to the deletion of women's forms of life writing from the canon. Extremely popular since the Vociani, the lyrical prose fragment flourished among artists in the Ronda (1919–1925) and Solaria (1926–1936) literary circles. Although the inspiration for the *prosa d'arte* frequently derived from the author's reflections on self and lived experience, the Rondisti and Solariani transfigured autobiographical content, aspiring to create a work of poetic beauty, memorable for the stylistic brilliance of its linguistic effects. This ideal is reconcilable with the highly influential Crocean concept of autonomous art, whereby art must transcend the personal, social, and historical spheres if it is to attain poetic beauty and truth. Thus, traditional accounts tend to interpret the "private" nature of such writing and its insistent concern with stylistic refinement as a withdrawal into the self, away from the social and political realities of daily life during the dictatorship.

The gaps in such conventional constructions of autobiography's development in the 1900s become evident by rereading literary works by women and commentary by critics written in the twenties and thirties, the latter of which is concerned, if not preoccupied, with the autobiographical practices employed widely by female authors. The responses that female life writings elicited clearly inscribe the divergencies between the poetics of autobiography elaborated by women and that of their male counterparts, while identifying the so-called pathognomonic features evidenced by forms of female self-representation and expression. Since the study of autobiography as a genre is a fairly recent development, it is understandable that critics of the interwar period did not make entirely systematic distinctions when applying the term *autobiografia*. When commentators speak of *l'autobiografia femminile,* they frequently refer to the common practice of using autobiographical materials for literary creation in fiction and poetry. Such general observations are valuable nonetheless. They provide a critical framework for examining the conditions in which women produced their autobiographies and for assessing how their narratives relate to the dominant autobiographical discourse shaped by the Vociani, Rondisti, and Solariani.

For critics of the interwar years in general, but particularly for those propounding the tenets of pure art, the most polemical aspect of women's autobiographical practices is the authors' tendency to reveal too much about themselves and their experiences of female being in its sexual, psychological, and emotional dimensions. The sustained endeavors of literary women to speak veraciously of modern female identity with images and expressive forms of their own devising purportedly break the rules of decorum and art, raising issues about the nature of artistic sincerity and how it functions in autobiography and as a measure of literary value. Examining this complex subject, Giuseppe Ravegnani brings to light how the female writers' conceptualization of sincerity in autobiography transgresses the dominant, Crocean concept of artistic sincerity. In fact, Ravegnani's discussion recalls Croce's arguments on the distinctions between artistic sincerity (one and the same with art) and personal sincerity, a state or quality in daily life that Croce elaborated in his 1906 article on Negri's poetry, titled "Ada Negri." There, he insisted on the autonomy of art from other disciplines and human activities, concluding that pragmatic values kill art, and therefore literary writing intended to critique forms of social injustice is unartful and artistically insincere.

Like Croce, Ravegnani cautions those who mistake a kind of "excessive, unnecessary autobiographical exhibitionism" for literary sincerity.

The tendency to privilege the ideal of creating a veracious portrayal of the full range of lived experiences and emotions blurs the distinction between life and art and also confuses the criteria for assessing a work's aesthetic value, especially, he points out, when the writer is a woman. Using Sibilla Aleramo's writing as a representative example of the concept of sincerity elaborated in women's literature of the interwar years, in the following discussion Ravegnani explores the problems raised by women's writings of self:

> In some cases, this documentary and cruel sincerity, through the effort put into being and remaining a crystal clear, precise mirror of the I moving it, most often ends up achieving negative meanings and results. That is, in the strong-willed excess of this effort, sincerity tends to become both unnatural and decorative. In fact, sincerity, and especially every form of female sincerity, can turn out in art like any ornamental motif of rhetoric.... The entirely feminine, narcissistic courage to confess something that is perhaps perverse or secret, or even physiological, doesn't at all exclude the dangerous existence of a real, typical rhetoric of sincerity. (1930, 60–61)

On the surface Ravegnani speculates about the risk of producing a rhetoric of sincerity, which women's narratives run by insisting on veracity on all occasions, with little or no simulation. He is also ruffled by Aleramo's unabashed writings about her love affairs with prominent artists of the time. More important, Ravegnani's characterization of female self-representation (cruel, perverse, secret, and so on) registers a general uneasiness provoked, I suggest, by the textual body of desires, experiences, and aspirations that women's life writings put into plain view, which impugns the idealized image of woman and, likewise, the binary logic of gender difference on which feminine and masculine roles depend. In his introductory remarks, Ravegnani notes the disturbing tendency of women's literature to "put on pants" instead of arraying itself in the romantic garb of traditional femininity (55–56). Moreover, the reader's expectation for truth in autobiography—a form of truth that denotes a faithfulness to the particular story of self told by the author more than facticity—strengthens the authority and transformative power of women's autobiography.

In addition to "excessive" self-disclosure, the most significant issues raised in commentary that differentiate the aesthetic of female life writings from prevailing trends in autobiographical discourse between the wars include the authors' attention to the material conditions within and against which women forge their identities, and the pragmatic value of their literature. While writings by the Rondisti and Solariani tend to employ private memories and thoughts to illuminate "universal" themes, pursuing the beauty of pure poetic expression, the confessions, remembrances, and intimate reflections composed by women writers generally focus on concerns specific to the female-gendered subject and her relationship to society. This model of life storytelling led such critics as Croce, Pellizzi, and Ravegnani to claim that women's autobiographical narratives were bound to the materiality of female being and thus flawed by a failure (or refusal) to transcend.[6] But the different practices of autobiography employed by Aleramo, Guglielminetti, and Negri, for instance, can also be interpreted as modes of challenging the conventional literary imperative of the universal, which destabilize the notion of the universal human subject and the aesthetic preserving its authority. These writers, among others, create a space for putting into discourse alternative perceptions of life and society, embedded in personal history. Such representations of female self-knowledge, as Sidonie Smith and Julia Watson (1992) explain, "have the potential to celebrate through counter-valorization another way of seeing, one unsanctioned, even unsuspected, in the dominant culture surround" (xx). The stories that women writers tell of female self-creation, undertaken in the face of institutionalized mechanisms of gender and class oppression, articulate possibilities for personal and social change, a purpose that distinguishes their autobiographical projects from those of male authors of their time.

Matrilineal Genealogies: Lifelines of Women's Making

Although writings by male commentators voiced hostility toward the autobiographical practices of women's literary production in general, Negri's *Stella mattutina* received unanimous acclaim among critics and readers alike. Following its original publication in 1921, this autobiography became a best-seller during the years of Fascism, with three Italian editions published between 1927 and 1932, and an English translation in 1930. While praising Negri's autobiography as a "masterpiece" of Italian literature, scholars reached remarkable consensus about the qualities of the work that fulfilled the ideals of sincerity and truth, as they conceived of them. Pellizzi (1929), for example, applauds the "sense of loss and honest, sincere sadness" permeating Negri's contemplation of her life (75), while Stanis Ruinas (1930) presents this "nontraditional autobiography" as an example of "sweet, profound poetry" (78) that, in his estimation, appeals to all readers. Similarly, Ravegnani's extensive analysis of *Stella mattutina* credits the author with creating a "miraculous" union between the humble content and style, concluding that with Dinin (whom he calls Ninin), "alongside human truth, Negri also found the reunited truth of style" (1930, 85).

Also worthy of remark is the 1921 review that Mussolini, then an accomplished journalist and aspiring political leader of the National Fascist Party, wrote for the newspaper *Il popolo d'Italia,* which he edited. This assessment, and more so his foreword to the 1940 edition of the autobiography (republished in 1945 and 1952), indicates a greater undecidability than we might expect among the positions articulated by Mussolini in his inventions of Fascist ideology, political practice, and private life. Indeed, these commentaries, separated by nearly twenty years, brim with praise for the delicate portrait of the woman's struggle to overcome personal and socioeconomic adversities and to succeed as an author. We must also remember that Negri became Mussolini's friend and correspondent and was the first woman member of the Academy of Italy, an influential Fascist cultural institution.[7] The exaltation of the mother figure, poised atop a pedestal crafted in the architecture of Fascist rhetoric, makes it fairly easy to understand the appeal that Negri's delineation of her mother continued to hold for Mussolini in 1940, more than a decade into the demographic campaign. However, the substantive discursive space that Negri dedicates to individualism and nonconformity as significant principles of self-fashioning and her critique of gender and class injustice hardly seem reconcilable with the notion of the female collective prescribed in the regime's programs and propaganda. In like manner, Negri's support of Mussolini, as friend and a leader for Italian political life, denotes ambivalence shading the author's politics of daily living and literature. Certainly, in speeches, in social welfare organizations, and in leisure-time groups Mussolini ostensibly designed roles for modern women's incorporation into the national public sphere. But these discursive and material apparatuses also encompassed unmistakably conservative models of woman and femininity, of the kind that Negri opposed in her activism for feminist and socialist causes at the turn of the century and consistently critiqued in *Stella mattutina,* as well as her short fiction.[8]

As I intend to show, Negri's representation of her mother and her recollected self transgresses the patriarchal model of the woman-mother constructed in scientific discourses of the late 1800s, later theorized and disseminated in Fascist writings. Hence, I want to suggest that the narrative strategies that this autobiographer crafts to achieve a contemplative voice and delicate tone mask the subversive components of her life story, which could induce changes in the body politic. The veil of calm self-reflection is created largely by the form of narrator chosen. Though Negri, like the majority of authors in the interwar years, frequently uses a first-person narrator in prose and poetry of an autobiographical nature, here she speaks in the first person only in the unforgettable opening lines, "I see—back in time—a little girl. Thin, standing straight, agile. But I can't say what her face really looks like" (1966, 217).[9] She then shifts to the third person for the remaining narrative. Negri's adoption of the third person strengthens the authority of voice and creates the sense of reflective distance between the narrator and the content that critics of the twenties and thirties found so appealing. It also tempers the stylistic lyricism, as well as the narrative intensity created by the author's use of the present tense for her story, broken only on rare occasions. Most notably, this occurs when the narrator retells the stories that the girl heard from her mother about Donna Augusta and Donna Teodosia, and in the passages that flash forward, beyond the autobiography's chronological frame (the 1870s and 1880s), giving us a glimpse of her brother's dissipating life and lonely death. Negri's choice of narrator also draws attention to the process of re-creating this particular story of her childhood and to the difference between the narrator and the girl of her past as a distinct persona, a phenomenon of doubling that is common to autobiography, regardless of the form of narrator.[10]

The structure that Negri creates to organize her autobiography executes a radical project of female entitlement as she locates her own development within a matrilineal genealogy constituted by her grandmother, a poor servant, and her mother, a worker in a woolen factory, whose legacy Negri then passes on to her own daughter Bianca in the book's dedication. By structuring the story of her childhood and adolescence in this manner, Negri alters the conventions of autobiography and history. As the Milan Women's Bookstore Collective points out in *Sexual Difference* (1990),

> the root *gen* in words such as *genus, genealogy, generation* characterizes words traditionally associated with birth as a social event, and, strictly speaking, it refers to the legitimate birth of free male individuals. In our culture ... the representation of the mother-daughter relationship is missing; a mother always carries a son in her arms. (25)

Negri's inventing of the mother-daughter relation as a vertical axis and thematic matrix thus reconfigures the space of autobiography, breaking the patriarchal interdictions of culture and society, a point I will elaborate shortly.

Stella mattutina belongs to the tradition of autobiography by successful literary figures who narrate the story of their formation as writers. But this text is also a valuable example of female working-class autobiography that engages directly with interwar politics of gender and class. Theorizing the workings of memory and supplement, Luisa Passerini (1987) provides a critical framework for assessing the interconnectedness of the personal and collective histories that Negri re-presents. "Memory," Passerini explains, "gives prominence to moments of individual and collective decision-making. . . . Memory tends, in fact, to elaborate what is narrated until it becomes meaningful in a contemporary context" (127). As Negri wrote her autobiography between 1919 and 1921, Italy saw volatile gender and class warfare as numbers of young demobilized soldiers and male degree-holders attempted to recapture labor positions lost to women during World War I and to win over new ones.[11] Amid embattled competition for employment, outright aggression toward women workers ranged from verbal to physical attacks, as Mariolina Graziosi (1995) documents in her study of writings published in the press in the years following World War I. Articles in daily newspapers and women's publications reported such slogans as "Women's employment is causing men's unemployment," "Women go home, because home is the place where you belong," and the pithy "Down with women"

(Graziosi 1995, 28). In addition to demonstrations staged by men to protest women's employment in banks, post offices, and even public education, in some cases threats of violence made it necessary for women to have escorts to and from the workplace. The violent tenor of both gender and class relations was compounded by the spread of Fascist *squadristi* in urban and rural sites. Gauging the material effects wreaked by Fascist attacks, Alexander De Grand (1989) notes that from January to June of 1921 alone, Fascist groups destroyed "119 labor chambers, 107 cooperatives, and 83 peasant league offices" (31).

Thus contextualized, Negri's personal history exhibits clear associations with collective sociopolitical issues. Her autobiography, spanning three generations of women, illuminates the intersections of gender and class struggle with identity formation as she reelaborates the hardships and injustices defining the relations of grandmother, mother, and daughter to the upper-class land and factory owners they serve. The importance the author attaches to her working-class origins is clearly indicated by the name she chooses to denote her childhood self, Dinin. Described by Anna Folli (1988) as "little more than a clear sound" (184), this name bears the inscription of the child's class on her identity; it resonates like the Italian word denoting the sound of a doorbell, *dindìn*, a constant reminder that the young girl must open the gate for the masters of the estate. Negri's earliest recollections of her childhood also bring to the foreground her location in the hegemonic class structure. As she plays games with the estate owners' three "beautiful" girls (with three "beautiful" names!), Dinin is driven by the desire and need to win, precisely, Negri tells us, because she is poor. In the estate garden, while Dinin takes in the beauty of blooming lilies, the mistress of the house intrudes and forbids the child to touch the flowers, implying that the little gatekeeper has stolen something, the appreciation of beauty, to which she is not entitled. The double marginalizations of Dinin as a female and a member of the working class converge on the subject of writing, when Negri recalls the rich woman's accusation that what the girl has written contains words stolen from male authors. This indictment leaves a lasting impression; Dinin feels as if she will always have the heavyset woman there to "tear the notebook out of her hand and tell her: This isn't yours! You lied" (224).

Negri's strategic contrasting of traditional and anticonformist female images forces us to reassess the conventional critical position that she, and women writers in general, merely reproduced patriarchal models of femininity in the interwar years. It is accurate to say that the autobiographer portrays dominant feminine roles. Yet her depictions create a rather dismal tableau, showing the need for inventing a different range of social models. This aspect of Negri's work is best illustrated by the suggestive dream sequence where Dinin loses her way and encounters characters representing traditional life paths: Daria, the way of passion; Augusta, the way of love; and Drusilla, the way of wifely affection. Valorizing her own talents, hopes, and aspirations, the heroine refuses to conform with such roles and chooses to embark on a path of her own making.

In both the genre of autobiography and in the broader context of literary discourses produced in the twenties and thirties, the life model of the mother created by Negri also appears extraordinary. First, from its beginnings the autobiographical tradition conceives the claim to the authority of authorship—of self and literature—in a paternalistic scheme; the process of reimagining the autobiographical "I" is played out in relation to the fathers, real and symbolic. Therefore, Negri's manner of designing her formation of literary identity in terms of filiative recognition of her mother, Vittoria, represents a significant innovation. Certainly, the resultant genealogy is not "positive" in some essentialist way, by mere virtue of its matrilinearity. However, the meanings that Negri draws in the portrait of her mother illustrate the crucial role of the maternal figure as a primary referent for the author's sense of corporeality and "symbolic placement." In contrast to the image of the mother in Deledda's *Cosima*, this autobiographer's re-creation of the mother-daughter relationship offers an example of feminine psychic and artistic generativity, whose features recast the traditional markers of passivity and self-sacrifice associated with the "cult of the mother."[12] By paying tribute to the mother, this autobiography may have appealed to more conservative readers. At the same time, the nuances of the maternal image show how the narrator attaches value to the woman's industriousness, intelligence, artistic power, and lively spirit, which belie her physical appearance, prematurely aged by years of hard physical labor and economic hardships. Also noteworthy is the way in which the author recasts the mother as a sexual subject whose body and potential desires register not fear in the daughter, but a sense of connectedness.

This is not to say that the mother-daughter relationship is unproblematic for the autobiographer. The narrator reflects ambivalently on whether the mother has given too much, and whether she can ever repay her, echoing one of the concerns that Aleramo examined so acutely in *A Woman*.[13] Yet by looking at the "minimal" differences as they emerge in Negri's representation we see how the memories and imagery she employs recast the maternal model. In Aleramo's autobiography, for example, the mother, likened to the Madonna, performs a key function as she exemplifies how maternal self-sacrifice and silence perpetuate female submission and servitude, embedding destructive tendencies in both male and female offspring. Vittoria also makes sacrifices for Dinin. Yet the mother's acts of devotion, aimed at fostering Dinin's concept of self, do not appear to threaten the terms of Vittoria's personal and social identities. For example, she provides economic support so that Dinin can complete her education to become a teacher and attain financial and intellectual independence. Vittoria thus makes it possible for her daughter to pursue the vocation of writer, a profession that was still quite exceptional for women in Italy of the late 1800s, though by the 1920s many working women shared this dream.[14] Negri's images of the mother-daughter relation seem to recognize filiative ties while maintaining the integrity of differences between women, as highlighted in the following passage:

> Her mother is the only one who can come into her reality without upsetting her. So unlike her, but she needs her for her sense of being in the world; together they form one of those monotonous but harmonious duets, third note high and third low, that, sung by the common people, fill the countryside with peaceful happiness. (236)

The autobiographer thus avoids collapsing diversified determinants of female social identity into the category of the feminine or the maternal.

Negri problematizes the contradictions between the life's vocation she shapes for herself and socially mandated female gender roles with parallel structures that dramatize the resultant sense of duality. Fashioning metaphors engendered by the female body and life course (perhaps one

of those specifically female, physiological "confessions" to which Ravegnani alluded), the autobiographer blurs the boundaries between life and
literature through the sequencing and representation of the girl's passage into womanhood and passage into poetry. Dinin's experience of approaching menarche is evocatively foreshadowed with water imagery as
she and her mother watch the River Adda rise and flow over its banks, an
image that has multiple connotations—the flow of menstrual blood and
fertility, the passage of time, a sense of loss and fear, as well as cleansing
properties suggesting the potentially ongoing re-creation of self. Indeed,
at the sight of her own blood, "purple, thick, warm, with a smell that
almost makes her crazy" (245), Dinin rebels against the female script of
romantic love, wifehood, and motherhood conventionally symbolized
by this passage. Shortly thereafter, Negri portrays another transformation, heralded by Dinin's "penetration" of poetry "blood and soul," and
articulates a different range of female possibilities for wealth, joy, love,
and birth made possible by artistic life.

As is common in formal autobiography, Negri vividly describes the
influence that such classic poets as Homer, Giacomo Leopardi, and
Dante had on her formal education. Yet against this glorious history of
literary creation she invents a different form of intertextuality, privileging the lessons of art and life learned from her mother, whose traces are
embedded in the literary identity that Dinin fashions for herself. The
writer puts to the printed page the stories she heard her mother tell over
and over. Anna Folli (1988) has pointed out the significance of these stories as representations of differences between the relations to language of
the three generations of women. The grandmother speaks primarily dialect, whereas the mother tells her stories in clear, spoken Italian, and the
daughter expresses her stories with the written word, contributing to literary Italian. The female images and influence of Vittoria's storytelling
also merit attention. The narrator tells us that all of the stories recounted
by Vittoria are about real people she has known or heard about. In these
life stories, powerful for their verisimilitude, Vittoria brings alive such
women as Miss Vivien Hall, the courageous Lady Teodosia, and Donna
Augusta, who each refashion, if not break, normative gender roles. The
image of Donna Augusta is particularly complex, for though she gives
herself to passion, she transgresses the symbolic laws of the castle through

her love affair and then wills herself to die. Negri's employment of such rebel figures in a network of female identification makes new positions available to women in the symbolic. The artistry of Vittoria's storytelling shapes her daughter's literary tastes and refines her consciousness of social injustice and suffering, as symbolized by the wail of Donna Augusta, a wail that "her mother gave her. . . . she planted it in the roots of her soul" (267). These elements are articulated in Negri's own aesthetic, which confers value on lived experience as a source of art in her poetry and prose. Likewise, the autobiographer elucidates the origins of her socialistic notion of writing with an episode from her mother's life. The sense of injustice that Dinin feels when the factory owners fail to give any compensation for an injury Vittoria sustains at work inspires the young writer to compose a poem, "Mano nell'ingranaggio" (Hand caught in the gear). One of the few references to her own writing, this passage dramatizes the creative process of transforming experience into poetry, a project that she conceives as a socially useful practice (278).

In the conclusion of *Stella mattutina*, as Negri depicts Dinin's impending departure from people and places of her childhood, she elaborates motifs associated with the journey, which function at the literal and symbolic levels of interpretation. The images arising from Dinin's quest for knowledge about herself and who she is in the world form a divided subject: the woman and the other "true" self, whose nonunitary character is conveyed by the fragmented linguistic forms employed. Negri's representation of the artist's persona that Dinin carries within her creates an exceptional metaphor for the female writer with the image of lava, as we see here:

> The Other One. The True One. That no one can see in her face, not even her mother: inviolable, inviolate: without a beginning, without an end: rich with an inextinguishable heat equal to subterranean flows. Misfortunes, humiliations of every kind can happen to the pale, poor Dinin; but the Other One, the True One is above everything and everyone else: she's the queen incognito whom nothing can hurt. She feels her, sometimes, reveal and impose herself over the circumscribed breathing walking person, with the power of a jet of lava. (283–84)

While recalling the flow of water and menstrual blood that signaled the heroine's passages into womanhood and art, this explosive stream of lava

represents an indomitable power to create and to destroy. With its natural association with the volcano, the site where "the Elements of air, fire,
water and earth are intermingled and transformed" (Cirlot 1971, 361), the
lava may symbolize the woman writer as an unrestrainable agent of social change.

Complementing this introspective analysis, Dinin's journey to the
country portrays her understanding of selfhood in a metaphysical context. Throughout this autobiography, Negri employs the garden as a
structural artifice and symbol; from the *Giardino del tempo* (the garden
of time) of her earliest childhood memories, with its forbidden lilies and
inviting hiding places, Dinin travels to several gardens (at the cemetery,
in the story of Augusta, at her teacher's house).[15] With the passage of the
seasons in the garden, the author also expresses a cyclical notion of time
that resonates in her representation of cycles in the female life course,
and of generations of women reaching across time. Here Dinin reaches
an open landscape. As the woman gazes out over the countryside and
horizon, which spread before her with no boundaries and only the
morning star as guide, her declaration, "I'm me, I'm here," affirms her
way of knowing and being in space and time. Although this journey
marks the young woman's separation from her mother, the author celebrates the strengths of their affiliative ties through the representation of
the pivotal role the mother has played in the daughter's formation of identity in society and art. Moreover, I propose that Negri's autobiography,
when read through Freud's notion of introjection, creates a thought-
provoking system privileging the symbolic power of the mother. In contrast to identification, an original emotional connection between subject
and object, Freud (1921) theorizes introjection as the process whereby
the object is introjected into the ego. As Kathleen Woodward (1991)
points out in her discussion of Roy Shafer's work on this subject, "the
motive of introjection [is] *the continuation of the relationship* with the
object by putting the object inside" (104). Thus, in her analysis of Eva
Fige's *Waking*, Woodward suggests how, by internalizing the mother, the
daughter creates "a maternal supplement to her body and being" (107).
Along similar lines, in the process of autobiographical production,
undertaken by Negri soon after Vittoria's death, the author first internal-
izes the mother, performing a re-creation in psychic space sustained by

memory, desires, and needs, which she then projects onto the "immortal" space of literary discourse.

Reinventing the Terms of Rebel Identity

Grazia Deledda's autobiography *Cosima* represents an important model of interwar life writing for its indisputable artistry, and also for the invaluable opportunity it provides to examine the configurations of female subjectivity as constituted in the later years of the Fascist dictatorship. A remarkable example of old-age writing that belies the association of late life and waning creativity, Deledda's story about her childhood and how she forged her identity through a commitment to a literary vocation was first published with the title *Cosima, quasi Grazia* (Cosima, almost Grazia) in the journal *Nuova antologia*. It appeared a few months after her death in 1936, when the demographic and rural campaigns were firmly in place, proffering the figure of the prolific countrywoman as a paradigm of health and happiness, a code explored in detail in my study on the politics of realism (chap. 4). Therefore, the forms of self-representation that Deledda employs to reconstruct her identity formation can tell us much about how this influential writer positioned herself in relation to the conservative ideology of woman as exemplary wife and mother, as well as the values of civil duty and obedience structuring the image of the model Fascist female subject in the national collective. There exists a range of models for women's cultural and social roles formulated in the orbit of official Fascist politics, as recent work by Barbara Spackman (1995) unquestionably demonstrates. In fact, reflecting on her own experience as a young girl growing up in the later years of the dictatorship, Lidia Menapace (1988) argues that the Fascist regime specifically proposed modern models of the woman journalist, the athlete, and the movie star among young females in order to compete with gender roles developed by the Catholic Church and in women's publications. Yet it is also true that the model of the intellectual, writing woman became a target for some cultural commentators who represented the model as deviant, useless. In fact, as early as 1922, the critic Luigi Tonelli proclaimed,

> Woman must be encouraged to live the right way, not to write literature. She must be helped to be a good wife and exemplary mother, not to be-

come an empty, useless 'celebrity.' This is passé, I know, but man's future lies in the sweet, sorrowful lap of Mary, not in the sterile, furious lap of Sappho or Aurora Dupin. (cited in Mondello 1987, 180)[16]

The exchanges between sociopolitical discourses and literary commentary were rarely so overt in the regime. Yet Tonelli's paternalistic interdiction articulates a sexual politics of culture aimed to guide women from the territory of artistic labor to the domestic sphere of reproductive labor.

By the time Deledda wrote her autobiography she had far surpassed "celebrity" status. In the course of her career this Sardinian author wrote more than thirty novels (many of which were published during Fascism), and some 250 short stories that appeared in the daily press, literary journals, and women's publications, earning her international acclaim. She received the Nobel Prize for Literature in 1926, marking a momentous event for women and men among the literary community. Underscoring the importance of Deledda's achievements, the writer Amalia Guglielminetti stated, "Honorable men, think for a moment about the fact that this human being who is making our value emerge from the shadows, this creature of genius, is a woman" (in M. Guglielminetti 1987, 151). I want to develop the proposition that, when situated within the specific sociohistorical conditions of the 1930s, the story of literary identity formation written by Deledda, a woman bearing exceptional cultural authority, may be read as an outlaw discourse that breaks the prohibitions of Fascist gender arrangements: the autobiographer reinscribes her initial refusal to conform with patriarchal laws devised to govern female gender roles and male-female relations of the late 1800s. After locating the features of Deledda's autobiography in relation to conventions of the genre, my examination focuses on the elements of thought, representation, and structure that constitute a discursive space of resistance to normative demands of the autobiographical tradition and gender ideology during Fascism.

Like Negri, Deledda narrates the story of her girlhood and early literary successes in the third person. With the especially patriarchal structure of Fascism in mind, we could reasonably interpret the author's adoption of this narrative form as a way of negotiating the heightened difficulties of speaking in the first person about intimately gratifying accomplishments and stinging disappointments incurred by her unconventional choice to make herself into a writer. And we should keep in mind the generally antagonistic position that male critics adopted toward self-display in women's writings. Deledda did not hesitate, however, to write short autobiographical pieces in the first person, as illustrated by "La Grazia" (Grace), for example. Published in the collection *Sole d'estate* (Summer sun, 1933), this story provides an earlier account of an episode in Deledda's autobiography, where the author reveals her experience of humiliation, shaken self-confidence, and, ultimately, revindication, precipitated by a scathing critique of her writing. Therefore, I propose that we may also read Deledda's deployment of the third person as a means to subvert patriarchal authority inscribed in the history of the genre's conventions. By writing in the third person, the author recalls the form of intellectual autobiography of the 1700s, which, as Marziano Guglielminetti (1986) explains, represented "an incomparable occasion for defining one's own function as a *man of culture* in the context of the 'republic of letters'" (140, emphasis added). When Deledda situates her autobiography within the illustrious tradition of this genre, she claims the "objective" authority that it bears for the story of her own formation as a prominent *woman of culture* in Italian literary life and also disrupts it as she engenders a different epistemological category formed by a matrilineal system of knowledge.

Although the adoption of the third-person narrator in *Cosima* (and in Negri's *Stella mattutina*) goes against the prevalent trend of first-person narration in interwar autobiographical writings, Deledda employs several practices that were typical of life storytelling. For instance, in the opening description of the house and neighborhood where Deledda grew up, the narrative voice unites the writer, narrator, and reader with the first-person plural possessive, referring to "our house," and later, "our young schoolgirl." Likewise, the narrative features a parsimonious use of personal interjections as well as language and temporal modes that call attention to the importance played by memory as the autobiographer reconstructs her history. The author emphasizes the process of remembering through deft shifts between verb tenses, which include the preterit, indicating events that belong chronologically to the distant past, having relatively less psychological or affective bearing on the autobiographical subject; the present perfect; and the present indicative, used to describe both historical events in Cosima's past and actions or states at the time of writing. In some cases these temporal modes serve to blur the distinctions between writer, narrator, and heroine, as illustrated by the following passage, which begins with the verb *knocked* in a tense denoting the remote past, and then, with the verb *remember*, suddenly shifts to the present:

> Six nights after Santus left someone knocked repeatedly on the door, very late. After a half century Cosima still remembers that beating little drum announcing a terrible event. She hears it still, pounding inside her heart; it is the most terrible sound she has ever heard, more mournful than one announcing death. (Deledda 1988, 52)[17]

Whereas verbs in the remote past enhance the magical atmosphere surrounding the "enchantments of childhood" and an archaic time with its own customs, beliefs, and stories, the shifts to the present tense convey a sense of immediacy and thereby capture the reader's attention. Thus, Deledda's use of tenses may indicate the relative importance that she attributes to events in her formation of identity. The majority of episodes portrayed in the present tense concern the author's literary and sexual growth, central poles of her developing self-concept. Among the most notable scenes are those about beginning her education at school, having her first idea to send a short story to the fashion magazine *Ultima moda* (Latest fashion), writing her first novel and stealing a liter of oil from her family in order to pay for mailing her manuscript, receiving the critical letter on her writing, being infatuated with Antonino in her girlhood, and having her moonlit interlude with Fortunio.

If, as some critics have argued, Fascism represents an exceptionally virulent type of patriarchal cultural formation, then it should not seem unreasonable to propose that Deledda's critical rewriting of traditional female roles upheld by the laws of patriarchy shaping social life in the late 1800s in the rural community of Nuoro assumes important political connotations in the Fascist regime of the 1930s. In the depictions of her mother and peasant women, Deledda inscribes the signs and symbols associated with the idealized model of wife and mother, yet she attaches new meanings to them. In the matrilineal line of descent created by

Deledda, which consists of her maternal grandmother, her mother, and herself, the mother embodies values traditionally prized by society and promoted during Fascism. But she also may be read as a nonproductive female model in much the same way as Aleramo's portrayal of her mother in *A Woman* (1906). Directly questioning the dominant values of female self-sacrifice and dedication to family and home, Deledda depicts the maternal figure as a "dutiful" wife and mother, whose scrupulous dedication to domestic responsibilities alone leaves her life intellectually and emotionally barren. Pale, her mouth withering, and her face no longer able to register happiness or sorrow, the mother becomes progressively withdrawn as she loses her children to death, disease, and a world vulnerable to the changes of modernity. While insisting on the importance of sexual development in all women's lives, a subject repressed in Fascist ideology, as Maria Antonietta Macciocchi argues (1976, 1979), the writer attributes her mother's state to a range of unfulfilled needs and desires. Joined in an affectionate, yet seemingly passionless marriage, the mother is infected by a sadness born mysteriously from, the narrator speculates,

> the fact that she had married without love a man twenty years older, who surrounded her with attention, who lived only for her and their family, but who could not give her any of the pleasure and sensual satisfaction that all young women need. And she wasn't able to get any outside the domestic circle: unable because of inborn sense of duty, superstition and prejudice, or also because of the absolute lack of opportunity. (29)

The mother is paradigmatic of other women sketched in the autobiography who tell their troubles to Cosima, imprisoned by the hopelessness of their immutable daily lives. This monotony, states Deledda, "of days without hope for any notable change weighed upon her spirits like an unjust condemnation—the ancient condemnation of women of her race" (87). Such images of the heroine, as well as other women belonging to the peasant and middle classes, create the sense of a preordained, inescapable destiny passed from mothers to daughters.

   In a unique way, Deledda materializes the prevailing cultural construction of female gender in the architectural structure of the domestic space where she grows up. An episode in the opening scenes of the autobiography offers a particularly compelling example. While exploring the different rooms in her home, and the treasures hidden away—a crystal plate representing art and beauty, foodstuffs piled high, and the rich store of books located, significantly, in her brothers' room—the little girl pauses, taking in the enormity of two stoves that stand as a grim reminder of the future solidly designed for her in the furnishings of the top floor. As we learn, "the little dreamer thinks that someday she will have to get married, like her mother, like her aunts, and live up there, fixing food on those stoves for herself and her family" (17). In contrast to these solid foundations of domesticity and the housebound existence they foretell, Deledda crafts the imagery of birds and flying—typically feminine symbols, according to Hélène Cixous (1981) and other feminist critics—as metaphors to convey the vicissitudes in Cosima's affective and psychic life. For example, after being ridiculed for her nonconformist behavior, she feels as if she were a swallow flying into a storm; later, hemmed in by her little garden, she walks like a captured eaglet waiting for the chance to fly off. Moreover, Deledda directly associates her writing and creativity with flying when she describes her newly finished novel as a bird trembling in her hands, which she must set free. In an especially important scene describing the young writer's attitudes toward self and the spiritual as well as physical image that she wants to project in a photograph in her novel, she transforms her body into a symbol of the desire to take flight and transcend the earthbound confines of the destiny imposed by family and community:

> Cosima's head emerged from a large fan of black ostrich feathers she had opened over her thin chest. It emerged as from a wing, which could also be symbolic. And her eyes had their oriental languor, a little exaggerated, her face all sweet, sly, partly from her own efforts and partly from the intelligent photographer's ability, who understood in his own way what he was dealing with. (81)

As the narrator confesses, Cosima's pose is struck to seduce, artistically and erotically, creating an association between nonconformist desires in art and love. Indeed, the aspiring author is crestfallen when, we discover, the novel becomes a success among women with bookish loves and "pretend ostrich feathers that cannot fly" (81).

Against the stage of prescriptive cultural models of femininity, Deledda invokes the figure of the female rebel to reinvent her process of self-making. This representational strategy raises some complicated issues regarding the potential of autobiography to uphold or upset hegemonic power relations. Doris Sommer (1988) outlines the parameters of this problem as she questions whether autobiography is

> the model for imperializing the consciousness of colonized peoples, re-placing their collective potential for resistance with a cult of individuality and even loneliness? Or is it a medium of resistance and counterdiscourse, the legitimate space for producing that excess which throws doubt on the coherence and power of an exclusive historiography? (111)

In weighing these two possibilities and their bearing on the interpretation of Deledda's text, we must also ask whether the "cult of individuality" functions as a stable construct or a historically and culturally contingent one. In Italy of the 1930s Mussolini, as Passerini (1991) shows, occupies a privileged position as the primary signifier of individualism, marked male, fueling the "cult of the duce" with a surfeit of visual images in the mass media and even on the face of urban architecture dotting the cityscapes. Accessing this form of male entitlement, autobiographic writings by Gabriele D'Annunzio and the Rondisti celebrate the trend of male self-display. At the same time, the maternal figure assumes high visibility in dominant discourses promoting the "cult of the mother." Furthermore, collectivity, and not individualism, formed the primary term of national identity that the Fascist regime endeavored to construct in its unions, leisure associations, welfare organizations, and children's groups.

Therefore, what meanings might Deledda create when she explicitly names herself the *piccola ribelle* (little rebel), an act echoing with the regional tradition of brigands as a manifestation of political insurgence? What functions could her rebellious enactment of individualistic practices, disavowing the imperatives of sexual and social life, perform in the broader discursive field? Does the female rebel image fashioned by the author, a potentially strong symbol of resistance, decline into the negativity of the Other as Cosima is cast onto the fringes of community? In fact, the autobiographer describes childhood ventures in daily life, literature, and love as incursions that situate her as an outlaw in the community. The pressures consequently brought to bear on her are clearly outlined as she recalls the responses elicited when her brother Andrea and fellow townspeople come to know that she writes stories:

> When he found out that his little sister Cosima, that little fourteen-year-old girl, who appeared younger and who seemed as natural and shy as a baby deer, was instead a kind of rebel against all customs, traditions and practice of the family, and even of the human race, Andrea took her under his protection and tried to help her. . . . Since she had begun writing poems and short stories everyone began to look at her with a certain suspicious amazement, if not to openly make fun of her and predict a dire future for her. (58)

By putting words to the page, the young girl breaks prohibitions operating in the social and symbolic spheres. At the most obvious level of interpretation, Cosima's dedication of time to writing deviates from the normative occupations assigned to female children—taking care of domestic chores, learning to cook, sew, and manage the household. In the Nuoro community, Cosima's writing takes on shades of the criminal, a sign of almost pathological moral disorder that dashes possibilities for marriage. More important, she breaks with the tradition of orality as determined by gender, class, and ethnicity. Several passages in *Cosima* relate the stories and legends told aloud by peasant men and women. Her father was an accomplished poet, composing his works in a Sardinian dialect. But the townspeople, especially the older women, view novels as "forbidden books." To write stories, and to publish them for all to see, signals the girl's claim to symbolic expression, and her challenge to the Law of the Fathers.

Although structured on rebellion and nonconformity, the model of self-fashioning that Deledda envisions may avoid the negativity of a purely oppositional stance by positing an ethics of self-guidance and responsibility. Cosima pursues her own ambitions, assuming the authorship of her life and literature. The autobiographer represents writing as an important process of self-affirmation and growth, which enables Cosima to escape the narrowness of her experience. The following passage exemplifies the importance Deledda attaches to writing as a constitutive element of her identity and offers an interesting representation of autobiographism in the woman's creative process. While others tend to their chores, Cosima

> throws herself into the world of her fantasies and writes, writes, writes out of a physical need, like other adolescents run through garden paths or go to a forbidden place, and if they are able, to a rendezvous of love.
> Even she, in her writing, arranges love rendezvous. Hers is a story where the protagonist is herself, the world is hers, the blood of the characters, their naiveté, their innocent follies are hers. (78)

What this description also demonstrates is the intersection of creativity and sexual desire in the configuration of subjectivity, a topic I explore shortly.

Although Deledda's descriptions of her formation as a writer, including her early literary successes and admiring reception among female and male readers, largely create an image of a steadfast, satisfying dedication to her work, the author also reveals the turmoil produced by her defiant devotion to making herself into a writer. Most notably, the autobiographer recalls a long letter critiquing her fiction. The retelling of this episode is significant both for the meaning Deledda attributes to the letter and for the language she employs, which echoes conservative discourses on woman produced in Fascist writings. The anonymous critic admonishes the young woman writer to fulfill her "true" destiny:

> Go back, go back, my little compulsive scribbler, to the confines of your family garden to cultivate carnations and honeysuckle. Go back to making socks, to growing up and waiting for a good husband, to preparing yourself for a healthy future with familial affection and motherhood. (88)

The images invoked—home, family life, gardening, knitting—had unquestionably regained currency as staple ingredients of femininity in conservative circles of the Fascist regime. Although this experience shakes the woman's notion of self, a subsequent revelation—a familiar trope in the tradition of intellectual autobiography—fosters a renewed commitment to her own way of being and knowing, as she decides to rely on no one but herself.

This outspoken paradigm of individualism has significance for how we think about the text's relations to notions of the individual and the collective, and the reading public. First of all, as Mariolina Graziosi

(1995) argues, Fascist thinkers conceived of women's personal and moral development in terms of fostering a conscious commitment to collective goals sanctioned by the state, whereby they achieved citizenship in the regime. A 1929 article published in *Il giornale della donna,* a women's magazine that became an official publication for Fascist women's groups late in 1929, succinctly expresses the position on female individualism and the collective:

> In the Liberal paradigm an individual is nothing but an individual. We Fascists . . . must make every effort to transform this individual into a personality. This is what we all ought to strive for. And we have to convince women that they should not rest on their natural "individuality." Once their personality is achieved, we should not deny them the opportunity to act on the basis of all their potential. Once the personality is achieved, which is the ability to be part of the state, women can contribute usefully as well. (cited in Graziosi 1995, 39–40)

Thus, with the representation of Cosima's strengthened resolve to pursue her aspirations, fashioning a life based on her own talents and principles, Deledda sets a productive paradigm of female individualism against the fascistized model of subjectivity. Not merely an example of the "exceptional" individual, the image of the rebel individualist also has a purchase on the collective imagination, for it belongs to a long-standing oral tradition of "disorderly women," who, as Passerini (1989) tells us, "in some way overturn gender roles" (191). To assess the importance of such female images, Passerini continues, we must recognize "the symbolic, rather than simply reflective, character of representations, and, at the same time, . . . their potential influence on forms of actual behavior" (191).

Another important dimension of Deledda's life story concerns the writer's formation as a subject of outlaw(ed) erotic desire. Although the depiction of a girlhood infatuation with the handsome, educated Antonino largely conforms with idealized images of romantic first love, the attraction between Cosima and Fortunio can hardly be understood within the traditional conventions of romantic literature or modern sexual relations described in fiction or advice columns written for girls in the thirties. The narrator notes that Fortunio, illegitimate, too poor to pursue his education and thus to secure a decent job, was lame from birth, with a twisted leg weighed down by an "ironlike shoe." We should not forget, however, that Fortunio, also a poet of sorts, intuits the young woman's poetic sensibilities and recognizes her talent. Likewise, given the importance the author attaches to her rebel identity, the figuration of Fortunio, an outcast by birth marked by his physical difference (or "deformity," if viewed from the townspeople's perspective), as an object of desire makes perfect sense. After all, they are in some ways kindred spirits. But more significant, Cosima's sexual encounter with Fortunio, whose face is described in terms of a delicate, feminine beauty, highlights the intersection of eros and creativity in the writer's process of individuation. In an insightful analysis of this topic, Neria De Giovanni (1987) examines the special powers that Fortunio possesses precisely by virtue of his lame foot. This particular physical trait, she tells us as she draws on the work by Tilde Giani Gallino, links Fortunio with archetypal male figures—gods, mystics, magicians—whose limping gait sets them apart from ordinary men and may, for its rhythm, suggest the feminine cyclical principle associated with menstruation, the moon, and the seasons. Possessing an unexpectedly complex system of codes, the foot can also represent power and fertility. Thus, De Giovanni concludes, in the enchanting scene of sexual initiation, consummated by a kiss under the moonlit night, Fortunio functions as a "magical-erotic archetype" (1987, 40), thereby elucidating the relation between eros and creative life encoded in Deledda's construction of rebel identity.

The realm of magic, mystery, legend, and dream occupies a privileged position in Deledda's sense of literary identity, as situated in a network of affiliative and ethnic ties. In this respect, and as a specifically female structure of autobiography, Deledda's representation of herself as her maternal grandmother's granddaughter merits attention. In her initial description of how the grandmother appears to the child, the author associates certain physical traits and unique powers with this figure. The grandmother's small, childlike stature and mythic aura remind her granddaughter of the little women, or fairies, of local popular legend, said to inhabit prehistoric dwellings carved out of stone on the rocky Sardinian landscape. More important, the aging woman evokes a bodily sense of memories belonging to a past life, whose residues reawaken and recede into Cosima's subconscious mind. Later in Cosima's childhood and adolescence, the scent of newly opened flowers or the damp woods, and the images of age-old cooking utensils or peasant women spattered with newly pressed olive oil, evoke the same dizziness and sensation of remembering through the body, thus conjuring up the grandmother's spiritual presence and symbolic power. Furthermore, as illustrated by the two dreams where the grandmother appears to Cosima, this figure enables the writer to achieve a deeper understanding of herself and her art. A source of knowledge, she reveals the history of Cosima's grandfather, dispelling the myths surrounding his origins and life. And though the grandmother's eyes reflect the dream spirit shared by Cosima and her grandfather, she alone awakens in her granddaughter the world of imagination, legends, and memory. As Patrizia Zambon (1989) points out, these elements form the source of Deledda's literary creation (315). Here, then, as in *Stella mattutina,* the autobiographer appears to create, though in a strikingly different way, a female-gendered system of knowledge, signs, and meanings that inspires and distinguishes her aesthetic.

Although some critical commentary has characterized the open-ended conclusion of *Cosima* as unsatisfyingly reticent, Deledda's decision to end her autobiography with memories of her journey to Cagliari in 1899 has significant ideological implications.[18] Certainly the scope of Deledda's work, to focus only on the part of her life best illustrating how she achieved her success as a writer, conforms with a common practice in autobiography that, according to Franco Fido (1986), dates back to the early 1800s (170). At the same time, the author refuses to provide traditional forms of closure, for instance, with her marriage in 1900 to Palmiro Modesani. Instead, Deledda's autobiography retains its power as an outlaw discourse, by rupturing conventional Oedipal and social scripts with a form of what Rachel Blau DuPlessis (1985) calls "writing beyond the ending" (x). She represents her journey as both a literal flight from the restrictive town life of Nuoro, and also as the beginning of a lifelong quest for personal and artistic growth. The heroine looks out over an open horizon of future possibilities, with the sea symbolizing a transitional phase in Cosima's life. Though the young writer's realization of her desire for greater involvement in the world of art entails separation from her mother, Deledda portrays the ongoing affective and psychic importance of her relationship with her grandmother and mother. At the sight of a man with "oriental" eyes, the young woman experiences the sensations produced by her grandmother's spiritual presence. Moreover, Deledda presents her act of self-affirmation as a new, productive model for fulfilling the daughter's wish to please her mother, by succeeding in her chosen vocation.

This exploratory examination suggests how the reading of autobiographies by literary women provides a new perspective on the genre's complexity, enabling us to see different codes and functions elaborated in female life writing, which, as Domna Stanton (1984) speculates, likely derive from the "tension between conventional roles and the unconventional self" (14–15). In *Stella mattutina* and *Cosima* the authors' forms of self-representation and the issues that they problematize seem to support Stanton's theory that the contradictory position of the female autobiographical subject constituted by "the act of writing itself" represents perhaps the fundamental difference between female and male autobiographies, a difference termed *pathological* by some critics of the interwar years. With their fashionings of strikingly different rebel female figures, Negri and Deledda reinvent their formation of literary identities, challenging the laws of gender and genre. Although we cannot employ the forms of self-representation fashioned by Negri and Deledda as universal models of female subjectivity, their discourses create alternative paradigms that transgress the conservative figures of woman circulated in literary and political discourses of their time. They thus occasioned the opportunity for communities of women readers to identify with nonconventional roles, perhaps inspiring different ways of thinking about the self, the labors of life and art, family, and society.

Furthermore, Deledda's work in particular belies the notion that by the late 1920s the trend of self-revelation in women's literature gave way to conformity with dominant values of duty and family, clearly showing the necessity to do further study on the multiple forms of autobiography and autobiographism elaborated by women in the interwar period. A dialogic project examining the representations of self-formation by writers adopting more or less mimetic narrative practices such as Tartufari and Negri, as well as avant-garde authors, Maria Goretti, for instance, would produce more nuanced paradigms of female subjectivities and the range of strategies designed to constitute them. Likewise, we should begin to construct a frame for exploring the intertextual relations—the points of convergence, tension, and transformation—between life writings by both women and men as they endeavor to re-create literary identities in the sea change of modern Italian life and society. By so doing, we could perhaps pose new questions about such important autobiographies written during World War II and in the postwar era as *Ritratto in piedi* (Standing portrait, 1971) by Gianna Manzini, *Family Sayings* (1963) by Natalia Ginzburg, *Cristo si è fermato ad Eboli* (Christ stopped at Eboli, 1945) by Carlo Levi, *Se questo è un uomo* (If this is a man, 1947) by Primo Levi, and *Althenopis* (1981) by Fabrizia Ramondino.[19]

THREE

Aeroromance: Reconfiguring Femininity, Fantasy, and Fascism

> The success of a work of commercial literature indicates (and it is often the only indication available) the "philosophy of the age," that is, the mass of feelings and conceptions of the world predominant among the "silent" majority.
>
> ANTONIO GRAMSCI, *Selections from Cultural Writings*

In his 1974 film *Amarcord*, Federico Fellini offers viewers a sequence of images that gives powerful cinematic representation to the linkage made in some camps between Fascism, female desire, and fantasy. At center stage, framed by girls and boys in uniform along with the townspeople who have turned out for the event and wait in growing anticipation, a Fascist government official emerges from a dusty cloud, almost magically. After some brief stock phrases exalting the glorious destiny that Fascism holds for Italians, the *federale*, accompanied by uniformed functionaries, sets out at a comic trot in tune with the marching band, putting the regime's virility and vigor on display. As the procession comes closer into view, the camera shifts from a wide angle and focuses in on Gradisca, bedecked in her fashionable red outfit, hat attractively tilted on her head of coiffed short hair. Against the general enthusiasm of the crowd, our attention is directed to the intensity of Gradisca's gaze, locked captivatedly on the Fascist official, as she exclaims, "He's so handsome! He's so handsome!" This scene underscores her (female) susceptibility to the allure of this male symbol of the regime's power, which gains force through absence; we see only the woman fervently looking, but the object of her gaze is off-camera. Although Gradisca appears equally lured by the popular images of the Hollywood star Gary Cooper, something more is at stake here: the way we think about modern female subjectivity and desire in relation to Fascism.

This issue finds its fullest theoretical analysis in Maria Antonietta Macciocchi's *La donna "nera"* (1976).[1] This influential study proposes to show how both the forms of self-presentation deployed by Mussolini, using his manliness and virility as window dressing for mass consumption, and the modes of address to female audiences seduced women into investing their desires in Fascism, issues that I examined in the opening chapter. Here I want to review a few of her other points from a different angle. Briefly, Macciocchi suggests that Mussolini solicited Italian women through a feminine semiotic system constructed on the idealized image of woman and her purity, goodness, and "immaculate" essence, familiar terms in Christian ideology that had a purchase on the female unconscious. Thus at the symbolic level, Macciocchi argues, the duce charmed women of Italy, who, as they exchanged their gold wedding rings with Mussolini, receiving an iron band in return, enacted "a sublimated marriage . . . : women married the father and the sacred husband, and the consummation of the marriage was mystical" (Macciocchi 1979, 75). While this line of inquiry works to show the erasure of female sexuality in Fascist discourse, Macciocchi also devotes substantial space to representing Mussolini as the virile sex symbol of the twenties and thirties who set the fantasies of historical women aflame. Among the elite, it seems, resemblances between "so-and-so's" baby and Mussolini provided the hottest topic of cocktail conversation, as socialites proudly speculated that the child could perhaps be the duce's offspring. To further support her position, the author relates an account of a conversation that transpired between Clara Petacci and the partisan Pedro when she was arrested with Mussolini, her lover, in April 1945. Macciocchi tells us that Petacci "said something that honors romance literature of all periods, and especially the romance fiction of Mussolini's time: 'To become the duce's lover,' Claretta confessed to Pedro, 'had become the ambition—whether secret or confessed—of almost all the high-society women he frequented'" (1976, 42). Certainly, general conclusions drawn from the words of the devotedly loyal Petacci about the intimate desires of upper-class women present more than a few problems. What interests me is the suggested figuration of desire in Macciocchi's parallel construction of relations between hero-heroine-story and duce-woman-history, which depicts the romance genre and Fascism as fitting bedfellows.

The correspondences, if not collusions, between the ways in which feminine and masculine models are constructed and plotted respectively in Fascist discourse and in romance novels written during the dictatorship form a more or less constant component in critical studies on the genre's development. Although the prizewinning literary works written in other genres by women in the interwar period have been largely overlooked, scholars have dedicated substantive attention to romance fiction, likely because the boom in this genre's success coincides with Fascism and offers a cache of information about the tastes and interests of women among the emergent mass readership. In 1953, the novelist and critic Anna Banti was among the first to take stock of the romance novel's fortune in the regime, as part of an overview of the genre's history. Her assessment established formative issues for subsequent genre criticism. She focuses particularly on the tendency among some women romance writers to show a faddish devotion to the male myths of virility, heroism, and aggression, and to female myths of "admiration for the male warrior," willing submission, and the importance of motherhood, concluding that this narrative form served to dim "the consciousness of individual women and the entire female class" (1953, 33). Since then, critics have tended to glean something dictatorial about romance heroes of the twenties and thirties. Antonia Arslan Veronese (1987) puts an interesting spin on this idea when she suggests that the images of self that Mussolini exploited in his address to women were modeled on heroes of popular literature:

> The myth of Mussolini is then constructed on a rougher male image, composed of traditional stereotypes that had already been thoroughly assimilated . . . : a conqueror yet paternal, the Duce satisfies the "natural female desire" for protection, drives away subversives, protects the good people and punishes the bad. He is a kind of Superman, a strong man, a Dominator, like the heroes in the popular novel, like the protagonist of so many romantic fables. (24)[2]

It is equally tempting to make comparisons between the image of the ideal woman designed by Fascist thinkers and the typical heroine—a good, innocent young woman whose pride, spirit, and budding sexuality become tamed by Mr. Right, as she assumes her role of the devoted woman-mother at the marriage altar.

Although the romance novel undergoes changes during the interwar years, which I will discuss shortly, the generic conventions of character and plot predate the advent of the Fascist movement. Nonetheless, since the idealized images of femininity and masculinity in romances appear to conform with the patriarchal institutionalization of the sex-gender system, the resultant conservative ideology raises more troubling questions when read within the context of the Fascist regime, which sought to reclaim male authority in the economic, social, and sexual spheres. As the argument goes, and here critics reach remarkable consensus, this genre's conservative value operates in support of the prevailing hegemony—dominated in this period by Fascism—and, according to generic laws, must confirm the readers' values and myths.[3] Otherwise, the reading act would not produce pleasure, which brings me to a related debate of concern here: the meanings that some scholars attach to the functions assumed by the structural system of romance under Fascist rule. Much of the pleasure of reading formula stories, whether detective or romance novels or so on, derives from the repeated discovery of what the reader already knows and anticipates, as conflicts, which may be aroused at both the textual and subjective levels, are then engaged and finally resolved in a satisfying manner at the story's end. Therefore, romantic "escape" theoretically operates in a consolatory fashion and allays fears about potentially real problems in life and society. This process may thus make readers disinclined to engage in political practices to improve the oppressive conditions that make the utopian promise of romance novels so alluring. Lino Pertile's (1986) comments on how Fascism unwittingly found an ally in mass literature, written by Liala and Lucio D'Ambra, for example, best represent this position. He claims that the booming market of escapist novels responded to the needs of readers who felt dissatisfied in daily life, by offering

the "*frissons*" of high life and adventure, moderate sensuality and sinfulness, together with the blissful comfort of a happy ending. This kind of literature, with its ability to adapt closely to all changes in conformist ideology, contributed considerably to the consolidation and preservation of

Fascism by releasing tension, depoliticizing the masses and feeding them
with ready-made myths and dreams for instant consumption. (178)

The reader can hardly miss the parentage of this idea, which aligns with
the theory of mass culture as an apparatus that manipulates passive
consumers and exhausts their revolutionary potential, elaborated by
such thinkers in the Frankfurt School as Theodor Adorno and Max
Horkheimer.[4]

Indeed, the associations that Adorno made between fascism and mass
cultural forms as formulaic, homogenized and homogenizing systems
have retained a certain currency. Therefore, it is useful to take a careful
look at how Adorno formulates the relations among fascist discourses,
the culture industry, and potential audiences. Addressing this issue in
"Freudian Theory and the Pattern of Fascist Propaganda," Adorno (1973)
contends that fascism has ready-made consumers:

> It may well be the secret of Fascist propaganda that it simply takes men
> for what they are: the true children of today's standardized mass culture,
> largely robbed of autonomy and spontaneity, instead of setting goals the
> realization of which would transcend the psychological *status quo* no less
> than the social one. Fascist propaganda has only to *reproduce* the existent
> mentality for its own purposes;—it need not induce change—and the
> compulsive repetition which is one of its foremost characteristics will be
> at one with the necessity for this continuous reproduction. (99–100)

Although Adorno bases his arguments on the postwar generation that
grew up with the proliferation of mass entertainment, he implies that
the culture industry shares a ground and structure with fascism, as exhibited by the prevailing psychological formation. Thus, fascism need
not produce something new, which, from Adorno's perspective, would
be impossible anyway. What concerns me here is the way that fascism
operates as a timeless "floating signifier" and, by so doing, as Michel
Foucault (1980) suggests, appears to be a diffused power system of super-
human dimensions, lacking any specificity. Moreover, by evacuating social
and cultural history, Adorno overly homogenizes both forms of mass
entertainment (romance novels and cinema, for example) produced, by
implication, during Italian Fascism, and Fascist cultural theories and
practices. He overlooks the inventiveness of Fascism, and thus the het-

erogeneity constituting part of its power. Ironically, Adorno's tendency to privilege high culture and disparage the deleterious influence of mass culture aligns with the position adopted by elitist factions of the Fascist cultural regime.

Another influential element of Adorno's model, which, however, weakens its effectiveness for exploring the potential exchanges between mass literature, Fascism, and reading publics, concerns his representation of the relationship between text and audience as simple "consumption." Cultural critics of the Birmingham School have since problematized the complex engagements between social subjects and dominant discourses. Stuart Hall (1973), for example, proposes three response models, elaborating "dominant," "negotiated," and "oppositional" relations to textual codes and meanings. Similarly, as suggested in my discussion of the short fiction published in the daily press, Michel de Certeau's formulation of practices of daily life (reading, walking, and dress) also enables us to examine the complexity of secondary usage where dominant signs may be incorporated, challenged, or transformed (1988). However, taking the specific case of romance novels produced during Fascism, scholarship in Italian studies tends to present the reading act as passive consumption and to focus on the genre's conservative value, paying scant attention to the conflicting feelings and ideas raised by the narrative about the changing forms of sexuality, gender relations, and social mores brought about as Italy becomes a more industrialized, consumer society. This research also suffers from an undertheorized notion of reader identification, assuming that female readers easily identified with the traditional heroine, and thus the values, myths, and desires that she embodied. Yet in the thirties, a prominent romance convention set the model of idealized femininity against contending female models exhibiting emancipated behaviors and attitudes toward work, sex, matrimony, and motherhood. More important, as Teresa de Lauretis and Cora Kaplan have demonstrated, the reader does not simply identify with characters of her own gender. In "Desire in Narrative" (1984a), a study including a rigorous analysis of the complexities of female identification in narrative and cinema, de Lauretis insists, first, that identification must be understood as a process and movement *actively* engaging the subject. Applying Freud's paradigm of male and female development toward the Oedipal stage to narrative movement, she argues that the positionalities of femininity and masculinity—respectively indicating the passive or active relation between the subject and desire—are produced in discourse with "the masculine position as that of mythic subject, and the feminine position as mythical obstacle or, simply, the space in which that movement occurs" (143). Based on this principle, de Lauretis posits a theory of how narrative and cinema solicit the female reader/spectator, proposing a process of double identification "with both the subject and the space of the narrative movement," which "would uphold both positionalities of desire, both active and passive aims: desire for the other, and desire to be desired by the other" (143).[5] This psychoanalytic model casts light on the different desires and meanings made available by romance novels during Fascism, which narrate, with a variety of embellishments, the Oedipal story of the adventures and misadventures that the young girl must negotiate on her voyage into womanhood, achieved when she marries the man of her dreams.

Following a similar line of thought, Cora Kaplan's article "*The Thorn Birds*" (1986) examines the operations of female identification specifically within romance narrative, though the author proposes a slightly different model that works on the concept of shifting (as opposed to simultaneous) identifications with the active and passive positionalities of desire. Historical romances, in particular, solicit reader identification across the lines of sexual and class difference, Kaplan speculates, by enacting a variety of scenarios in the fictional fantasy. She supports this thesis with a meticulous analysis of the distinctions and connections between fantasy as psychic structure and fantasy as romantic narrative, using the theory of fantasy developed by Freud and expounded on more recently by Jean Laplanche and Jean-Bertrand Pontalis. For a reconsideration of Italian romance fiction, two points especially merit attention. As Kaplan explains in her discussion of the nature and operations of original and unconscious fantasy—the site and process where sexuality and subjectivity are constituted—the subject does not occupy a stable position. Instead, she maintains, in fantasy as scenario "the shifting place of the subject is a characteristic part of the activity." She supports this argument with observations by Laplanche and Pontalis, which bear repeating:

Fantasy is not the object of desire, but its setting. In fantasy the subject does not pursue the object or its sign: he appears caught up himself in the sequence of images. He forms no representation of the desired object, but is himself represented as participating in the scene although, in the earliest forms of fantasy, he cannot be assigned any fixed place in it. . . . As a result, the subject, although always present in the fantasy, may be so in a desubjectivised form, that is to say, in the very syntax of the sequence in question. (150)

While Kaplan takes into serious consideration the different registers of fantasy—original fantasy scenario (seduction and castration, for example), daydream, and conscious narrative fantasy—Freud's insistence on the interrelations between unconscious and conscious fantasy structures grounds her proposition that the fluid movement between active and passive subject positions in psychic fantasizing may function analogously in romantic fantasy fictions. The deeper critical understanding of fantasy articulated in Kaplan's theoretical discussion and textual analysis provides a useful departure from the one-track thinking about the relation between the female reader and heroine, expanding the field of inquiry to the variable engagements of active female desire with both the images and syntax of fantasies created predominantly by women authors for women among the mass reading audience.

In this study I want to work through the theories of multiple female-reader identification elaborated by de Lauretis and Kaplan, in an exploratory rereading of Liala's romance novel *Signorsì* (Yes, sir!), a blockbuster published in 1931. Their critical models are particularly suited to exploring the configurations and syntax of romantic fantasy in *Signorsì*, since the text's structure, metaphors, and symbols highlight the movement—material and figurative—of desires. Liala creates a site where female readers may indulge in forbidden desires articulated, in part, by the rich fashioning of the flight metaphor. Evoked with frequent images of wings, eagles, airplanes, and flying itself, the metaphor of flying assumes different valences, for instance, encompassing sexual abandon, adventure, freedom, nationalism, and, more important, mastery over new technologies. Given this genre's explicit address to women readers, an examination of the terms of identification constructed in the narrative movement and images enables us to chart the terrain of fantasy life where female desire and subjectivity are inscribed. Therefore, my discussion speculates about ways for rethinking the performative functions of romance fiction among communities of women, as well as the entrenched associations made between femininity, fantasy, and Fascism. How do the models of femininity fashioned by Liala relate to the myth of a "natural" female desire to be defended and protected? Which features are embodied by the male object of desire, and how do they pertain to the traditional markers of the masculine hero as warrior—aggressive and dominating? In what ways might the psychical subject appeal to women who, after the years of open gender struggle in the wake of World War I, had achieved increased socioeconomic and intellectual independence— advances they would not willingly relinquish in their daily lives? And last, thinking in broader terms, is it possible that such forms of mass entertainment as the romance novel may have productive exchanges with Fascism, but not because they both ostensibly "colonize" the masses with homogeneous, repetitive formulas? On the contrary, perhaps popular literature and cinematic genres, which raise topical issues and conflicts, challenge the inventive power of Fascism, forcing the regime to constantly modernize and vary the images that it projects.

Romance Italian Style: Its History, Conventions, and Con-tensions

The publication of *Signorsì* heralds both the debut of Amaliana Cambiasi Negretti as a romance author and a hallmark in the development of the romance genre in Italy. Recognized by critics as the novel that signals the beginning of the modern romance form in Italy, *Signorsì* tells the story of a quest for the ideal, "authentic" woman, which Furio, the Duke of Villafranca and Monleone and a flying ace of national fame, embarks on and finally consummates in a passionate, yet ill-fated union with Renata, a heavenly woman of unrivaled beauty and purity. The book attracted thunderous applause among the mass readership and literary celebrities alike. In fact, Gabriele D'Annunzio immediately wanted to meet the woman who had made her mark as the author of the first Italian airplane novel. Years later, Liala fondly recalled that encounter, when D'Annunzio invented her suggestive nom de plume, fashioned on the word *ala,* or wing, in Italian. He stated, "You'll call yourself Liala. A wing fits perfectly in the name of a woman who writes about flying" (cited in Gregoricchio 1981, 10). Christening the birth of Cambiasi Negretti's literary persona, D'Annunzio gave her an autograph with the inscription, "To Liala, a winged, insolent companion" (in Gregoricchio 1981, 10). Until her recent death in 1995, Liala continued to captivate a broad audience with her more than seventy romance novels and the regular reprints of her works dating from the thirties.

In order to assess the potential associations between romantic stories of female fantasy, their readers, and Fascism, I want to situate *Signorsì* within the tradition of romance and its changing conventions in Italy during the interwar years. The malleability of the romance genre in Italy, as elsewhere, resists rigid definition. Yet the *rosa* (romance genre) follows some generic rules that should suffice here for a working definition. Most important, the romance tells a love story, generally written and read from women's perspective, where the heroine most often assumes the role of protagonist and navigates the tempestuous forces frustrating her union with the hero, the love of her life, which she ultimately achieves. The story's satisfying conclusion, which may or may not focus on the rapprochement and blissful marriage between heroine and hero, is an equally indispensable narrative feature; it fulfills the contractual agreement between author and reader that the story will deliver the pleasure promised, allaying whatever emotional tensions it elicited and bolstering the hope that there may be a "happily ever after." Yet throughout its development, the romance also displays a full range of diachronic elements composed from sociohistorical trends and its complex symbiotic relations with such popular literary forms as the detective and adventure stories and the feuilleton.[6]

In the Italian romance genre tradition, whose mixed lineage has been traced back to the late 1700s by way of the sentimental novels by Neera and Matilde Serao and the gothic novels by Carolina Invernizio, the 1920s and 1930s represent a transitional period. According to Silvana Ghiazza's (1991) excellent historical study, the modern romance novel as we know it was established in Italy in the early twenties, when the publisher Ettore Salani founded the first series, which featured works written primarily by foreign authors, including Delly (Jeanne Marie Petit-Jean and Frédéric de la Rosière), Elinor Glyn, and Baroness Orczy. The iconography and design of the cover art made the product easily recognizable. The novels' covers blushed in shades of pink and featured the illustration of a rose on an open book. Although foreign authors dominated the growing romance industry in the twenties and thirties, a culturally specific form of romance writing also emerged, fashioned by Italian authors and stories. Belonging to the latter line of romance, *Signorsì* exhibits narrative traits that predominate as the genre becomes more codified, as well as some atypical stylistic practices. A refined, elegant milieu occupies the story's center stage, creating spaces and occasions for readers to luxuriate and to enjoy respite from the problems besetting day-to-day existence. Liala employs the technique of what Daniela Curti (1987a) has termed "hyper-description," portraying in detail places, characters, and fashions.[7] She thus encourages the reader's easy indulgence in a fantasy where every particular takes visual shape, dimension, and color. Likewise, frequent rhetorical questions, exclamations, repetitions, and summary make fundamental textual meanings self-evident. The linguistic system that Liala crafts in *Signorsì*, however, also incorporates models and vocabulary drawn from the high Italian literary tradition, along with an evocative use of metaphor and symbol, which all but disappear in later novels. The resultant literary aura, which does not interfere with the accessibility of the language, may thus address a broad audience made up of upper-middle-class readers, likely familiar with high literature, as well as readers among the urban working class, perhaps aspiring to that refined milieu.

Since the development of this Italian branch of romance coincides with the rise and consolidation of Fascism, which staked a claim on mass culture, scholars tend to assume the texts to be irreparably tainted. It is true that the regime established new policies and institutions for the management of mass culture, among them a program to revamp the educational system, spearheaded by Giovanni Gentile in 1923; the establishment in 1925 of the Fascist Institute of Culture (sponsoring libraries and public lectures); and the creation of leisure-time organizations. But the rocky progress of mass media industries, with the exception of the press, and the lack of a clear program impeded any prospects of building a coordinated system of cultural production and surveillance, until the 1937 founding of the Ministry of Popular Culture, formerly the Ministry of Press and Propaganda (1935). Prior to 1938, most Italian filmgoers viewed foreign, predominantly American, feature films, along with the obligatory newsreel produced by LUCE (Union for Educational Cinematography), an organization that was nationalized in 1925. And radio did not figure prominently for the diffusion of propaganda until the midthirties.[8] It should come as no surprise, then, that Fascist cultural politics did not develop a coherent program for mass literature, least of all for the romance. Furthermore, as Ghiazza (1991) maintains, the panorama of romance fiction displays no overt support for such specifically Fascist undertakings in women's culture as the youth groups or leisure organizations. Thus, she concludes, this genre "crosses the regime, but remains substantially impermeable to its appeals and cultural directives, following its own generic laws, which sanction its particular metahistorical and ideal continuity, beyond the direct subordination . . . to a historically determined political system" (139).

However, the apparent lack of open relations between women's fictions of romantic fantasy and Fascism hardly speaks to the issue of their potential complicity as sites of ideological production. As we see from *Signorsì*, the narrative system of romance and its position in the hegemonic discursive field exhibit more complexity than we might expect. For example, Liala's novel voices a strident nationalism from the opening scene, set in the final year of World War I, right up to the last sentence, where the hero transforms his pain into strength and answers the call to duty with a resounding "Yes, sir!" The many thrilling descriptions of the "flying eagles" in the Italian air force and their high-thrust aircraft evoke images of a nation pioneering frontiers of space and technology, where duty and incredible feats are performed, not for personal gain but for the glory of Italy. At the same time, the repertory of male and, more particularly, female models and the sites where they play out their roles dramatize a crisis in subjectivity. We see the upheaval of Italian social subjects casting about in the crosscurrents of tradition and modernity. Hence, Furio, who exudes an intriguing mixture of virile sensuality, sensitivity, and sweetness, sets out in Italian sports cars and planes, which reduce entire communities and the distances separating them to a speck, trying to find the woman of his dreams, who is, in his words, "beautiful, healthy, honest" (59). This ideal of the "authentic" woman—signified by a beauty canon of long blond tresses, skin unspoiled by the sinful guise of makeup, and retiring manners—resonates with the naturalized version of woman promoted in Fascist discourse. But the notions of love and marriage clearly propose contending values. Furio searches not for a woman who will give him a family, but for someone who will share interests, understanding, affection, and the pleasures that love offers. Moreover, throughout the first half of the novel, the dispositions toward modern trends of behavior and beauty displayed by the women Furio encounters in flirtatious dalliances, one-night stands, and brief affairs make it appear that his dream woman may be just that. Liala gives us a kaleidoscopic vision of these changes across classes with her female portraits: the refined, blue-blooded woman, a wife and mother who calls Furio a cad because he will not return her advances; the popular author Lery, emancipated in her professional and sexual life, yet also jealous and clingy; aspiring dancers and actresses, whose bare breasts and thighs highlight their artificiality; Perla, a girl from a middle-class family now boasting a newly made fortune, whose wiles belie the innocence and purity reflected on her face; and town girls, assuming names like Frilli and Popò, with peroxided hair and caked-on makeup that clash with the idealized image of the natural, healthy, industrious countrygirl.

There is little room for doubt that Liala presents these predatory female models as undesirable from the hero's (male) perspective, causing a sense of confusion, anxiety, and inadequacy, a point also made by conservative thinkers in the regime. For subtly different reasons, however, Fascist cultural commentators and the Catholic hierarchy condemned escapist literature for women, outlining the dangers that it posed. General charges lodged against romantic fiction before and during the regime hold this genre responsible for the decay of traditional values and the sacred institutions of love, marriage, and motherhood. In 1920, prior to the establishment of the dictatorship, Ferrucchio Vecchi denounced the dishonesty of authors who, by trafficking in this cocaine-like substance, offended all that was decent in life (cited in Meldini 1975, 131). In the early 1930s, Manlio Pompei traced the problem of growing materialism among Italian youth to the influences of writers, bemoaning the changes in their hopes and aspirations. For girls, he tells us, "love is something from the Middle Ages; all they dream about is having a car" (in Meldini 1975, 204).

Most important, Fascist writers denounced romantic literature for the way that its emotionally charged images exalted hedonistic, "sterile" love, thereby undermining both traditional family values and the demographic campaign (announced in 1927), the bedrock of the regime's sexual politics.

Paolo Araldi's analysis, published in his 1929 work *La politica demografica di Mussolini* (Mussolini's demographic politics), typifies the major arguments of conservative circles in the regime. The writer opens his diatribe by accusing literature, art, and fashion of spreading antinationalist propaganda, targeting a group where it is ostensibly most effective—women. Singling out the representation of love in foreign literature, with a description that applies equally well, if not better, to the romance, Araldi charges that such novels have "introduced Italian women, and even sweet young girls, to the justification of childless love and made the complex, delicate, exquisite, and aphrodisiac subtleties of artificial, sensuous, and emotional complications available to readers of all levels of intelligence" (in Meldini 1975, 161). For Araldi, the influence levied by this different notion of love, along with socioeconomic factors, has wreaked havoc reaching from the heart of domestic life and the family to the spheres of community and national life. For the traditional Italian woman—a model destined to extinction in Araldi's eyes—love represented a noble mission that gave essential meaning to her life and illuminated her home with angelic light, creating a sanctuary for the family. In contrast, the modern Italian woman makes men hesitant to cross the threshold. Araldi's discussion hinges on the following points. Immodest and forward, woman now employs the latest devices in beauty and fashion, creating illusions and false forms of love, which is to say, relations whose scope lies beyond procreation. Worse still, she flaunts her "arts of seduction" on the public streets, creating a presence that disturbs mature businessmen, young men who hold Italy's future in their hands, and children. By unleashing these instincts, modern female behaviors encourage ephemeral, hedonistic relations that corrupt the institutions of matrimony and motherhood. Hence, Araldi concludes, art and literature that "propagandize sterile love, the battle against births, or at least the limiting of them," commit nothing less than a crime against the fatherland (in Meldini 1975, 162).

Catholic writings of the interwar years exhibit a perhaps unexpected openness to adapting Catholic female models to the modern changes in work, volunteerism, courtship, and marriage.[9] Nonetheless, the hierarchy persisted in its censure of sentimental, romantic stories for women, as well as works by critically acclaimed authors that sounded the subterranean recesses of passion. For example, in the midtwenties the Catholic Book Index, intended to guide the general constituency's reading choices, included novels by Grazia Deledda on the list of forbidden works. The church's opposition to sentimental literature and its efforts to entertain and edify female readers by providing wholesome stories in its publications failed to dampen interest in romantic fiction. In response to reader requests, such Catholic magazines as *Fiamma viva* (Burning flame) began publishing stories written about themes related to love and emotions, which, however, as Elisabetta Mondello (1987) notes, worked within the parameters of traditional Catholic beliefs and values.

Within the hegemonic system predominated by Fascist institutions and the Catholic Church, which promoted models of femininity dedicated to the role of wife and mother, cast respectively as political and sacred, the romance novel, and mass culture in general, represented an alternative authority on modern canons of beauty and fashion, etiquette, and love. Italian studies on romantic fictions produced during the dictatorship tend to overlook the value that their encyclopedic information had in female social relations. They adhere instead to the concept of romance reading as passive consumption, a form of "consent," as Ghiazza (1991) words it, whereby the female reader lets herself go in a flight of fantasy.[10] Critical theories on the textual relations between women and mass-produced romantic fantasies, developed in *Loving with a Vengeance* (1982) by Tania Modleski, *Fantasy and Reconciliation* (1984) by Kay Mussell, and *Reading the Romance* (1991) by Janice Radway, amply demonstrate different ways that readers engage in an active negotiation of the images, information, and meanings put at their disposal. For young Italian women of the working and lower-middle classes, De Grazia (1992) proposes, the romance and other mass cultural texts offered a form of social empowerment: "Alienated from their families and isolated in the face of repressive Catholic and antifeminist ideologies, they turned to the stories, advice columns, illustrations, and jokes to comprehend and master new sexual manners and social practices of their society" (133). In *Signorsì*, Liala's detailed descriptions of everything from women's toilette to different kinds of kisses bear out this claim. The author does not provide a mere inventory. On the contrary, her information instructs us on the new devices for female self-fashioning and how to use them artfully to create a tasteful, attractive public image.

Even in contemporary times, Liala prided herself on the instructional value of her novels. Drawing a distinction between literary knowledge, gained from reading widely, and practical knowledge for daily living, she declared, "My books are educational nonetheless. I teach good manners and cleanliness. Liala arrived before deodorant" (cited in Gregoricchio 1981, 12). In the thirties, Fascism unquestionably set increasing occasions for women's public appearances at processions and rallies in the piazzas, but Liala, Lux, and Revlon furnished women with the tools to create their own impressions. Indeed, with a technique not dissimilar to *Glamour*'s "Dos and Don'ts," the author parades a variety of female images before the reader's eyes, drawing attention to the importance of personal hygiene, the secrets and errors of applying makeup, and choosing clothes and accessories to fit the occassion. The beauty canon constructed by Liala epitomizes the fashion adage "Less is more," as she gives advice on how to achieve a look that is unaffected and elegant. For those who do not possess the flawless, natural beauty gracing Renata, the heroine, Lery represents a more achievable aesthetic model. The impression she makes on Furio testifies to her skills in the art of makeup and dress: "Extremely elegant, slender, with curly, short tawny hair, she had wide, intelligent, lively eyes that were the color of graphite, knowingly highlighted with a shade of light green eyeshadow" (19). When Lery meets Furio for their first date, he is struck by her tastefully assembled spring outfit, as the narrator notes, "Every detail, from her hat down to her dainty shoes, from her parasol to her charming purse, was exquisitely elegant, and everything about her was bright and joyful" (21).

Although the fashionable accoutrements at Lery's disposal clearly belong to an economically privileged class and social milieu beyond the reach of the mass female readership, a narrative trait fulfilling an important operation of the fantasy, the author suggests that fashion know-how provides the most valuable currency for good taste and is available to all. Using Furio as a guide in the semiotic field of style, Liala makes biting assessments of breaches in taste, ranging from the indecorous advances that a rich woman, noble by birth, makes toward the hero, to a parvenu's vulgar display of a brooch, broadcasting the kind of wealth only money can buy. The narrative exhibits a different attitude toward girls from the lower classes, cautioning against the misguided excess in makeup and clothes that makes them resemble brightly plumed flies on a fishhook hoping to bait the first eligible man who comes their way.

If the critical temptation looms to dismiss these supposedly frivolous everyday preoccupations, the publicity campaigns launched by the growing fashion and beauty aid industries show us that it was serious business. Taking, for instance, the advertisements appearing in La stampa, a nationally distributed daily newspaper published in Turin, we see frequent promotions for mass-produced brands of toothpaste for whiter teeth, of shampoos for soft, manageable hair, soaps, perfumes, and makeup, amid ads for such luxury items as record players, radios, and Fiat sports cars. The female aesthetic presented in Liala's romance novels of the thirties resonates with the promises on which new feminine beauty products are marketed and sold. The ads for Lux soap and Tokalon makeup best illustrate this point. Promising women "Skin as delicate and soft as the petals of a flower," the ads for Lux feature close-up photos of such famous movie stars as Bebe Daniels and Evelyn Brent, who along with major Hollywood directors—King Vidor of Metro-Goldwyn-Mayer and Irvin Villat of Universal—sell the idea that women must have soft, smooth, radiant skin, and Lux will deliver it. In fact, the ad boasts, 417 Hollywood actresses have chosen Lux.[11] Emphasizing the high value placed on the "natural look," Tokalon powder, a Parisian brand, markets itself with the following description, headed with the caption in bold print:

WOMEN WHO ABSOLUTELY MUST BE BEAUTIFUL: High society women, actresses and movie stars absolutely must be beautiful. For success and prestige you have to have fresh color, a youthful looking face, and skin that is soft and beautiful. Women who must be beautiful, like women who desire to be so, think Tokalon powder is priceless.

The ad goes on to claim that this powder corrects your shiny nose and oily skin, protects your skin from the wind, cold, rain, and sun, and, most important of all, "it is so light, soft, and delicate, you can't see it on your face." And further, although Liala presents long hair as the ideal for attracting men, it is interesting that the vogue of short hairstyles prompted the development of products marketed specifically for new problems created by modern fashion. For those times when the sharp lines of a precision cut "alla garçonne" need touching up along the neckline, the women's shaving cream Lampocrema will prevent skin irritation and unsightly red blotches.

Flights of Fantasy: Reconfigurations of the Masculine and the Feminine

Liala's novel addresses the interests and concerns among communities of women, creating a popular discourse on love and guiding readers of the thirties and today through the maze of commercial culture, with its uses and abuses. I now want to speculate about the different ways in which Liala's narrative practices may engage female readers in the movement and syntax of the romantic fantasy, making available active and passive positionalities of desire. The concept of multiple identification affords an approach that is particularly helpful for examining *Signorsì*. Unlike the vast majority of romance novels, Liala's story, told through third-person narration, features a male protagonist, who, however, as the woman author's invention, represents the male as both the subject of male desire and the object of female desire. The entire first part of the novel (some 140 pages) is devoted to the hero's relations, aspirations, dreams, and disappointments. Furio displays a provocative set of characteristics and behaviors that conform with some aspects of traditional masculinity, while destabilizing others. Strikingly handsome, with a tall, slender body and tanned skin that sets off his blond hair, Furio cuts a dashing figure in and out of uniform. Although this character primarily occupies the active position within the textual movement, Liala creates a suggestive image of the specular male body, as the hero and his closest friend Mino stand before a mirror, where "two tall men, dressed in elegant white uniforms, were reflected, and smiled at each other in the crystal" (51). While enjoying the privileges of noble birth and wealth, Furio, perhaps as a sign of the changing sociopolitical values caused by the Fascist paradigm of producers and parasites, has chosen not to dissipate his time and money. Instead, he dedicates his life to duty and honor in service of Italy and distinguishes himself as an air force pilot whose skilled bravado in war and peacetime has made him a national hero.

Although Furio's strength of body, mind, and character recalls the dominant construction of male virility, the narrative also highlights his ability and pleasure in nurturing. In relations with his parents (especially his mother), friends, and the young pilots he trains, the hero freely gives of his sensitivity and kindness. And he adores children! In some of the most moving scenes, we see the ace pilot satisfying the whims voiced by little Elma, the daughter that Mino shares by an affair with a married woman, as he helps her name a new doll or emerge victorious from battles fought amid pillows and blankets. Moreover, the ideal of love that Furio wants to realize challenges the notion of a dominating, self-sufficient, and purely sexual male desire, as demonstrated by the following conversation between the hero and Mino: "'If you only knew how much I need love!' Furio whispered, 'but not a sensual kind of love; I need gentleness and caresses; I need a woman who can comfort me a little and say tender things to me. This need for tenderness even numbs my senses'" (79). In this woman's fantasy, the needs and dreams articulated by the hero, who, we must remember, is loved by women and men alike, posit terms of male and female desire that differ substantially from the model of masculinity commonly associated with Fascist discourses, exalting, for instance, dominating power or aggressivity.

The substantial discursive space dedicated to exploring Furio's thoughts and feelings works to enlist the reader's sympathies. More important, however, the active positionality occupied by the hero as he embarks on a mythic quest for a woman who embodies and can sustain his ideal image of the "authentic" woman incites our desire to read further, to discover who he will find, and what will happen. This process derives from the mechanics of narrative elucidated by de Lauretis, who reminds us that "the productivity of the text, its play of structure and excess, engages the reader, viewer, or listener as subject in (and for) its process" (1984a, 121). In the episodes logging the hero's search, the female figures are for the most part static icons—obstacles in the form of false images that the hero must overcome. Indeed, as the hero "looks" everywhere, the narrative focuses attention on woman as the object of the gaze. The protagonist's seemingly endless encounters with characters representing a variety of female models, which I summarized earlier, fulfill two important functions. With this episodic series, the author modulates the text's affective pitch between expectation, elation, and disappointment, in a course of deferment that heightens reader anticipation. These involvements also sharpen Furio's knowledge and perception, enabling him to discern the meanings signified by changing female manners.

Two relationships play particularly significant roles in the protagonist's education in the modern art of love. Just as he begins what will become a herculean task, Furio receives his first lesson in female devices and desires from Lery Poli, as you recall, a successful writer, possessing remarkable beauty, too. The author's description of the direct, self-assertive approach that Lery takes on her first date opens the eyes of those of us who may entertain illusions about the originality of the sexual revolution in the sixties. She tells Furio where to drive, negotiates with the hotel owner herself, checks in, and assures the young man that his "dream is real." In the conventional romance language of sexual euphemism, we learn that the night flew by, leaving Furio dazed and happy. To dispel any doubt as to what transpired, in the space of a sentence our characters have changed from the formal *voi* address to the more intimate *tu* form. Moreover, suggesting a scenario where a woman seduces a man, the author pictures Lery leaning over Furio, who lies supine in a state of languor as she caresses his hair.

Lery clearly represents the emancipated female model popularized in mass publications and censured in Fascist writings. She appears to have a mind of her own, which, along with her exceptional intelligence, beauty, and sensuality, distinguishes her from other women and captivates Furio. Yet Liala implies that liberated sexual manners do not necessarily indicate a marked difference in women's notion of self and male-female relations. Lery falls prey to an obsessive jealousy that, in Furio's eyes, makes her just like all the other women. Soon after he breaks off the affair, the fantasy register moves into high melodrama. Amid both raging storm and emotions, Lery returns to beg Furio's forgiveness. But this woman scorned differs from those in romantic tales and life of yore. After a chaste night, our hero answers his former lover's plea for a farewell kiss. As he leans over Lery, she fires a revolver, just grazing him, thanks to the medal on his chest. Lery projects her rage toward the male, not inward, in a revenge fantasy exemplifying Modleski's proposition that women's romances may exert subversive power by expressing female desire for vengeance against patriarchy. Liala employs the romance technique of summary to underscore further the scene's paradigmatic significance. Furio, thinking back on what happened, concludes that the times really have changed because "in the past, women killed themselves, but now they kill . . . if they can" (107).

This cautionary tale defines a central dilemma raised in *Signorsì*, which concerns the ways in which the unstable, equivocal dimensions of female sexual difference threaten disruption, if not destruction, in personal and social life. It would be unwise to dismiss Liala's representation of sexual conflict in the thirties as pure fantasy. In the first place, part of the genre's appeal derives from the portrayal of heroines successfully resolving problems that have a direct bearing on women's lives in patriarchal society, as the critical studies by Modleski, Radway, and Mussell have shown. Furthermore, working through the concept of "subtext" elaborated by Fredric Jameson, we see that, like other artifacts of mass and high culture, romance novels rewrite preexistent social contradictions in the very process of creating a symbolic resolution and thereby actively engage "the real." Describing the relations among text, history, and reality operating in subtext, Jameson (1981) maintains:

> The literary work or cultural object, as though for the first time, brings into being that very situation to which it is also, at one and the same time, a reaction. It articulates its own situation and textualizes it, thereby encouraging and perpetuating the illusion that the situation itself did not exist before it, that there is nothing but a text, that there never was any extra- or con-textual reality before the text generated it in the form of a mirage. (82)

Thus, we may read Liala's fantasy as a restructuration of the contradictions, fears, and anxieties elicited by the ambiguity of gender roles, accelerated by the socioeconomic advances that working women gained in Italy during World War I. Similarly, in their insightful analysis of the broader social conflicts raised through representations of feminine models in Italian romance fiction of the thirties, Pietro Cavallo and Pasquale Iaccio (1984) maintain:

> In this period of changes and jumps, the figure of woman, more so than any other, is where appeals and tensions intersect, deriving from a society in profound transformation and from a political regime that, for the first time in Italy, tries to manage not only the "public" but also the "private." (1153)

Furthermore, the apparatuses designed by the Fascist state to discourage emancipated behaviors associated with the model of the crisis woman and to reengender traditional manners more becoming to woman suggest that modern female practices in life and culture became a matter of increasing sociopolitical concern.

Thus contextualized, Furio's search for the ideal woman may be interpreted as a symptomatic response to the confusion and puzzlement over nontraditional gender roles. Caught in a maelstrom, where new manners and beauty canons symbolize the trappings of femininity, the hero seeks an untainted, natural image of woman as a transparent mirror to the soul. Enter Perla, one of three daughters and a son belonging to the Rosivi family, which has just made a killing in cheese and represents the nouveaux riches. The image of innocence, her face is sweet and pure, framed by long chestnut-colored braids. Casting a net of coy charms, Perla seduces the young man, first with a voyeuristically portrayed game of footsie played under the dinner table, just beyond her parents' watchful eyes, and then, with her lavish mane and "knowing caresses." She soon, however, dashes his dreams. Perla perfunctorily announces her impending marriage and reveals that she engaged in the last month of nightly assignations only because she wanted to know what it was like to kiss a duke. The crassness of her motivation sends Furio into a tailspin of doubt and despair about his inability to read images of female self-fashioning. As he confesses to Mino, "These perverted, pretty girls hurt other women, too, the good ones, the honest ones. How can you tell the pure women from the other ones now, if they appear with eyes modestly cast down and even know how to deceive the people who live with them all the time?" (92).

The tension created by the drama of mistaken identities is momentarily alleviated when, in part 2, the narrative shifts focus to Renata, who, in addition to personifying the features Furio has dreamed of, possesses several characteristics typical of romance heroines. A paradigm of guileless beauty, Renata unassumingly carries her tall, perfect body and has a face that shines with "the purity of a Madonna," crowned by a head of long curly blond hair. As the narrator tells us, she is "compliant, intelligent, good, and extremely beautiful," as well as an accomplished harpist. Although raised and educated in Milan, Renata lives with Zianna—an aged, loving aunt, wise to the ways of the world—in an idyllic country villa draped in wisteria. As the reader discovers, tragic childhood events have caused the heroine to live this cloistered life. She is haunted by memories of the pain and anguish that her mother's affairs wreaked on her father, until one day he caught her with another man and killed her, and then himself. Liala's portrayal of the heroine's Oedipal past accomplishes two other important purposes. It introduces the themes of heredity, transgression, and guilt, associated with the fantasy of origins, foreshadowing the possibility that the sins of the mother may be visited on the daughter. Renata's fear that her mother's tainted blood courses through her own veins also explains her initial cold politeness toward Furio, who must then win her over.

In contrast to romantic tales of old, in *Signorsì* the prince does not ride up on a white horse but falls from the sky, reining in a massive, rumbling silver bird. The author's depiction of the seduction fantasy, from courtship to honeymoon, invents what I shall call an aeroromance, refashioning traditional tropes of romance for a new age of speed and technology. Every day, Furio circles his plane above the villa, perfectly following the rules of etiquette as he begins to court Renata, waving to her from the cockpit, sending his first salutation, "Good morning, sunshine," and then throwing her a bouquet of roses with a card that declares his love and asks for permission to land. In a manner worthy of my subject, I shall defer analysis of the seduction scenario for the moment, in order to examine how the author's development of flying as a structural metaphor and symbol creates opportunities for identifying with the active principle of culture and for engaging the subjectivity of historically situated women readers.

In *Simians, Cyborgs, and Women* (1991), a groundbreaking study on the relations between discourses of science as discipline and fiction, and social reality, Donna Haraway demonstrates both the power and plea-sure that stories of technology exert as public myth, inventing popular meanings in daily life. For readers in Italy of the 1930s, Liala could not have chosen a more powerful object of myth than aviation. Amid the general fascination with planes and flying, the possibility to navigate ever-widening horizons had a particularly strong purchase on female-gendered imagination and practices. As we see from the historiographic materials unearthed by Michela De Giorgio (1992), the daily press and women's publishing of the twenties gave extensive coverage to what was called women's "flying fever."[12] Following the example of such pioneer-ing Italian women aviators as Rosina Farrario, who earned her pilot's li-cense in 1913, and Clelia Ferla, increasing numbers of upper-class women took to the skies. They sought the pleasure offered by this new pursuit as a vocation or a daring sport that created the possibility to demonstrate their skills in competition. For instance, Carina Negrone Di Cambiaso captured the 1935 women's world record for the highest altitude reached in a seaplane. The heart-stopping feats accomplished by female aviators, proving their intelligence, talent, and courage, obviously contradicted traditional dualisms reinforced during Fascism—man/woman, public/private, technology/nature. By so doing, such feats provoked growing debate in the press. In a defensive response, one commentator cautioned members of the "fairer sex" about taking over the controls of a plane, arguing that woman's weaker constitution, "easily shocked and given to light-headedness" cannot withstand the "extreme demands flying puts on the nervous system" (cited in De Giorgio 1992, 256). Similarly, some writings represent women's aviational achievements as an example of female vanity, in an attempt to trivialize the enterprising spirit and ambition driving the pilots to do what had never been done before and to surpass records in distance, altitude, and speed. Mussolini's own re-sponse was unequivocal. In a telegram sent in 1934, Mussolini requested the prefect of Bologna to inform the director of the Aero-Club, which had published an ad inviting women to enroll in flying classes, that

> in Fascist Italy, the most Fascist thing women can do is to pilot a lot of children, something that doesn't prevent them from taking a plane when they have to, or for pleasure. But piloting a plane is another very serious

matter that must be left to men, who, at least in Italy, are not in short supply. (De Felice 1974, 155)

However, perhaps attesting to the failure of attempts to ground women with a discursive battle over the skies, some writers co-opted the triumphs of civilian flyers, while constructing a nationalized model of the Italian female pilot that reconciles this "virile" pursuit with the overriding imperative of femininity. Typical in this respect is one of the many articles reporting the death in 1932 of Gaby Angelini, a young woman pilot from Milan who captivated the minds and hearts of Italians. The first woman in Italy to complete a trans-European flight, for which she received the Golden Eagle medal, she embarked on a flight to the Orient but died in a crash en route. Paying her tribute, the *Corriere della sera* reported that "although many foreign women have revealed how extremely strong and virile they are, this young Italian girl showed how females can be daring and not lose any of their truly exquisite femininity" (in De Giorgio 1992, 258). The journalist goes on to applaud the way that Angelini brought the grace and harmony of classic dance to the highly competitive arena of aviation contests. In deed and word, she became an inspirational hero, particularly for women, as we see from her comments on the fame bestowed on her by Italians: "But I didn't do anything special. I'm a girl who likes sports and went on different kinds of vacations. A lot of other girls could do what I did, and see some of the world in just a few days, live, and learn. All they need is strong nerves and a little courage" (in De Giorgio 1992, 258).

An examination of how Liala's aeroromance encodes flight gives a different perspective on the meanings and forms of psychic exchange that the author constructs for her women readers. The representations of flight span different registers ranging from technical to fantasmatic. Throughout *Signorsì*, Liala integrates scientific language and information about aeronautics with descriptions that are so precise and plentiful that they prompted one critic from the *Corriere della sera* to think the author was a man (Gregoricchio 1981, 10). Indeed, we learn about different kinds of aircraft and their special quirks and capabilities, controlling the high-tech instruments during takeoffs and landings, training exercises, and performing acrobatic stunts in the skies—all conveyed in aviational terminology. The text thus creates a sense of mastery in the discourse of this new technology. Likewise, for women among the reading public whose economic conditions made taking a train to the city (let alone flying in an airplane) the dream of a lifetime, the detailed sensorial depictions of air travel foster a priceless illusion, as if their bodies, and not just their imaginations, were taking flight. Exciting all the senses, the author evokes the smell of fresh air and fuel, the feeling of wind rushing against the skin, the sounds of the thundering engines that make their own sort of music, and the pit deepening in the flyer's stomach as a seaplane performs the circle of death, threatening to dive to the ground just before it reaches the peak of the somersault.

More important, Liala highlights how airplane flight alters the perception of space and time, as illustrated by the following passage, which describes how Furio and Renata perceive the panorama from aloft:

> Genoa disappeared, dazzling with light, and speeding along below them, Rapallo and Portofino passed by, the ancient, abandoned tower of the Villafrancas—perched on a bare, peaked hill over the Moneglia Gulf—passed by, Pietrastella passed by.... Deiva appeared with its green and rose-colored marble and white gravel, Levanto came up, sprawling on the ground, the little towns of Cinque Terre appeared, clinging to the rocks, then Vernazza came into sight, looking, from above, as if it were under water, and ever onward, to Portovenere, where the houses were all bunched together, and looked like a herd of frightened sheep. (216)

In contrast to passages simulating the bodily sensations produced by the motion of flying, here Liala creates the impression that the landscape flashes past a fixed point of vision. The cumulative series of sights appearing one after another, in what seems like moments, telescopes both vast spaces and time, thus representing new modes of perception in Italian technological society. This altered state of aerial vision and temporality does not allow the observer to take in the details of the scenery, providing instead impressionistic images of the landscape's most visible features. But there is no sense of Heideggerian discontent with the changes of modernity here. On the contrary, Liala exalts the technological possibilities of the modern age.

Liala's evocative representations of aerospace and the aviators and aircraft navigating it also merit attention for the symbolic codes that she creates, beckoning women into a fantasy of flight. The figurative language in *Signorsì* unites traditional symbols of flight, which are modernized for the industrial age, with new metaphors. As we would expect, the writer exploits the aircraft as a symbol of Italy's technological advancement. However, she also develops an aesthetic of the machine, gendered through metaphors traditionally associated with femininity. The significance of this narrative strategy can best be assessed with the help of Gillian Beer's work "The Island and the Airplane" (1990), which examines the impact of aviation on political, economical, sexual, and literary relations of the 1930s. Most important for this analysis, as Beer points out, in the early 1900s Freud began to note and analyze the increasing incorporation of flying machines into dreams. Not unexpectedly, Freud adapted the new dream technology to a phallocentric interpretative model. Freud, Beer summarizes, "identifies 'the remarkable characteristic of the male organ which enables it to rise up in defiance of the laws of gravity' as the reason for its symbolic representation as a flying-machine" (265), and thus a woman who has dreams of flying does so, in Freud's words, out of her "wish to be a man" (265).

Liala encodes flight and aircraft in a more ambivalent system of signs. The massive giants become objects of beauty, admired as much for their high-powered engines and strong gleaming metal as for their gracefulness, evoked through typically feminine metaphors of butterflies and birds. The relationship between machine and pilot at times assumes a strong sexual character, as the writer employs the strategy of anthropomorphizing the planes and drawing analogies between flying and sexual relations. For instance, when Furio tries to comfort Renata, he says, "Rest here, quietly, try to sleep. I'll caress you like this, very softly, the way I caress the wheel of my red plane. A seaplane obeys tender caresses, but it rebels against sharp movements. Be like a plane; obey, go to sleep" (323). Woman occupies the passive position in this passage; she becomes (like) the aircraft. But Liala's representations of flying as a transformative, emancipatory experience solicit engagement with the syntax of the narrative and symbolic movement. The eagle, rejected by the futurists as an outmoded figure of flight, operates as the dominant unifying symbol of aviation and assumes nationalistic and metaphysical valences. The golden-eagle medals shine as a tribute to the feats of valor and duty performed by the aviators for the Italian nation. Pilots are described as young, talented "eagles" who carry the Italian flag to far-off lands (113). At the same time, the eagle symbolizes the adventure and freedom made possible by flight, interestingly encoded in domestic imagery, as illustrated by the following description:

> When the eagle, in full command of its own wings, prepares for its first flight, it doesn't think about the nest it is about to leave but casts itself blissfully into space and serenity, sure that further on, or higher up, it will find another nest where it can rest its tired wings. (12)

What this passage also highlights is the way that Liala evocatively depicts ascent as a form of transcendence. Elsewhere, the skies represent a heavenly reign of peace, purity, and solitude, offering escape from the problems of daily living.

I also want to suggest that Liala's fashioning of aviation provides ample reason to question the critical tendency to split high and mass culture into binary forms. The symbolic meanings that Liala makes available in her treatment of flying exhibit exchanges between mass literature and avant-garde futurist texts. Certainly, at the dawn of the twentieth century, F. T. Marinetti and his fellow futurists primed the Italian imagination for a modern poetics of the machine, executed, ideally, among the masses, with artistic devices of their own making in manifestos, music, poetry, and painting. Keeping pace with the development of new technologies, in the late teens and early twenties such futurists as Mario Scaparro and the aviator Fedele Azari elaborated forms of aerial performance, which gave rise to experiments with aeropoetics in poetry, painting, sculpture, and food, which I will examine more closely in my analysis of avant-garde women's poetry. In an interesting way, the futurist poetics of flight and Liala's aerial fantasy in *Signorsì* both draw on the boom in aviation as science and myth. Although the futurists in their founding manifesto of 1909 proclaimed their desire to murder the moonlight along with the romanticized ideals of woman and love—in other words, everything that the romance genre glorifies—such aeropoems as "L'aeropoema del Golfo della Spezia" (The aeropoem of the Gulf of La Spezia) by Marinetti (1935), "Decollaggio" (Landing) by Pina Bocci (1933), and "Foligno" by Leandra Angelucci Cominazzini (from the unedited text "Umbrian futurist aeropoem," 1939) exhibit features that intersect with, as well as diverge from, Liala's aeroromance. These include, for instance, renderings of the sensations, perceptions, and emotions produced by flying, the glorification of technological progress, and the fashioning of aviation as a symbol of boundless freedom, power, adventure, and, ironically, escape from the economic and social conditions that make technology and mechanical production possible. Moreover, though we must keep in mind the significant differences between the innovations authored by Liala within the romance tradition and the experimental linguistic and visual practices developed by, in particular, futurist women aeropoets and aeropainters, both parties encode aviation as a powerful female symbol of freedom. For women futurists, as Claudia Salaris (1982) explains, the gendered poetics of flight also had political implications: "All of their artistic practices, which are also based provocatively on male models, always contain a strong will for emancipation from the behavioral stereotypes attributed to woman and are proposed as alternatives to the ordinary conditions that woman occupies in everyday life" (201).[13] Likewise, I suggest, Liala's exhilarating images of flight expand the horizons of women's fantasy lives.

When we last left our hero and heroine, Furio was waiting for Renata to grant him permission to land. In the seduction scenario, Renata occupies the passive positionality in relation to desire; she is both figuratively and quite literally part of the landscape—a flash of golden splendor that first caught the pilot's eye. The purity and innocence emanating from this "blond Madonna" and her life in the pristine countryside, represented as a haven from urban moral decay, echo motifs shaping the female model of the countrywoman disseminated by the regime in its rural campaign. But the likeness seems to end here. Liala's depiction of the romance heroine lacks any sign of stout rural industriousness. Her body, Furio tells us, was created for love, not labor. But, as you will remember, the trauma that Renata experienced as a girl fostered such deep-seated distrust and fear that she dismisses any thoughts of marriage and permits the pilot to land only as a favor to her aunt. As the object of desire, the heroine now represents a resistant space that the hero must overcome if he is to attain his dream.

In relation to the description of Furio's courtly attempts to sweep Renata's heart away on the wings of flight, their actual encounters receive surprisingly little space. Only the first meeting and the proposal scene are developed. The author provides essential information through summary, while encouraging the free play of imagination with a few suggestive remarks. The first time that Renata and Furio meet announces the dawning of the heroine's sexual awareness and of the life the hero could only dream about until now. Thereafter, the narrator informs us, Furio steals away from the base every evening in a shroud of secrecy, until the night he asks Renata to marry him. In the context of the romance genre's conventions, the hero's proposal and especially marriage generally promise the resolution of conflicts and misunderstandings that have thwarted ideal romantic coupledom. Liala uses this scene, however, to heighten the affective tensions between desire, guilt, and fear in a dramatic struggle of wills. Furio prevails but merely breaches Renata's defenses. Although she professes her love for the hero, she first refuses to marry him, later giving her consent out of concern for his immediate well-being.

The episodes depicting the marital life shared by Furio and Renata develop the heroine's psychological complexity while conducting a substantial social critique of patriarchal male-female relations that scholars have virtually ignored. The author examines the issue of family abuse as the hint of jealousy exhibited by our otherwise gentle, sensitive, irresistibly attractive hero becomes a nightmarish obsession. From the moment when Furio hides his new bride in a secluded house far away from family, friends, and the city, Liala makes it clear that jealous mistrust, and not a misguided wish to protect, motivates his actions. The representation of escalating psychological and physical violence also demonstrates the objectification of woman. Initially, Furio takes preventive measures to ensure that the heavenly beauty personified by his wife, whom he renames Beba, will remain for his eyes alone: he discourages Renata from going out alone and permits only rare visits from guests, which he watchfully surveys; on the few occasions he takes his wife out, he dictates what she wears down to the last detail, even chiding her about the shade of nail polish she chooses. Later, when a doctor must administer a shot to Renata, Furio, crazy with jealousy, bites her shoulder, marking her as his possession. It is fair to speculate that the representations of Furio's displays of irrational outbursts and physical victimization of Renata disengage the reader's sympathies. As Mino, the voice of conscience, states, "What kind of hero would strike a woman?" (262).

As Furio's heroic stature diminishes, Renata conversely acquires depth as she progresses from an obedient, childlike bride to a woman who expresses her desires and the right to have the respect she deserves, albeit within the circumscribed logic of patriarchy. The glimmers of intelligence and independence that she exhibits in social relations with friends and acquaintances, which are repressed in the domestic sphere, surface in a burst of rebellion after Furio accuses her of being attracted to other men:

> But what am I then? Why shouldn't I suffer? . . . What am I, indeed? A pretty young girl to take when you're tormented by desire, and to insult when desire is quenched. That's just what my life is like, Furio. Kisses and beatings. When you're not throwing me on the bed, you push me to the ground, your hands torturing me. . . . To live like this, like this forever, no! I'm not an animal, I'm a woman! I have a soul, pride, a heart! (253)

While critiquing male behaviors and attitudes that position woman as sexual object, this scene also foregrounds the issue of female sexuality. The significance of Liala's representations of the female as sexual subject, within the narrative and the broader discursive field, should not be underestimated. In the interwar years, hegemonic discourses effectively repressed the subject of female sexuality. Fascist discourses designed to solicit women as heroically pure reproducers of the nation invoked immaculate, sexless figures—the Virgin Mother and the angel of home and hearth. As Maria Antonietta Macciocchi claims, "The body of fascist discourse is rigorously chaste, pure, virginal. Its central aim is the death of sexuality," which castrates both women and men (1979, 75). Similarly, Catholic writings sought to manage and discipline female sexual inclinations and manners, with threats of a host of physical ills, ostensibly brought on by everything from lipstick to masturbation. Although popular publications diffused advice on acceptable forms of flirting, choosing a future husband, and setting up a household, as De Grazia points out, little practical information about sex was available. Liala therefore speaks the unspeakable, giving narrative representation to female sexuality. Although the author presents Lery and Perla as negative cultural models of active female desire, her characterization of the heroine appears to reconcile polarities constructed in Fascist and Catholic ideology: she endows Renata with the goodness, purity, and beauty of the Madonna as well as sexual desires and agency.

In the 1930s, Liala depicts sex, Italian style, in euphemistic and sometimes pointed fashion. Surprisingly, given the conventional importance of the heroine's sexual initiation in romance, the narration provides meager information about the bride and groom's first night of lovemaking, telling us only that Furio later watched Renata as she slept, peacefully smiling. Everything else is left to our imaginations. Thereafter, however, the narrator and other characters frequently note the telltale signs of passions spent—dark circles under the eyes, pallor, trembling hands, and physical exhaustion. Hence, fearing his friend may loose his life if he flies in such a state, Mino appeals to Renata's sense of reason, telling her, "It's up to you to rein in that magnificent horse's gallop" (171). The narrative also represents a wealth of popular psychology and attitudes toward female sexuality. For example, during one of his outbursts Furio questions his wife's fidelity, maintaining that the first lover merely sparks the pleasure that others will flame—expressing the notion of women's insatiable sexual appetites, which, according to De Grazia, was popularized in jokes of the time. In contrast to such euphemistic language, other depictions of female sexuality speak quite candidly. Again, Mino, noticing the increasingly sensual demeanor that Renata assumes during her pregnancy, recalls the intimate information his own lover once shared, confessing that "some women, when they get pregnant, become frigid, and making love turns into something painful; other women can't live without that pleasure" (289). He concludes that Renata is among the latter group. Here, and in a following scene where Renata—"happy, intoxicated, yet not satiated"—seduces Furio, the text breaks a double taboo. Fashioning a counterfigure to the Fascist model of the virgin mother, in this fantasy the sexual subject is female and an expectant mother—a state generally portrayed by dominant culture as asexual and "purely" maternal.

The visions of the romantic heroine as an agent of desire, which the author elaborates in a plot twist mobilizing fantasies of origins and seduction, invite the readers to engage in forbidden dreams and, at the same time, arouse general psychosocial conflicts about female sexuality. Liala prepares us for the plot complication with subtle clues whose meanings become clear in an emotionally compelling scene. While Renata anxiously searches the skies for the planes flown by Furio and Mino, she faints at the thought that Mino, and not her husband, has crashed. The subsequent loss of her unborn son figures as a punishment for what has thus far been only an unconscious, emotional betrayal of her husband. While this development creates pleasure by confirming the suspicion that a tragic fate borne by the mother's accursed blood would befall Renata, the shift in the heroine's affections reconfigures the terms of masculinity as the object of female desire. Through self-reflexive commentary, the heroine calls into question the mythic, seductive power of the domineering "superman" constructed in the Fascist ideology of masculinity; she charges Furio's overbearing and abusive behavior with alienating her love. Instead, she comes to desire Mino, represented as an affectionate, attentive, and, most important, gentle confidant. These contending male models point to the undecidability of what masculinity means during Fascism, despite the regime's attempts to measure the ideal modern man in terms of the will to dominate, sexual prowess, fatherhood, familial authority, and combativeness.

Examining a related phenomenon in early-twentieth-century representations of the male body, Maurizia Boscagli (1996) argues that the years from the turn of the century through the 1930s saw a crisis in the configurations of masculine subjectivity and generated new visual markers of a male body responding "to a range of cultural imperatives from mass consumerism to a new economy of gender. Through the new corporeality, the western male subject was deftly inserted into the new circuits of commodity culture and consumer desire" (1). Read against the trends of masculine self-display analyzed by Boscagli, which include futurist and fascist models, among many others, Liala's reconfigurations of masculinity provide a different register for examining the New Man. Important here is an episode narrated in the provocative voice of romantic fantasy, where the author envisions the heroine as feminine image and sexual initiator. At Renata's request, Mino takes her out in a rowboat on the moonlit lake. Although Mino at first resists Renata's advances, he ultimately lets himself be seduced. The language that Liala employs casts a tender, innocent light on this sexual interlude, as "the boat swayed back and forth in the water, gently cradling their love" (317). Yet the sound of a train rumbling overhead on a bridge breaks the magical dream, leaving the lovers awash in the guilt and shame of betrayal.

In keeping with the generic conventions of romance, Liala spares no feelings in her representation of the toll exacted for Renata's transgression of the values structuring male-female relations. The heroine dies by her own hands, availing herself of modern technology to deliver, not defy, death. She takes one last flight in her plane during a climactic denouement that was heart-wrenching even for this reader, who approached the romance text as an intellectual enterprise. Although tragic, Renata's suicide fulfills the genre's imperative of a "satisfying ending" because, as Daniela Curti (1987b) explains, her death confirms the system of moral values represented in the narrative, restoring order to the symbolic space disrupted by the heroine. The conclusion thereby assuages the readers' anxieties. Read within the conventions of the genre, the text amply supports this interpretation. But I question whether the final scenes suture the multiple rifts in the representations of femininity and masculinity so seamlessly. First of all, as illustrated by the following passage, the author's depiction of Renata's death creates a seductive image of escape from and transcendence of what she perceives as a world with no clear paths or answers, a "small, confused, cloudy" world visible below:

> Oh, how that small silver plane rebelled, how it reacted, how it clung to the serene sky in order not to fall! Decisively, Beba shut off the gas, pushed the lever, and dove the plane headfirst into the ground. The air whistled, screamed, and sang all around her, then all of a sudden there was silence. And in that silence, Beba felt herself becoming lighter, as someone pulled her out of the dying plane, and carried her high above and far away. (326–27)

This ending, perhaps the only one imaginable for the guilt and torment of an impossible desire, may recontain the transgressive force articulated in Liala's representations of female sexuality. Essentially, we have come full circle, returning to the scenario where women kill themselves. At the same time, by providing this form of closure instead of successful family formation—the conventional conclusion to the romanticized Oedipal script—the narrative may also suggest that the institution of family cannot resist the pressures brought to bear by modern female desires.

As noted above, *Signorsì* features some narrative traits that become codified in the modern romance, as well as atypical ones, and thus should not be read as an exemplary text representing the broad horizons of romance fiction published during Fascism. However, given the novel's phenomenal success among the mass audience, it is reasonable to speculate about how the romance engages readers. And if, as Antonio Gramsci (1985) contends, commercial literature inscribes the traces of the dispositions, fears, and fantasies of "common" men and women in their affective, psychic, and social dimensions, then romance fiction in particular, which by generic imperatives draws on topical conflicts to be negotiated, offers an invaluable terrain for examining sexual and social relations in the process of transformation. Indeed, the mobile gaze that Liala constructs and the hypervisualization of multiple terms of femininity and masculinity resist fixed notions of the sociosymbolic relations between the body politic and material bodies. Moreover, this romantic fantasy creates a whirl of competing, potentially disorienting codes that puts into question the commonplace notion of uniform(ed) mass culture and its unproblematic "consumption."

FOUR

Continental Drift: The Politics of Realist Aesthetics and the Novel

> Fascism politically is a realist doctrine. . . . Practically it aspires to re-
> solve problems that it poses historically by itself, and on its own finds
> or suggests the solution. To act among men, as in nature, one must
> enter into the process of reality and master its forces.
>
> BENITO MUSSOLINI[1]

Since the establishment of the conservative coalition government in
Italy, headed by Prime Minister Silvio Berlusconi and including right-
wing members some would call neo-Fascists, the topic of Italian Fascism
has gained amazing currency in the news and popular media, as journalists avail themselves of the latest-breaking bulletins, news clips, and especially photographs in an attempt to explain what Fascism really is to
readers in the United States.[2] A photograph accompanying one such article on the contradictory body of right-wing Italian politics, titled "The
Ghost of Mussolini Keeps Rattling His Chains" (Cowell 1994, 3), illustrates this point. The photographic image, an "analogon" to reality, as
Roland Barthes (1977, 17) cautions, captures a group of young white people standing with faces cast toward someone or something to their left,
beyond the camera's eye, a few with arms hanging relaxed at their sides,
others making the stiff-armed salute, clearly visible above a banner
marked by a swastika. Most of the men have shaven or closely cropped
hair, a style graphically expressing the term *Nazi-skins*, which Italians
have drawn from the English vocabulary to name them. Both the men
and women (the latter of whom are somehow excluded from the cap-

tion) are darkly clad, from their fatigue boots to jackets. In the context of Italian fashion tastes, the labels could be Levi's, Benetton, or, though unlikely, Armani. But the color is black, worn as if the bearers had arisen from a bygone era. Undoubtedly, this photographic image must evoke many different associations among readers, depending on their age, sex, race, religion, and nationality. At the most immediate level, the rhetoric of the image selected by the photographer deploys familiar symbols and aesthetics to convey the meaning of Fascism. (Not by chance, I would hazard to say, the heavyset, brutish male figure dominating the center foreground space resembles, through the shape of his neck and clean-shaven head, Mussolini. Or perhaps my own mind is playing tricks.) As we know, however, the photograph also distorts reality, as it isolates these individuals from the spectacle of the larger group and from the context, reducing everything to a flat, black-and-white surface. Furthermore, aside from a small, vaguely foreign abbreviation appearing in the left corner, nothing in the photo indicates Italianicity. Indeed, if it were not for the caption identifying the site as a rally of neo-Fascist extremists in Vicenza, this could be a shot of what we refer to as "skinheads" in the United States, Germany, or elsewhere.

The revival of the aesthetics and politics of Fascism gives new relevance to the cautionary message that Susan Sontag conveyed in her article "Fascinating Fascism" (1974), though we must make an initial distinction. For the men and women pictured in the recent newspaper photograph, a historical consciousness and political agenda anchor their employment of Fascist symbols—the fashion and color of dress, hairstyles, the salute, the swastika—for they have gathered to pay tribute to the memory of Benito Mussolini and Adolf Hitler. Sontag's treatment of fascist aesthetics, written more than twenty years ago, tackled a different order of problem. Her analysis warns readers about the unpredictable vicissitudes of popular and elite tastes that may unknowingly work to revive fascist artifacts and styles, even making them fashionably au courant. She makes this danger material to postwar life by re-presenting as an object lesson the artistic production in film and photography of Leni Riefenstahl, also the subject of a recent film, *The Wonderful Horrible Life of Leni Riefenstahl* (1993). Thus, Sontag's initial analysis resituates Riefenstahl's acting and filmmaking career within the specific historical context of her early success, German Nazism and the Third Reich, skill-fully exposing the inaccuracies, lapses in memory, lies, and inventions on which, the critic maintains, this artist's rehabilitation rests.

Then, from an examination of the thematic continuities running through the filmic and photographic texts that Riefenstahl produced during the years of Nazism and thereafter, Sontag undertakes the enter-prise of identifying thematic concerns and structural devices that consti-tute a category of fascist aesthetics. These include the sustained attention to such themes as domination and submission, the ability to master pain, and the objectification of people, frequently staged in spectacular demonstrations that exalt the bending of the multitude to the will of a magnetic, virile figure (or "force"), exhibiting epic strength. As Sontag is quick to admit, these traits appear not only in works that are created and presented under the name of fascism, but also in texts produced in "free" artistic marketplaces of liberal democracies and in communist states. To negotiate the bind of somehow distinguishing between communist and fascist variants of totalitarian cultural production, Sontag falls back on a familiar notion, stating that "features of fascist art proliferate in the offi-cial art of communist countries—which always presents itself under the banner of realism, while fascist art scorns realism in the name of 'ideal-ism'" (91). The idea that fascism adopts a hostile stance toward realism, a premise on which much cultural criticism on realist and modernist movements of the interwar years hinges, clearly recalls the position elab-orated by Georg Lukács as he refined his project of a critically reflective realism. In his essay "Expressionism: Its Significance and Decline" (1934) and subsequent writings fueling the "realism debate"—a struggle among such titans as Theodor Adorno, Walter Benjamin, and Bertolt Brecht over the performative political value of realist, modernist, and avant-garde aesthetics—Lukács presents fascism and realism as mutually ex-clusive terms. Clarifying his position in a letter written to Anna Seghers in 1939, Lukács minces no words as he identifies fascism with a reac-tionary, irrational decadence exemplified by what he calls "the Marinet-tis and D'Annunzios," and proclaims his conviction in "the connection between realism, the popular character of literature, and anti-fascism" (1981, 196–97).

As an Italianist working on what appears to be a highly complex discursive field in Italy during Fascism, with a full range of positions on high and mass cultural forms that constantly shift and compete for dominance, I cannot help but be struck by the way in which Lukács invokes F. T. Marinetti and Gabriele D'Annunzio in his construction. I would speculate that for many scholars investigating the critical theories of popular culture, the avant-garde, and modernism as they arose from the intellectual sparring over the politics of realist and experimental aesthetics in the 1930s, this detail seems so minor as to not qualify as part of the debate at all. In fact, it is apparent that Italy exists only on the margins of this controversy, a liminal presence at best. Though certainly not the only nation cast in this light, Italy is re-called, I wish to propose, as the Fascist Other against which critics representing different currents of thought may define themselves. In the thirties, Lukács declares battle against decadence as the literary expression of fascism, using a strategy typical of war. He depersonalizes the enemy, Marinetti, D'Annunzio, and, by association, the "other" Italian writers of the time that they are now called on to represent, by making their patronymic names into object nouns, in the plural no less, as if the dream of self-sufficient male procreation that Marinetti envisioned in *Mafarka, le futuriste* (1910) had become reality. Similarly, as shown by Russell Berman's (1990) salient analysis of Walter Benjamin's influential essay "The Work of Art in the Age of Mechanical Reproduction," Marinetti is again invoked to support Benjamin's theory that fascism typifies the aestheticization of politics. True, a well-chosen quotation serves to substantiate Benjamin's thesis. Nonetheless, he evacuates the historically specific location of Marinetti and his text in the highly diversified range of political and cultural production during the Italian Fascist regime.[3]

Critical rereadings of the ideas and paradigms proposed by Lukács, Benjamin, and other writers participating in the discussions about the political and symbolic functions performed by realist versus antirealist aesthetics have examined the weaknesses, gaps, and strengths of their arguments. As a result, we have gained a more productive understanding of different aesthetic forms as equivocal systems, neither intrinsically subversive nor complicitous with the hegemonic system surround, whose textual politics can best be assessed by examining their performative value within the specific sociocultural conditions of their making.[4] However, in a substantial amount of criticism published in the American academy on artistic currents during the interwar years, the Lukácsian invocation of Marinetti remains intact. Here I am speaking about major works that have structured how we pose and think about issues concerning modernism and realism. Take, for example, the influential collection *Modernism: Challenges and Perspectives* (1986), which includes no less than eighteen essays on a wide variety of subjects.[5] Though no Italian artists appear in the titles, the index of this anthology shows that there are some references to them. Moreover, in the essay "Modernism and Ideology" (1986), Matei Calinescu proposes to test the notion of commitment in modern art and the theory that modernism and fascism may be closely related, two central issues in Italian studies on the relation between interwar and postwar culture. Given the dominant identification of modern art in Fascist Italy with Marinetti, it is not entirely surprising that the engaging line of questioning that the author adopts as he analyzes the potentially revolutionary power of art in formulations of "form-oriented" and "content-oriented" commitment does not veer into Italian terrain.

So let us look, just for a moment, at how Calinescu, ostensibly writing against the conventional Anglo-American position, represents the bearing that Italian artists may have on the second problem. At the outset of the section subtitled "Modernism and Fascism," Calinescu summarily states:

> The fact is that in Europe, with the exception of Mussolini's Italy (where people such as Marinetti's futurists or more independent modernists such as Papini or Pirandello supported fascism), few writers whom we could call modernist favored the various extreme right-wing movements that swept the continent in the 1920s and 1930s. (83)

While most scholars select a field of inquiry and textual objects according to their expertise and interests, frequently explaining the reasons why a study concentrates on one set of problems instead of another, Calinescu does something quite different. In the first place, Italian Fascism holds the distinction, perhaps dubious, of providing a model that exemplifies, during the 1920s and 1930s, the engineering of sites and apparatuses for the institutional articulation of fascist ideology in culture and society. Yet in a supporting clause Calinescu dismisses the case of Italian Fascism as a subject worthy of critical attention. In an equally troubling manner, he oversimplifies the relations among Marinetti, futurism, and Fascism, as well as the different forms of modernism elaborated under and outside the auspices of official Fascist culture, problems that I examine in the following chapter. To be fair, Calinescu notes a few other exceptions, limited however to individual authors who had alliances with fascism, for instance, Arnolt Bronner and Martin Heidegger, and to Céline, an "enigma." But representing Italy as an exception has fundamental importance for Calinescu's thesis, for only by doing so can he conclude that "given all these exceptions and certainly others (less spectacular and therefore easier to ignore), continental modernism, including the avant-garde, was *not* attracted to fascism" (84). This lapidary assertion authorizes his position that Lukács's critical theory of the distinct ideological implications of realist and experimental aesthetics affords the only, and in his opinion, weakly formulated, basis for making any connections between fascism and "*European* modernism" (emphasis added).

Recent scholarship has begun to weaken territorial borders demarcated in debates about the relations between the politics of fascism and aesthetics, questioning the critical drift authorizing them. Such works include the volume dedicated to "Fascism and Culture" by the *Stanford Italian Review* (1990), Richard Golsan's *Fascism, Aesthetics, and Culture* (1992), whose international perspective incorporates two provocative examinations of modernity, modernism, and futurism written from the vantage point of Italian Fascism, Andrew Hewitt's *Fascist Modernism* (1993), and Lucia Re's "Fascist Theories of 'Woman' and the Construction of Gender" (1995). These studies offer differentiated analyses of the heterogeneous, unstable discursive positions adopted toward Fascist ideology by female and male protagonists shaping modernist and avant-garde movements in Italy. While pursuing the direction in critical thought opened up by this body of work, here I plan to veer into relatively unexplored "peninsular" formations and literary practices of realist aesthetics in the Fascist regime. Although some cultural critics have tended to underestimate, if not deny, the capability of Fascism to produce original theories of art, the debates among Fascist intellectuals about realist and avant-garde aesthetics as vehicles for a cultural revolution show, first, that the relation between Fascism and art warrants serious attention, and second, that we cannot approach Fascist aesthetics as an abstract or fixed category.[6] Therefore, in light of Lukácsian commentary, the first part of my study provides an extensive reappraisal of the paradigms proposed for realist art by canonized Italian writers, some working within the orbit of Fascist culture, and others working against it. My intent is neither to defend nor to disprove Lukács's model of realism or its subcategories as an implicitly antifascist aesthetic. The analysis serves to draw out the complexities of assessing the political meanings and assumptions attached to aesthetic systems.Therefore, I hope to construct a more nuanced account of the theoretical and literary range of realist production in Italian culture during Fascism, inspiring perhaps new questions for which no ready-made answers exist.

The initial assessment of the formal properties of realist aesthetics and the social and symbolic functions that they are called on to perform within the specific juncture of Fascism also constructs a necessary comparative framework for my examination of two novels by female writers, which is intended to theorize the location of women's textual politics of realism. For this latter section of my inquiry, I have chosen to reread *Maria Zef* (1936) by Paola Drigo and *Nessuno torna indietro* (1938) by Alba De Céspedes. At the time of their publication, both novels attracted widespread critical and popular acclaim. An overnight international best-seller, De Céspedes's novel was translated into thirty languages, including an English translation published in 1941 as *There's No Turning Back* and later adapted for a television movie in 1987.[7] In 1954, Luigi De Marchi directed a film adaptation of Drigo's novel, followed by another film, which the Italian broadcasting corporation RAI produced for television in 1981. Attesting to the continued interest in *Maria Zef* among general readers, Garzanti reprinted the novel in 1982, and in 1989 it appeared in English translation.[8] Nonetheless, from an overview of Italian scholarship on the novel and realist forms of representation developed during Fascism, it appears that these novels, among many others written by prizewinning women authors, did not survive the postwar editing of the canon.[9] Therefore, an essential aim of this study is to propose how a consideration of women's novels would substantially alter our view of the canonized history of the novel, currently constructed on the genre's fortunes and misfortunes among men authors. My textual analysis of the novels by Drigo and De Céspedes focuses on the "performativity" of their realist discourses, a concept that I employ in Judith Butler's sense of "a specific modality of power as discourse" (1993, 177). Although some artists in the regime lay claim to a full spectrum of experimental and realist forms as a foundation for elaborating a Fascist politics of art designed to create a truly Fascist subjectivity, I want to suggest that by examining the discursive effects constituted by Drigo and De Céspedes we can see an oppositional space subverting the very patriarchal structures of power that realism is generally assumed to reinscribe. Specifically, their ways of plotting and of representing forms of female self-fashioning among characters belonging to different socioeconomic classes and locations contend with the epic myths of woman, rural life, community, and nation—key elements of Fascist politics in everyday life and culture.

The Physiognomies of Realist Aesthetics during Fascism

From its inception, the ideal of a cultural revolution, the brainchild of Mussolini and fellow thinkers, drew talented intellectuals and artists into salient debate about the materials, aesthetic qualities, and performative functions of art in general and, in particular, of an "authentic" Fascist art, to this day ill defined. The aesthetic theories and practices proposed in the 1920s and 1930s chart the multifarious, often competing, and undecidable positions on forms of literature and the arts to be inaugurated under the sign of Fascism, as paradigmatically illustrated by the inquiry spearheaded by Giuseppe Bottai (1885–1959) from 1926 to 1927 in the Fascist journal *Critica fascista,* which he founded and edited.[10] In these debates about what constitutes the spirit and principles of Fascism, and which artistic current may best express them, such avant-garde artists as F. T. Marinetti and Anton Giulio Bragaglia championed futurism as the only logical contender for a "fascist style." Working on the generally held premise that Fascist art is in essence Italian art, Marinetti promotes the revolutionary aesthetic of "futurist fascist art" as "extremely Italian because it is virile, bellicose, joyous, optimistic, dynamic, synthetic, simultaneous, and colorful" (cited in Schnapp and Spackman 1990, 262). Ardengo Soffici, a former futurist, makes his case instead for the *Novecento* movement, proposing a poetics that "draws its inspiration and its elements from the observation and the study of living, current, functional reality" to be transformed by a process of synthesis, revealing "the lyrical spirituality and the stylistic will of the author" and "the poetic qualities of nature" (in Schnapp and Spackman 1990, 241). Though painters and writers working in the *Novecento* circle hoped to march in their program as the official art expressing the new age of Fascism and certainly benefited from Margherita Sarfatti's patronage, they also demonstrated lively interest in diverse poetics elaborated by authors associated with other currents of European modernism, and even by anti-Fascists.[11] For example, among the editorial board and contributors for the journal *Novecento* (1926–29), cofounded by Massimo Bontempelli and Curzio Malaparte, we find such artists as James Joyce, André Malraux, Rainer Maria Rilke, and Alberto Moravia. Whereas Soffici quickly distinguishes his concept of synthetic realism from an objective, "veristic" narrative, Mario Puccini urges fellow artists "to become simple, homey, provincial, realistic, perhaps even crudely and roughly realistic" (in Schnapp and Spackman 1990, 259). He presents this project as a medicinal purge of the symptomatic tendencies toward affectation, immorality, decadence, and "false aestheticism" spread during the liberal era. The cure he prescribes, if followed, would produce a strong, ethical, and virile art, guaranteeing the author citizenship in the Fascist nation of letters.

This brief overview highlights some of the main coordinates forming the physiography of directions proposed for executing a Fascist program of cultural renewal. It would be a mistake, however, to assume that these different positions, and the artists constructing them, remained fixed during the *ventènnio*. In actuality, even at the moment when proponents announce their respective poetics, they articulate sets of internal variables that accommodate seemingly irreconcilable bearings, as Jeffrey Schnapp and Barbara Spackman (1990) point out. Thus Soffici claims that Fascist art is "both materialistic and idealistic," able to encompass the past and future. Likewise, the painter Cipriano Efisio Oppo, a fellow *Novecentista*, characterizes Fascist aesthetics as both populist and universal, "revolutionary and traditional at the same time, new and old together like the magnificent, acceptable contradiction that is the history of Italian art" (in Schnapp and Spackman 1990, 265).

After years of implementing new cultural organizations, institutions, and forms of artistic patronage with prizes and monetary awards, ideologues still hesitated to define the relation of Fascist art to the Italian artistic tradition and to the experimental poetics of modernity, as clearly illustrated by the 1939 essay "Modernità e tradizione" (Modernity and tradition), written by Bottai, one of the leading figures in the regime's politics of culture. Bottai, who esteemed the veristic writings by Giovanni Verga, artfully negotiates the controversy, suggesting that "like some rivers that hit impenetrable strata in the earth, tradition may suddenly run deep, and after taking a subterranean course, may abruptly resurface where least expected, perhaps even beyond the geographic borders of the nation where it was born" (1992, 170). Further elaborating this point, he states that for all reckless diviners who might deny the forward reach of the past, an analysis of the river waters would verify how "within the twisted subterranean channels other geological strata—more ancient and yet richer with salts and denser with archaic earthly memories— new enriching substances, which didn't exist on the freely flowing surface, may have dissolved" (171).

The way in which Bottai likens the affiliations between Fascist art, tradition, and modernity to a river underscores a common rhetorical strategy that accomplishes several purposes. Clearly, the fitting analogy he draws plays on the river as a rich symbol of creativity and time's passage, whose waters can carve an unpredictable course, pulling the most disparate substances into its currents while dissolving others. The multiple meanings and associations evoked by this metaphor deny precise definition while naturalizing artistic relations that are culturally constructed. The Fascist state's refusal to identify itself exclusively with any particular avant-garde, modernist, or realist current or to define its aesthetic in specific terms evidences the thesis, advanced by Schnapp and Spackman, that Italian Fascism is best understood as "an unstable and deeply paradoxical ideological formation held together with an often slippery aesthetic glue" (1990, 237).[12] By maintaining an open set of shifting variables within the general category of Fascist art, conceived as an authentic expression of the Italian race, morally committed and virile—a signifier of dynamic, productive, creative principles—the regime afforded itself the opportunity to co-opt critical and artistic works, regardless of the author's political allegiance and subjectivity. For instance, the novelist Curzio Malaparte praises Benedetto Croce's *History of the Kingdom of Naples* as a truly Fascist work, though Croce outspokenly opposed the regime and authored the "Manifesto of Anti-fascist Intellectuals" in 1925. Eligio Possenti employs a similar strategy in the article "Volontà costruttiva e realtà nazionale nella letteratura fascista dell'anno XIII" (The will to construct and national reality in fascist literature of the year XIII, 1935). Written to pay tribute to the rich terrain created by Fascism for the flourishing of artistic life, the article boasts a lengthy inventory of authors and poets, including such anti-Fascists as Alberto Moravia and Marino Moretti, thus appropriating their voices. The heterogeneous features of the aesthetics that Fascist cultural politics aimed to create or co-opt show the difficulties of constructing a workable category defining typically fascist themes, structures, and modes. Furthermore, developing Richard Golsan's (1992) observations about the implications of fascist modernism's lack of specificity, the way in which Fascist aesthetic production works across critical/political boundaries between realist and experimental paradigms means that its practices may be dispersed more easily in subsequent forms, even, I would add, in those that claim an oppositional stance.

Postwar debates, reaching from the forties to the present day, about Italian neorealism's status as an oppositional aesthetic to Fascism exemplify this problem. A variety of artists and scholars contributed to the now-towering body of work in critical theory, literature, cinema, and the figurative arts that instantiated the hegemony of neorealist conventions as "committed" sociopolitical practice and as a founding myth of an anti-Fascist national identity. By so doing, they, like Bottai's reckless diviners who overlook the particles swept along in deep-running waters, forestalled questions concerning the relations between postwar and Fascist conceptions of art. In this sense, it is little wonder that cultural critics working outside the field of Italian studies tend to overidentify literary production during Fascism with F. T. Marinetti and futurism. A few scholars, however, have broached the problem. Most notably, in the early eighties Alberto Asor Rosa noted the elaboration of a realistic aesthetic in the theoretical and literary works produced by young leftist Fascist intellectuals. Romano Luperini proposed (by way of G. Quazza) a critical approach focusing, not on a rupture between the Fascist regime and the liberal republic, but on potential continuities.[13] Adopting a similar paradigm, the recent work by Ruth Ben-Ghiat provides the most extensive analysis and documentation of the endeavors among a new generation of left Fascists to theorize and practice a "new" realism, clearly operating within the sphere of officially sanctioned culture in the 1930s.[14] Tracking the development of this aesthetic in writings by such figures as Elio Vittorini and Vasco Pratolini, published in a variety of journals, Ben-Ghiat convincingly demonstrates how many of the notions of a neorealist thematics, systems of address, textual performativity, and authorial roles formulated as a Fascist cultural intervention were then rehabilitated as part of an oppositional aesthetic deployed by the Left in postwar Italy.

Recently published scholarship on the realist paradigm articulated by populist Fascist intellectuals forces us to reassess the assumed aesthetic territories colonized by Fascism. Reconstructing the genealogy of this emergent form of realism, signified by the term *neorealism,* along with its narrative ideals and practices, critics trace its origins to Italian commentary written in the late twenties on the contemporary Russian novel and to articles of the early thirties on the novels by German authors participating in the *Neue Sachlichkeit* movement.[15] In the thirties, such writers as Carlo Bernari and Elio Vittorini also rallied for a contemporary Italian realist aesthetic, designed specifically to serve populism, collectivism, and social change—ideals constituting the radical face of Mussolini's Fascist revolution. As artists affiliated with Fascist cultural politics theorized a new form of Italian realism, they distinguished their poetics from those advanced by Russian authors and, because of what they (like Lukács) saw as an excessive focus on angst, from German writers as well. Likewise, they rejected the positivist, deterministic forms of Italian *verismo* and naturalism, arguing instead for an interpretative, realistic representation of the individual actively engaging in material social relations, which would lead to transforming life and society. In his 1932 article "Del romanzo" (About the novel), Mario Pannunzio underscores the artistic value of this new realism: "The way that a fact . . . is interpreted, transformed, and even deformed through foreshortened, perspective observation has greater importance than the documentary value of the fact that is narrated" (435).

The proponents of neorealism, as well as such magical realists as Massimo Bontempelli, reconceived the role of the artist as a "committed" producer of art as sociopolitical practice, a notion not lacking precedents. Ada Negri, for instance, articulated a similar idea in her project to devise a socially committed form of poetry at the turn of the century, and Giuseppe Antonio Borgese specifically employed the image of the artist as builder in the early 1920s. Yet this formulation also echoes the opposition between producers and nonproducers structuring Fascist discourses and the regime's corporate system. Hence, challenging the aims of this revised notion of commitment, Pasquale Voza (1981) reads the Fascist-aligned attempts of young neorealist intellectuals to present themselves as active agents in modern reality as signs of "an ideologically transparent need for self-identification in a terrain of initiative and intervention, which animated and adapted the realist tensions and projects of those years" (77). However, as demonstrated by such model novels as *Tre operai* (Three workers, 1934) by Bernari, and *Il capofabbrica* (The foreman, 1935) by Romano Bilenchi, neorealists advocating a Fascist proletarian revolution dedicated substantive attention to the critique of working-class conditions and of empty bourgeois values.

It is highly significant that Fascist officials overseeing cultural organizations, publications, and policies supported neorealist artists and, as Ben-Ghiat (1991) maintains, even canonized their aesthetics as the product of a "movement which best embodies the anti-rhetorical and activist stance of Fascism" (157). Nonetheless, we must keep in mind that the discursive field of neorealism encompassed a broad variety of practices, developed by artists with different political affiliations, including Borgese, Moravia, and Corrado Alvaro. Furthermore, in some cases where social critique posed clear ideological challenges to the regime's image and practices, the state intervened to censure or sequester literary works. While Fascist commentary reproached Moravia's bleak portrayal of Italian bourgeois alienation in *Gli indifferenti* (Time of indifference, 1929), the regime sequestered his novel *La mascherata* (The masked ball, 1941) and prohibited him from publishing his writings in newspapers, to which he had been a major contributor. Even Vittorini, a member of the left-wing Fascists, drew criticism for the ideological implications conveyed in *Il garofano rosso* (The red carnation, 1948), first published in the journal *Solaria* (1933–34).

In order to theorize the relations between the textual and sexual politics of realism during the regime, we must situate the program developed by artists working under the sign of Fascism in the diversified field of realist aesthetics cultivated by men and women writers operating beyond circles sanctioned specifically by the state. By so doing we can see tensions between the differing redactions of realist aesthetics that have been largely overlooked. Indeed, the efforts among young left Fascist intellectuals to elaborate a new populist poetics of realism participate in a broader project articulated by men writers to revitalize realistic narrative, along with the Italian novel, as a means for committed artists to speak to greater numbers of readers, by addressing the interests and concerns arising from modern social reality. Therefore, genre, as an interpretative category, has useful applications here for understanding aesthetics as a site where different sectors of literary women and men struggle for expressive possibilities to create social and symbolic meanings for their reading publics. The category of genre is critical for appraising realist fictions within the context of changing attitudes, expectations, and tastes bearing on the writing and reading of texts.

The artist and critic Giuseppe Antonio Borgese best represents the changing perception of realism and the novel among the male literary establishment. In his suggestively titled work *Tempo di edificare* (1923), which indicates that it is "time to build or edify," playing on the meanings of *edificare*, Borgese theorizes the concept of the writer as socially productive and morally committed and outlines a project to democratize the elitist sphere of Italian literature by retooling the thematic scope, narrative practices, and linguistic properties of the novel. This undertaking emerges as a militant response toward the decadentism of D'Annunzio and the experimental poetics developed by the Vociani and futurists, to whom Borgese, among other writers, attributes the decline of the novel and of Italian literature in general:

> The beautiful, sumptuous edifice of Italian literature written as the past century drew to a close and the new one began has broken apart, as if it were a building for a grandiose world exposition, leaving behind a dusty

cloud of debris; the great personalized lyric has become pulverized and the fragmentary word chases after a sensation without a subject. (22)

A brief overview of the poetics and commentary produced in the early 1900s by the Vociani testifies to their invention of an aesthetic suited to conveying the flux of thought and being in its immediacy—a representational ideal that, from their perspective, the novel's "inferior" models of expression could not even approximate. Thus, in such exemplary texts as *Un uomo finito* (1913) by Giovanni Papini, *Il peccato e altre cose* (1914) by Giovanni Boine, and *Ragazzo* (1919) by Piero Jahier, the authors create a self-reflexive, delicate web of musings on metaphysical and existential motifs, diaphanously fashioned in lyrical, expressionistic prose, most prized for its stylistically brilliant effects. Similarly, authors sharing the artistic tenets advanced by the literary circle connected to the publication *La ronda* (1919–22, 1923), which argued for the autonomy of art from the social, political, and historical spheres, rejected the novel, aspiring instead to the "pure" aesthetic value of the "prosa d'arte," the lyrical prose poem or fragment. Aesthetic choices, however, seldom concern matters of purely artistic inspiration. In this case, critical writings of the time suggest that we can also read the cultivation of experimental, lyrical prose forms among esteemed men of letters as a defensive strategy elicited by the way in which women made the novel their own, artfully developing expressive forms that earned the acclaim of critics and the emergent mass readership.

Although more vehemently misogynist than most critics of his time, Giovanni Boine represents the general symptoms of male anxiety, as we see in his review of Clarice Tartufari's novel *All'uscita del labirinto* (On the way out of the labyrinth, 1914). At the outset of his assessment, Boine quickly nods in agreement with the critical community, stating that Tartufari's novel is excellent. Indeed, the fine way that she represents the characters and events, with a "precise sobriety" and "solid sincerity" tempts him to characterize her writing as "manly." He resists, however, and launches into the reasons why the work actually displays "womanliness":

This novel's qualities—the good qualities—transported into art, are the same ones that make your wife so good at keeping your home in order, and at balancing your budget, when it's in shambles, with so much wise scrupulousness and so much patience and, yes, with such punctilious courage and self-sacrifice. (Boine 1914, 258)

Boine employs this description along with Otto Weininger's notion of the woman-mother as "grounding" for his theory that "women's sense of order and their logic are of a mathematical nature, absolutely lacking the lyrical" (258). Hence, applying this essentialist idea of sexual difference to the field of genre, he maintains that such womanly traits are remarkably suited to the novel, which he demarcates as female-gendered space.

Yet at the same time, Boine deprecates the novel's artistic value for two important reasons. Regardless of the artful skill the novelist may display in giving form to creative inspiration, the process of novelistic narrativization produces, in his view, a still shot of life, a suffocating "photographic refinishing (a repeating of life)" (1914, 259). In an intriguing way, Boine's perspective on the novel aligns with recent theories of the central function that repetition plays in organizing narrative. In *Reading for the Plot* (1984), for example, Peter Brooks adopts the psychoanalytic model of the fort/da game to interpret narrative repetition as a process of coping symbolically with the lack of the mother, whereby fathers and sons endeavor to gain mastery. Although Marianne Hirsch (1989) argues that Brooks's narrative theory is irreparably bound to male psychosexual models and examples, Boine perceives this feature in women's novels and thus opens some interesting questions concerning women's reelaborations of realism. Are the plotting structures of the realist novel fixed in masculine models designed to achieve mastery? Does this genre then function exclusively to reproduce forms of patrilineal affiliation? How, if at all, can women authors create a space for representations of female subjectivity and sociability in the literal and symbolic dimensions? If so, what can we say about the broad success of women's novels among reading communities prior to and during Fascism? Boine, for instance, feels no allure and spurns the general readers who do. "Do we eternally have to work to entertain the paying public and to spin fables so that they can pass the time away?" he rhetorically asks (259). Assuming a position on high art not unlike Adorno's, Boine defends the lyric as the last bastion of true art against the growing swell of mass readers and the authors who seek to contribute to their cultural formation. Not surprisingly, Boine stakes a claim on the lyric as privileged territory for the expression of male subjectivity. He exhorts his fellow *letterati* "to be real men. . . : Let's leave literature aside and do poetry" (259).

The attitudes toward the novel, the lyric, and mass art that Boine so lucidly expresses represent prevailing notions of artistic values among esteemed men of letters and explain why Borgese, writing in a 1920 essay, assumes a tone of feigned embarrassment when he begins to evaluate the novel's status:

> I've read some novels: a confession that can't be made without slightly blushing because if someone wants to earn the indulgence of certain brotherhoods, he should abstain from writing as well as reading novels. . . . The same malevolence that was first directed toward the epic poem was then transferred to the novel, its firstborn son. But not only against the novel. Against the short story, the drama, and books in general, against every form that had a beginning, a middle, and an end, a meaning and a structure. (in Borgese 1923, 79)

I don't question the accuracy of this assessment of the novel's status among men writers. But if we expanded the evaluative field to women's novelistic production of the early 1900s, would the novel appear to suffer the dire crisis represented in much critical commentary of the interwar period and in literary histories written in the postwar years? In the late 1800s, following the early enterprises undertaken in the epistolary novels *Lettere di Giulia Willet* (Giulia Willet's letters, 1828) by Marquise Romagnoli Sacrati di Cesena and *Lettere d'un'italiana* (An Italian woman's letters, 1825) by Baroness Carolina Decio Cosenza, women writers had a firm hand in shaping the Italian novel, ranging from the potboilers written by Carolina Invernizio, undoubtedly the most widely read Italian author of her time, to the critically acclaimed novels by Neera. Many of the prizewinning female writers who made their literary debut in the 1800s produced some of their most powerful novels after the turn of the century. A few examples should suffice. Readers of this period saw the publication of *Suor Giovanna della Croce* (Sister Giovanna of the Cross, 1901) and *Ella non rispose* (She didn't answer, 1914) by Matilde Serao (1856–1927), applauded for her incomparable attention to the customs, beliefs, and socioeconomic conditions of Neapolitan life among the middle classes. Grazia Deledda (1875–1936) wrote *Elias Portolu* (1903),

Canne al vento (Reeds in the wind, 1913), and the internationally acclaimed *La madre* (The mother, 1920), each among her masterpieces,
according to the critical establishment. Clarice Tartufari (1868–1933),
who possessed, in Benedetto Croce's esteemed opinion, true genius as a
novelist for her critical interpretation and concise, engaging portraits of
modern life, published *Il miracolo* (The miracle, 1909), *Eterne leggi* (Eternal laws, 1911), and *All'uscita del labirinto* (1914), among other works.
Carola Prosperi (1883–?) authored her first novel, *La paura di amare*
(The fear of loving, 1911), winner of the Rovetta literary prize, *La nemica
dei sogni* (The enemy of dreams, 1914), and *L'estranea* (The estranged
woman, 1915), which earned the writer critical recognition for her realistic portrayal of the lower and middle classes struggling with materially
and ethically impoverished conditions of daily living in urban and rural
communities.

Although it is beyond the scope of this study to explore the intersections and divergencies among the poetics that these women authors
executed as they contributed to the novel's development, many continuing to write well into the years of the regime, a few points bear highlighting. First, these writers' narrative practices demonstrate the formulation of a populist aesthetic. Uniting the ideals of pleasure and cultural
edification, women's novels provide artistic representations of topical
subjects of interest arising from the quotidian. These include, for instance, the economic straits of factory workers, peasants, and even nuns
in the changing Catholic hierarchy; courtship and matrimony; the institution of family, sexual relations, and tensions between traditions and
emergent modern mores. An equally important part of this project concerns experimenting with linguistic models in order to fashion a literary
language suited to expressing the writer's particular perspective to a
broad audience, without sacrificing evocative power. Rejecting esoteric,
rhetorical models, the women's novels craft metaphors and symbols
belonging to the literary prose tradition yet increasingly make use of
constructions and vocabulary common to conversational Italian.[16] Some
writers, including Deledda and Drigo, weave selected words and expressions from regional dialect into the narrative gossamer, following the
self-styled mediation of the *questione della lingua* offered by the verista
Giovanni Verga.

Moreover, for this study's purposes, the representations of female cultural models created in novels by Tartufari, Deledda, Drigo, and later, De Céspedes inscribe signs of a politics of writing aimed at putting into literary discourse a fuller, more veracious range of women's intellectual and affective desires, experiences, and disillusionments. Theorized by Sibilla Aleramo and Amalia Guglielminetti as an oppositional discourse to literary and scientific writings on woman, this narrative project privileged women's lives as valuable subjects and proposed that women write from their direct experiences and observations in order to produce "documents of truth."[17] While this concept might seem to share the belief in positivism and a scientifically verifiable social reality, which anchored Italian naturalism and *verismo* in the late 1800s, the notion of veracity in woman's texts is conceived as creating literary visions that disclose as faithfully as possible the author's own *perceptions* of women's manners of knowing and being in the world. Furthermore, the substantive critique of the ways in which material conditions, societal beliefs, and institutions suppress female self-formation suggests an awareness of gender, not as a naturally given essence but as a sociocultural construction in patriarchy. In this sense, such works perform a feminist function as they challenge dominant codes and symbols of idealized womanhood and, following the broad definition provided by Rita Felski (1989), "reveal a critical awareness of women's subordinate position and of gender as a problematic category" (14). In *Nascita e vicende del romanzo italiano* (The birth and development of the Italian novel, 1939), the author and critic Maria Luisa Astaldi offers a provocative indication of the different meanings that such writers as Serao and Deledda create as they adapt realist conventions to their own designs. Astaldi writes against critics who attempt to read these two authors exclusively in relation to the master aesthetics of naturalism, *verismo*, and in Deledda's case decadentism, too. Instead, Astaldi argues that the Deleddian opus features highly personalized narrative practices employing realism and symbolism to represent, among other issues, "the conflict between the sexes as a woman has experienced it, not the kind of cerebral debate proposed by [Henrik] Ibsen, but the irreconcilable hostility of natures and organs" (98). In Serao's case, perhaps more difficult to evaluate in sweeping terms because of her experimentation with realist and gothic conventions, the critic draws an important distinction, maintaining that the author's attentive observation of Neapolitan middle-class life shares little with the impassive, scientific mode of observation posited for naturalists by Luigi Capuana. Instead, articulating an idea of the photograph that diverges from Boine's, Astaldi credits Serao with a "photographic" sensitivity to detail, whose modern sensibilities transform the print's flat surface, giving representational depth to the affective life of fears, sadness, and hopes enacted behind closed doors.[18]

Remarkable for the way that Astaldi attentively situates the works by a variety of women novelists within the genre's development, this study on the novel also tells us much about female authors first constituted as part of the canon and then deleted, and about critical attitudes toward the performativity of the novel during Fascism. Although Croce's conception of pure art insists on the autonomy of artistic production from the politics of life and society, Astaldi clearly joins the camp of critics who privilege the politically committed role of the artist in the regime. She underscores this stance as she closes her study with the call for a "violently national culture" and declares that

> we want to reaffirm that for us there exists an indissoluble connection between politics and literature, which is not to say an enslaved, adulatory form or one nourished on nauseous eloquence, but a literature addressing certain interests, tied to conflicts and burning with fire—beyond which the writer seems sterile, and exiled in his homeland. (284)

Significantly, Astaldi credits such writers as Flavia Steno, Bianca De Mai, and Willy Dias with contributing to the important development of the bourgeois novel—a term she employs to indicate "modest intent" and "portraying the vicissitudes of daily living," and notes the new directions charted in experimental novels written by Gianna Manzini and Paola Masino, and in new works by De Céspedes and Tia Celletti, among many others.

The figuration of the woman novelist in the popular female imagination offers another valuable dimension to critical perspectives on women's novels. During the *ventènnio*, in addition to professional female writers and poets—numbering some four hundred women, according to the 1936 registry of the Fascist Professional Women's Association—a virtual flood of women aspired to penning the great Italian novel.[19] The question of the day, posed by hostesses at gatherings for tea and enlightened conversation, was "Have you read my latest novel?", as Liliana Scalero reports sardonically in "Le donne che scrivono" (Women who write, 1937). Although the status of novel writing as a "female fashion" warrants circumspection, the idea that women authorized themselves to write in such a patriarchal regime does not lack significance and indicates as well the prominence that the model of the woman novelist had achieved in Italian culture and society. Moreover, the overwhelming response to works written by such established authors as Deledda and Drigo, and by a younger generation of women, including De Céspedes, attests to the success of their populist aesthetic as a cultural intervention in the literary formation of reading publics.

The breadth and success of women's literary production in the novel cast a different light on the writing project that male authors presented to "revive" the novel and to "create" a modern poetics of realism as part of a populist canon. If, as André Bazin (1971) claims, "realism can only occupy in art a dialectical position" always defining itself as an oppositional "reaction" to other styles, then for such anti-Fascist writers as G. A. Borgese and for leftist Fascists like Vitaliano Brancati and Elio Vittorini, this enterprise represents a reaction against the aesthetic developed by the Vociani, decadentists, and Rondisti (48). But we can also interpret this project as a general attempt to reclaim the novel as a site for reasserting male cultural authority. Indeed, some of the key notions proposed— the new role of the artist as a builder, and literary writing as a socially committed, productive activity, for example—seem devised to alter the enfeebled image of the elite man of letters in an ivory tower, composing esoteric musings for an equally elite circle of readers. At the same time, such left-wing Fascists as Bontempelli, Malaparte, Brancati, and Vittorini, who championed competing styles, perceived the novel as a vehicle to bridge the gap between elite and popular art and their respective publics, as part of a cultural intervention for the revolutionary age of Fascism.

The tensions between the diverse realist paradigms created by men and women writers, and the salutatory position adopted by the regime toward neorealism overall raise intriguing questions about F/fascism and the politics of aesthetics. Clearly, Fascist cultural politics contradict the assumptions about fascist hegemonic relations in art and society inherited from Lukács, who states that "a régime preparing for war, or a régime relying on oppression and confusion of the people, must necessarily—as Mussolini, Hitler and MacCarthy [*sic*] show—tend toward the suppression of realism" (1962, 101–2). This contradiction, in itself rather unremarkable since critical theory has exposed the more sophisticated apparatuses, beyond repression, constituting the Fascist hegemony, forces us to rethink the performative politics of aesthetic categories, the subjectivities of authors, and reading publics. Yet if we apply, for instance, Lukács's model of defining an aesthetic category and the functions it may perform irrespective of the author's subjectivity to the neorealist project advanced by writers of the left Fascist camp, the analysis highlights the instability of discourse. The ideals for a new realism intersect, in fact, with some of Lukács's prescriptive principles, among them, portraying the typical as opposed to deviance or angst, maintaining the dialectic between the individual and the "objective" reality of the social community, and, significantly, demonstrating "concrete potentiality" by delineating the means for future change. Though not a form of critical or socialist realism, the paradigm of employing realist conventions to represent a populist enterprise where each citizen assumes an important role in the collective struggle to ameliorate socioeconomic injustices could prompt us to ask whether the redaction of neorealism written as a Fascist enterprise creates a "fascistic" system at all, working within the parameters proposed by Lukács or Sontag. Or could such fictions, meant to found the Fascist nation and subjectivity, operate to enable the formation of different forms of subjectivity among socially differentiated reading publics? Furthermore, given such indeterminacy in the field of Fascist aesthetic production, how can we theorize potential locations and tactical strategies producing the effects of an oppositional politics?

Here, Homi K. Bhabha's work on the performativity of language in the constitutive relations between narration and nation, a central issue in the debate over aesthetics among Fascist intellectuals of different artistic orientations, suggests a useful approach to the problem. Proposing an understanding of the nation as an unstable, ambivalent discursive construction forever in the process of self-invention, Bhabha charts the sites and dynamics of cultural politics:

> The "locality" of national culture is neither unified nor unitary in relation to itself, nor must it be seen simply as "other" in relation to what is outside or beyond it. The boundary is Janus-faced and the problem of outside/ inside must always itself be a process of hybridity, incorporating new "people" in relation to the body politic, generating other sites of meaning and, inevitably, in the political process, producing unmanned sites of political antagonism and unpredictable forces for political representation. (1990, 4)

This paradigm appears particularly well suited to the instantiation of power relations during Italian Fascism as Mussolini, along with fellow writers and artists, produced a surfeit of signs to construct the idea of the Fascist nation yet refused to define precisely what they signified. Therefore, an examination of the images, metaphors, and symbols performatively constituting the urban and rural faces of Fascist national identity in relation to the expressions of affiliative communities and society elaborated in the novels by Drigo and De Céspedes may enable us to theorize the locations where their politics engage with and diverge, while working within the aesthetic of realist representation.

The ways in which Drigo and De Céspedes situate their visions of female formation of self and community within the tradition of novelistic realism have far-ranging symbolic and practical implications in the interwar years, as the Fascist state endeavors to invent its national identity and reconceive how citizenship may be achieved among different constituencies, while reasserting the patriarchal authority of a sex-gender system. From its inception, as Timothy Brennan contends, the realist novel has performed a particularly important role in fabricating the myths and symbols that constitute the nation as, in Benedict Anderson's words (1983), an "imagined community" (Brennan 1990, 48). The historically and culturally specific case of Italy bears out this claim. Indeed, with the publication of *I promessi sposi* (The betrothed) in 1827, Alessandro Manzoni authored the foundational fiction of an Italian national identity, which performed as an ideal of independence and unification until, following three wars of independence, the 1880 ratification of the Italian constitution brought together the dis-membered parts of the body politic, at least as a discursive formation.[20] Although the realist variants of *verismo* and regionalism appear to emerge as a measure of the gap between the ideal of an Italian national identity and the hierarchical situat-

edness of disparate communities within the nation-state, some intellectuals maintain that only tenuous ties obtain between the nation as narrative effect and verifiable realities, if they exist at all. The Peruvian writer
Carlos José Mariátegui (1971) represents this stance, declaring that the
nation "is an abstraction, an allegory, a myth that does not correspond to
a reality that can be scientifically defined" (187–88). To the extent that
this may be so, what better aesthetic than realism, with its tradition as
civic discourse, to construct "authoritative" myths of the Fascist state as a
virile, dynamic body engaged in the active building of social reality?
Fredric Jameson (1988) highlights the unique potential of realism, locating its originality "in its claim to cognitive as well as aesthetic status . . .
the ideal of realism presupposes a form of aesthetic experience that yet
lays claim to a binding relationship to the real itself" (135). Although the
aesthetic of a new realism developed during Fascism privileges the in-
tepretative value over documentary usefulness, this apparent purchase
on the "real" may authorize both dominant constructions of Fascist
community and "other" forms of affiliation generated at the "unmanned"
borders of realist narrative of the nation.

Maria Zef: The Discourse of Country and Its Dis-membering

The nature of the subjects that Drigo openly speaks about and her obdu-
rate critique of famine and disease among the subaltern rural class have
to make us wonder how *Maria Zef* ever reached the bookstores in 1936.[21]
A summary of the spare plot illustrates this point. While a widow and her
two young daughters make their yearly journey down from their mountain home in Carnia to sell household wares to the plains families and
make enough money to survive the winter, the mother fatally succumbs
to a debilitating illness. The orphans' uncle takes them back home where,
one evening when the younger girl is in town to receive medical treatment, he rapes the adolescent Mariutine, infecting her with syphilis. One
night, as her uncle Barbe Zef sleeps in a drunken stupor, Mariutine puts
an end to the cycle of sexual abuse, acting to defend her sister from a similar fate. She delivers a clean blow of an axe and chops off his head. Although such materials and plotting might be standard fare in the gothic
or adventure novel of the time, they represent striking innovations in the
neorealist paradigm. In contrast to Corrado Alvaro's short story collec-

tion *Gente in Aspromonte* (People in Aspromonte, 1930) and Carlo Levi's later novel *Christ Stopped at Eboli* (1945), each acclaimed as emblematic instances of the general (neo)realist aesthetic, *Maria Zef* does not offer visions of women with eyes like deep pools of archaic wisdom, as in the former case, or with eyes burning with passion, as in the latter; in Drigo's story, women's eyes are spent by hunger and by the misery of a slavish existence as the property of patriarchs. In fact, the author produces a serious literary treatment of sexual difference as *the* determining factor in the economic, social, and sexual oppression of concrete relations.

The writings by critics of the thirties clearly outline the original artistic contribution made by Drigo's novel to the emergent canon of neorealism, which was eclipsed in the postwar years by the paradigmatic shift valuating "antifascist" practices of war and resistance as a key trait of the neorealist movement and of Italian national identity. Besides earning the praise of such literary critics as Pietro Pancrazi and Arnaldo Bocelli, *Maria Zef* was represented in the 1939 anthology of Italian literature edited by Giuseppe Zoppi for foreign readers, titled *Antologia della letteratura italiana ad uso degli stranieri* (Anthology of Italian literature for foreigners). The scope of this anthology deserves note, for it focused on giving a "faithful image" of contemporary Italian literature with works by great writers that exemplified major trends and expressive originality. As commentators agree, several of Drigo's narrative practices situate her writing in the *verista* lineage of the realist novel. These include her mindful rendering of regional topography in the literal and figurative sense, as it shapes customs, beliefs, and the very texture of daily living as a palpable attachment to the community. In *Maria Zef* the signs of regional origin are also written on the body. Mariutine, as the narrator tells us, has "fair skin, intensely blue eyes, and fine features, as people of Carnia often have when young," as well as a tall stature and strong build, "with a mountain woman's broad shoulders" (76, 3). Likewise, the narrative lexicon fashioned by Drigo highlights the function of language to express both a sense of belonging to place and time, and of Otherness, a resistance to acculturation. She incorporates Friulian dialect for forms of address and endearment, objects typical of the region—the *scarputis*, for example, or cloth shoes worn in Friuli and Carnia—and in the regional songs that Mariutine sings.

However, Drigo shifts the bearings of the literary territory charted by Giovanni Verga and enriches the field of the new realism of the thirties. While giving representation to the disenfranchised subaltern class with a tenuous hold on day-to-day survival, she focuses on the female experience of alterity. Bocelli perceives the importance of female sexual difference in Drigo's realist aesthetic, as he comments in a rather enlightened way on her concern for "poor innocent women—victims of male violence or their own weakness or destiny's adversity" (1937, 466). Furthermore, Drigo's realist fiction does not confine itself to the ideal of impartial, ostensibly unmediated representation. Rather, the novelist offers psychological analysis and interpretation, a narrative practice that drew mixed reactions, shaped more or less by gendered constructions of textual pleasure. For example, the passages Bocelli finds most beautiful and appealing in *Maria Zef* depict female innocence, "preconscious sensibility," tragic pain, and resignation—terms that conform with the traditional notion of submissive femininity. Thus, precisely when the protagonist overcomes a culturally conditioned subservience in a willful act executed for justice and change, the text fails to produce pleasure for him. With such a "truculent resolution," Bocelli argues, Drigo "seems to obey a polemical, abstract desire for catharsis; she insisted on vindicating herself at the hands of Maria, her character. A moral, but not moralistic woman writer, she gave in, against her will, to a thesis; the woman took control of the writer" (467). Precisely! In his paternalistic comments, I suggest, the critic identifies one of the marks of sexual difference that distinguishes this author's politics of realist aesthetics from the projects proposed by leftist Fascists and anti-Fascist male writers; Drigo's critical interpretation of the relationship between the female and socioeconomic realities and the potential transformation she proposes reject the logic of the heterosexual plot, inventing new terms of community, a point I develop shortly.

Finally, the other major feature distinguishing Drigo's novel in the neorealist currents of the thirties concerns the treatment and evocation of affect. In this regard, Manara Valgimigli's assessment shows his attempt to recognize this difference, while situating Drigo's work within canonical ideals:

Drigo is really a manly woman. She is a virile woman writer. By saying this, I don't want to give her stupid praise due to stupid antifeminism. Rather, I want to grasp one of her qualities and try to make a distinction. The virile does not exclude emotion because it cleanses it of weakness and wipes all laxity away and because the virile doesn't find emotion just anywhere, at a tawdry price. It bores to the depths and elevates emotion, not dissolving it but building it; the virile doesn't melt emotion but hardens and solders it because it enobles emotion, giving it dignity and austerity. (1943, 206)

As Barbara Spackman (1990, 1995) cautions, we cannot simply take the term *virile*—commonly invoked in life, culture, and politics of the time—to signify a quality of the male sex. Yet in the specific context Valgimigli sets up, he appears to blur gender boundaries of writing. In praise of Drigo, he applies the less ambiguous word *manly* to her female person. Although his characterization of her writing as "virile" conforms with critical usage of the term to denote creative power and genius, he associates this ideal with the emotions, a traditionally "feminine" literary field, yet specifies that virilization creates strong, noble, and dignified emotion. While this argument, advancing a notion of strong, moral emotions versus weak, immoral ones, resonates with the regime's project to reform modern mores and to instill "morality," it may also provide a clue about how Drigo managed not only to have a novel published that presented a violent slaying of a man (not without his own poignant appeal) as the female protagonist's deliverance of and from male authority, but also to win readers over to the idea that it was the "moral" thing to do. For overall, critics received *Maria Zef* with overwhelming enthusiasm, applauding it as a "masterpiece," an example, in Pietro Pancrazi's words, of "fully achieved art," unique precisely for its moral strength (1943, 233).

With my reading of *Maria Zef,* I want to propose that the properties of Drigo's aesthetic create a space for a politics of sexual difference that, within the discursive field constituted by neorealist narratives, resists purely patrilineal forms of affiliation and the Fascist rhetoric of rural life. By approaching aesthetics, which construct notions of beauty and value operating through forms of artistic discourse, with Foucault's theorization of the equivocal relations between discourses of power and opposition, we can theorize sites of resistance constituted within the paradigm of realism, yet against the patriarchal authority it ostensibly exerts.[22] This situatedness has crucial significance for resistances, which, as Foucault writes,

> are all the more real and effective because they are formed right at the
> point where relations of power are exercised; resistance to power does not
> have to come from elsewhere to be real, nor is it inexorably frustrated
> through being a compatriot of power. It exists all the more by being in the
> same place as power; hence, like power, resistance is multiple and can be
> integrated in global strategies. (1972b, 142)

Drigo employs the mother-daughter relation to structure her novel. As a site for the production of ideology and symbolic meanings, this structuring device posits a notion of affiliation that resists the Oedipal organization of patrilineal society and the totalizing myths of Fascist national identity. Divided into four parts, the novel narrativizes the daughter's formation of self as a process involving the loss and subsequent recuperation of the mother through memories, experience, and ways of knowing. In part 1 the maternal figure initially emerges through shades of enigma, which, following her death, gradually gain depth and clarity as her daughter begins to piece together the story of her life; in part 2, as Mariutine assumes the role of mother, attending to the care of her younger sister and uncle, flashes of memory concerning her mother's changing appearance and behavior form a cloudy, disturbing prescience; in the third section, Mariutine is raped by her paternal uncle, experiencing through her own body what her mother had undergone; the concluding section portrays the daughter's coming to knowledge about the missing pieces of her mother's life, which link their histories yet also give Mariutine the strength to break the chain of victimization and create a different future for her sister and herself.

We can best understand the symbolic significance of Drigo's structuring device by referring to the frame that Luce Irigaray constructs to assess power relations in society and culture. Reminding us that both women and men comprise societies and different genealogies between mothers and daughters, mothers and sons, fathers and daughters, and so on—a fact that should be self-evident—she observes:

> Patriarchal power is organized by submitting one genealogy to the other.
> Thus, what is now termed the oedipal structure as access to the cultural

order is already structured within a single, masculine line of filiation which doesn't symbolize the woman's relation to her mother. Mother-daughter relationships in patrilinear societies are subordinated to relations between men. (1993, 16)

Through her representation of the relationships extending from mother to daughter and daughter to sister, in their literal and figurative sense, Drigo succeeds at giving symbolic expression to a productive matrilineal line of filiation in culture. By doing so, the author also constructs the notion of female "verticality," which Irigaray sees as essential to establishing a women's ethical order, a point examined more closely in the analysis of the role Mariutine adopts with her sister.

Drigo's adaptation of conventions associated with realism to portray maternal bonds as a transformative, ethical principle disrupts the notion of the paternal filiation of nation and narration fostered by the realist paradigm. Such studies as *Breaking the Chain* (1985) by Naomi Schor and The *Mother/Daughter Plot* (1989) by Marianne Hirsch propose that the representational practices developed in the nineteenth-century realist novel depend inextricably on the containment of the feminine and woman. Working through Freud's essay "Family Romances," Hirsch argues that in novels written by women in the 1800s, the specific repression of the maternal perspective

actually engenders the female fiction, a fiction which then revolves not around the drama of same-sex parent/child relations, but around marriage, which alone can place women's stories in a position of participating in the dynamics of ambition, authority, and legitimacy which constitute the plots of realist fiction. (57)

This would explain the plethora of plots that belittle, banish, or kill off the mother.

In *Maria Zef,* it is true that the plot depends on the mother's silence and death and thus at first appears to operate within the conventions of the realist novel as outlined by Schor and Hirsch. Indeed, with artful control of the omniscient narrator, in the opening descriptions the author draws out the mother's bewildering, elusive qualities, creating a sense of distance as she limits the point of view to Mariutine and outsiders. Her body broken by the ravages of poverty and disease, the maternal figure haunts us with her mournful eyes, "tired face, old, white lipped," her toothless mouth and, importantly, her form of self-exile conveyed when she irascibly alienates buyers for her wares and even begrudges her daughter's joyous gift for singing. Only one brief passage, in the free indirect style, gives expression to Catine, and it focuses exclusively on the searing pain and thirst wracking her body when she finally collapses in the road, like "a heap of rags," according to a passerby. As Hirsch (1989) also contends, a mother's silence about her own life story creates the conditions insuring that daughters will share similar fates, as tragically happens in *Maria Zef*, however, with a difference. For although Mariutine experiences events in a cycle of victimization that first entrapped Catine, Drigo invests the mother with symbolic functions as a source of meaning and value in the daughter's self-construction, which ultimately make a new ending possible. Therefore, this work may represent a transitional moment, a point of "hybridity" (Bhabha 1994) where terms of female identity and community emerge to envision a different plot and future.

Drigo poignantly represents Mariutine's re-creation of the mother through mourning, memories, and experience. When the orphaned girls and Barbe Zef near their mountain hut, it is as if the mother comes to welcome Mariutine, as different images of Catine flash before her elder daughter's eyes—first, a vision of strong, youthful womanhood, with the baby Rosùte in her arms, then somewhat haggard, her spirit and energy fading, and, finally, her body withered and drawn, convulsed by coughing. Yet her mother's presence seems to imbue the home and surrounding landscape with loving vigilance, as we see from Mariutine's perceptions:

> There came over her . . . a sense of comfort, of security. The dreadful emptiness of boundless solitude was no longer there: the mother filled it with her breath. . . . *she* had come towards her. All nature had her eyes, sad and deep; silence speaks with her voice. Here nothing will change. . . . Here the mother will exist eternally. (46)

But in the process of remembering her mother, the daughter catches glimpses of words, gestures, and scenes exchanged between Catine and Barbe Zef, which incite fear and anxiety, on the cusp of consciousness. Most important, on entering the cramped cabin—with a kitchen, one bedroom, and a room for storing tools and hens—for the first time after her mother's death, she recalls both how Catine unyieldingly banished Zef to the storeroom at night and her uncle's drunken abusiveness. These preoccupations, associated also with Mariutine's growing awareness of sexuality, gnaw at the girl throughout the text.

Drigo's representation of the daily life that Mariutine, her little sister, and uncle lead in the Friulian mountains, and their relation to surrounding rural communities provides a scathing critique of conditions in the country, which, when read within the specific political context of its production, engages with and undermines the idealized images of country living constructed by the regime as part of a major ruralization campaign. The peasant became a key figure in the imaginary of Fascist identity and in politics. Even Mussolini, though he donned various images for public appearances, frequently invoked his peasant roots, representing himself as a countryboy. Furthermore, as Ruth Ben-Ghiat (1990) tells us, he identified peasant life as a privileged locus for the reclamation of Italian culture, proclaiming in 1933,

> We need to honor the people of the fields, to consider the peasants as first-class members of the national community.... This political and moral reappraisal of the peasant and of agriculture will be more effective when it is detached from the Arcadian literature of those who know the countryside only from having seen it while traveling. (1990, 156)

Already in the late twenties, state thinkers and policymakers began plans to stem the tide of men and women abandoning the land, which threatened both the project to double the Italian population and the goal of achieving autarky. According to Piero Meldini (1975), from 1921 to 1938, more than one million peasants left agricultural areas in the south. Alexander De Grand's estimates on migration within Italian borders, which do not specify the numbers of peasants moving from rural to urban sites, show that some six hundred thousand Italians changed residences in 1923, followed by eight hundred thousand in 1926, and more than one million per year in the thirties (1989, 67).

The regime's endeavors to reruralize Italy included several initiatives. For example, a law of December 1928 made the return of migrants to their place of origin obligatory (though impractical), and in 1931 the government instructed the prefects of large cities to follow regulations to limit changes of residence strictly. Some ideologues proposed changes in the education system, as shown by G. Cocchiara's 1930 article "Perché i contadini abbandonano la terra" (Why peasants are abandoning the land). Contending that the curricula and textbooks used in rural schools actually inspire countryboys to strike off for the big city, he outlines a program wherein teachers would educate students in the rich tradition of peasant culture exemplified in books by regional authors:

> We need to exalt local life, and from it bring forth the spirit and soul to convince the adolescent peasant that the real fortune he and his people possess is there, in that field where his father works from morning to night, with a song on his lips and faith in his heart. This is the great usefulness of regional books. (cited in Meldini 1975, 175–76)

This passage also highlights the idealization of the countryside as an Edenic site of health, honesty, and joy in the fruits of labor, which Fascist writers opposed to the image of the city as a den of iniquity, disease, and deviance in a discursive battle of signs. The campaign to ruralize Italy dedicated particular attention to countrywomen, who, according to De Grazia, left agricultural sectors in even higher numbers than men.[23] Mussolini, for instance, glorified the country mother, representing her as the queen of her family and home, the safeguard of tradition and morality. Furthermore, Fascist organizers, with Regina Terruzzi at the lead, established the *massaie rurali* association in 1933 to educate farm wives about marketplace values of selling and buying so that they could run their family economies more efficiently, thereby improving their daily lives.

Nonetheless, the continued waves of migration to urban centers and the growing tendency to limit family size show the inefficacy of such endeavors to offset demographic trends motivated, in some cases, by the regime's own policies. Several commentators of the thirties note how the attempt to deproletarianize the poor rural classes by settling families on small plots of land actually sabotaged dreams of strengthening the large patriarchal family structure. Opening up opportunities for land speculation, the shift toward selling off land on wealthy farm estates, then parceled out, made the labor force of large-sized families, such as those represented in Bernardo Bertolucci's film *1900* (1975–76) or Ermanno Olmi's

Tree of the Wooden Clogs (1978), obsolete. Hence, in search of work, families broke up, some members emigrating, others working as day laborers, and girls going to the city to work in factories or as servants. Amid conditions of underemployment, malnutrition, disease, and isolation, the chance for better employment, welfare services, and entertainment offered by the city represented more than an alluring "mirage," as Fascist writers claimed. This was particularly so for women in the country, who, in addition to working in the fields from dawn to dusk while tending to their young children, also labored at the household chores. In the oral histories that Nuto Revelli (1985) gathered from countrywomen who grew up during the interwar years, hunger, deprivation, and constant fatigue form recurrent motifs. Maria Abello, a mountain woman born in 1897, who married at thirty-one and had six children, recalls

> The woman had it worse off than the man; she had the house and the field. . . . We'd arrive with the load of hay, using our backs to stop the sledge, or pulling it along, me pulling it, too, every evening. I'd get home. . . . I had to take care of the cows and the children, and after that take care of the hay so the ropes would be ready for the next day, to go back on the mountain, and the night passed by. Sometimes I was so tired I'd fall asleep on the hay, I'd fall over with sleep while he was untying the ropes on the sledge. Ah, if I sat down for a minute, I'd fall asleep. . . . I used to go to bed at two in the morning, and by four I was already up. He'd go up the mountain to harvest the hay, I'd prepare the polenta. (Revelli 1985, 215)

As Maria Einaudi, another mountain woman of the same generation concluded, "It was better to be born a goat than a woman" because at least the goats wandered free (219).

Although we must keep in mind the fictive nature of Drigo's realist novel—not a mere reflection of reality, but a creation of a system of meaning—her narrativization of themes and conditions of female mountain living resonates with those remembered by rural women of the mountain regions, whose way of life differed from that in the hills and the plains. In *Maria Zef*, Drigo does not portray peasants as a unified community, sharing similar economic capabilities, beliefs, and attitudes. Rather, her representations draw out differences based on financial means, sex, and geographic location, which form hegemonic relations among the rural classes and even create a hierarchy among the poor. The

Zef family belongs to the rural underclass, the most stricken by poverty. As the narrator tells us,

> Even among the wretched hovels of the mountain folk, their cabin was among the most wretched and bare and could not possibly have resembled the beautiful houses of the plain that she had seen—solid and well lit, with ample windows letting in the sun, and vast courtyards, barns and stables. (59)

The solitude of mountain life makes the pain of deprivation more acute. As carnival time approaches, Mariutine thinks about others who barely scrape by but, because they live farther down the mountain, can at least enjoy the company of other people, playing cards and roasting chestnuts: "Yes, even for the poor, winter was not the same all over. On a scale of privations and sacrifice there was still a bit of difference, fate still played favorites" (82).

Certainly, the author's plentiful descriptions of the daily tasks and hardships that the Zef family must overcome lay bare dimensions of peasant life repressed by dominant cultural discourses of the thirties. Yet through her use of spatial imagery, Drigo also powerfully symbolizes the dislocation from normative societal affiliations that derives from class and gender differences. First of all, the reader's initial pictures of the mother and her daughters show them relentlessly pushing onward with their cart of goods, without even stopping to eat, as they journey from one farm settlement to the next—never participating as a stable part of a community. Moreover, Drigo visually situates the widow and girls on the fringes of communal life and economy; they hawk their wares by daylight and sleep in abandoned shacks, near haystacks, or on porches at night. They lead a precarious existence that depends entirely on the economic well-being of homesteads on the plains. In times of plentiful harvests, farming families can buy the Zef's kitchenwares and perhaps invite them to share a meal and the after-dinner festivities, with Mariutine singing regional songs. In bad economic times, however, the households and settlements close in on themselves, for as one woman says, "to buy bowls . . . one must have something to put into them" (11). Even the dogs then bark hostiley at the outsiders.

The way that the novelist represents the behaviors and attitudes of townspeople following Catine's death exposes hypocrisy and biases that also marginalize the orphaned girls, even as the do-gooders purport to welcome them compassionately into the community. As we might expect, the death of the Friulian woman and the plight of her two daughters cause quite a stir, with a hint of scandal providing grist for the town gossips. While the men discuss the diagnosis at the local cafe, insinuating that Catine, like other "women tramping around" while their husbands emigrate to find work, died from a disease caused by "immoral" behavior, the womenfolk gather donations for the funeral and the girls' expenses. The depiction of the nuns who take in the orphans suggests that the church, ostensibly the heart of charity, compassion, and assistance, may primarily serve the interests of the privileged. In fact, when the nuns discover that Mariutine does not know how to sew or write and, more important, has not had first Communion—attending Mass perhaps only once a year— they condemn the mother "to the flames of hell for all eternity" (22). They fail, in other words, to appreciate the rigors of mountain life with its unending labor and physical isolation, which make church services a luxury. In fact, the nearest church is three hours away. Thus the mother, a victim of poverty, is criminalized by the religious and civic communities.

In Drigo's poverty discourse, the thoughts and behaviors attributed to Mariutine express an awareness of self as an object of exchange whose value consists of making herself useful in the economy of goods and services. Thus on her return home, as at the nuns' hospice, she immediately takes on all the adult responsibilities that her mother had managed, though physically and psychologically she is just a girl, as the narrative emphasizes. Within this context, the reader can understand her fear that Barbe Zef might send her to work for someone else, far away from her home and Rosùte, for whom she feels deep love and attachment. In actuality, the practice of hiring out girls and boys, as young as six years of age, to watch grazing herds or to gather flowers for the city shops was still prevalent among peasant families in the twenties and thirties. According to Maria Laugero's memories of what was called "la fiera dei bambini" (the exposition of children),

> They rented us out like calves. . . . Our parents had to rent us out. Everyone was poor, they didn't even have bread to give us. I remember that I

was there in the piazza with a lot of other kids, with my little bundle of raggedy clothes. . . . I was crying, I was embarrassed. The others were crying, too. We were children, who should have been kept at home, not rented out. (in Revelli 1985, lxii)

By discussing the dire conditions of rural family life—the plight of parents and children—the novelist also challenges dominant discourses designed to naturalize the traditional ideal of the countrywoman. Conservative commentators of the interwar years represented the rural woman as "retaining" the "natural" female gifts of "patience, docility, a calm spirit and emotional equilibrium," in the pediatrician Giulio Casalini's words (in Meldini 1975, 111). In contrast, Drigo represents how the pressures of class and gender imprint Mariutine's formation of self. She narrativizes the notion of female identity not as natural essence but as a performative construction, along the lines proposed by Judith Butler (1990), who contends that "there is no gender identity behind the expressions of gender; that identity is performatively constituted by the very 'expressions' that are said to be its results" (25). The adolescent girl's expressions of gender appear as products of economic and cultural conditioning, as well as strategies for survival. Hence, aware that her age, sex, and economic status make her entirely dependent on Barbe Zef, she adopts a servile and obedient attitude toward the elder male. Mariutine's thoughts about what she could do if her uncle insisted on sleeping in the bedroom convey an awareness of her inferior status in family power relations. Fraught with anxiety, she feels "diffident, weak, a child incapable of refusing to obey if Barbe Zef ordered her. 'My god. . . . The mari didn't want. . . .' If her uncle insisted, what should she do? . . . Her mother had dealt with him as an equal, but she, how would she be able to do that? . . . He was the boss, now" (55).

The subservient position that Mariutine occupies in the hierarchy of her immediate family may be read as a micropolitical site reflecting sex-gender relations in the broader social sphere. This perspective takes shape in a highly important section of the novel where the young girl becomes acutely aware of her family's material and emotional privations and of her body as an object of sexual exchange. Having left Rosùte at the town hospital, Zef and his niece spend the evening with the owners of a large estate, where they share, momentarily, in the plentiful abundance of space, warmth, food, sociable company, and apparent affection. Through her effusion of feelings intermingling estrangement, loneliness, and enjoyment, Mariutine experiences an uncomfortable awareness of the family patriarch's physical advances and lewd comments about her body. She feels diffident and cannot respond to Compare Guerrino because of his status as the master and the eldest male. Moreover, the narrator explains, "her extreme poverty had shaped in her even since early childhood the habit of compliance and almost servility with regard to anyone outside her own family" (121). This evening's atmosphere of gaiety virtually seems to smolder a sense of foreboding, evoked by Barbe Zef's uncontrollable drinking, male gestures of desire and sexual innuendo, and sets the stage for the tragic scenario played out when the uncle returns home alone with his niece.

Excavating the terrain of taboo subjects, Drigo dares to speak about brutal forms of female victimization—rape, incest, and sexually transmitted disease—which may be committed in the isolation and solitude of the countryside as easily as behind closed doors in the city. She dashes hopes and ideals about ties of blood and family constituting the image of the family in Italy of the 1930s and, I dare say, the image that many American readers of the 1990s still entertain.[24] With superb orchestration of metaphors and tone, Drigo presents a fast-paced sequence that evokes a full range of moods—from paternally protective to vaguely sexual, from playfully intimate to utterly cruel. With the imagery of a "game of cat and mouse," the hunter and the prey, the narrative delicately draws out Mariutine's girlish innocence and goodness, and fear, just as the unthinkable actually happens, and Barbe Zef, amid fumes of grappa, rapes her.

Critics of the thirties applauded Drigo for her portrayal of Zef, not as a melodramatic villain personifying evil, but as an outcast, victimized himself by the poverty of his miserable existence. Indeed, the sympathetic attention devoted by the novelist to the hard life that Zef tries to survive, making his livelihood by doing all sorts of odd jobs and never before raising a hand to the girls, makes the scene all the more powerful. The uncle's behaviors and comments, however, also suggest that he perceives Mariutine as property, her worth now defined by her sexual value. In fact, before the rape Zef tells his niece that Guerrino expects him to "play the pimp." At no time does the narrative express the uncle's ideas or feelings during the attack and its aftermath. But it appears reasonable that the rape represents in part a battle over property fought on the girl's body; he possesses her in the most absolute sense before his rival does. And we should bear in mind that in the thirties Italian society, for all its modern ways, still placed a high premium on virginity. The manner that Zef adopts toward Mariutine in the following weeks supports this idea. In what becomes a cycle of sexual abuse, Zef displays total indifference to Mariutine's person, avoiding her by day, yet cornering her at night when, "without seeing her face, without hearing her sobs, the way the male dog takes the bitch, he would take her, then let her go, and fall asleep" (151).

The representation of how Mariutine experiences and copes with the trauma of rape refigures, quite literally and symbolically, the notion of family, while proposing a new ethic of community. Initially, the rape destroys the girl's sense of connectedness, to her sister, her daily life of chores and responsibilities, and her hopes to one day marry Pieri, a young suitor now working in Argentina. As if no one and nothing else existed, the narrator specifies, "reality was that male body. . . . She felt entangled in one of those silences where it seems that nothing more can happen; where life, death, joy, and grief seem abolished forever—a silence unlike any other; definitive and final" (136). At first, Mariutine gives in to a resigned despair, compounded by the shame, humiliation, and fear she harbors, as well as the confusion created by the betrayal of her trust. Yet she also feels a surviving sense of gratitude toward her uncle who is "family and home" (141). However, when Mariutine learns that the same fate had befallen her mother before her, she begins to turn her anger outward, toward her uncle. The girl's awareness of the growing resemblance in appearance and spirit that she shares with her mother foreshadows the scene of discovery. Indeed, the psychological and physical abuse has worn her face and exhausted her energies in a prematurely aged image, as reflected in a piece of broken mirror. Thus, worried by the blisters covering her palms, a stubborn fever, and other symptoms she cannot explain, Mariutine embarks on a journey to see the mountain woman who had taken care of her mother and learns, among other things, that she has the so-called "French disease."

Drigo's use of venereal disease has complex metaphoric and historical significance. In *Sexual Anarchy* (1990), Elaine Showalter examines, among other topics, the discourses of sexuality and disease in the late 1800s, which directly concern normative notions of family and sexual behavior. Exploring the different meanings attached to the iconography of syphilis, she concludes that "to most late-Victorian feminists, syphilis was the product of man's viciousness and represented innocent women's entrapment and victimization" (197). The perspective that Drigo creates as she depicts the young girl infected with the disease reflects a similar position and, at the same time, challenges dominant discourses gendering disease. In Italy, the state had a relatively solid history of intervening in the sphere of sexuality to safeguard the health of the nation. In the late 1800s, as Mary Gibson (1986) tells us, "the defeat at Adowa in 1896 fueled fright about the effects hereditary diseases like syphilis might have on the fiber of the nation" (170). Medical and juridical writings singled out military personnel and prostitutes as the contagions of moral and venereal disease yet argued for stricter regulations on women, displaying class and sex biases. For example, one expert argued that in comparison with a woman, an infected man could spread the disease to fewer partners (in Gibson 1986, 176). During Fascist rule, the state initiated reforms on morality that introduced legislation on social hygiene and prostitution. Although reliable statistics on the number of venereal disease cases in Italy of the interwar years do not readily exist, in 1908 some 63,209 patients were treated at dispensaries. Peasants in the country, however, were more likely, according to Gibson, to visit a local healer, who administered such folk remedies as herbal drinks and even ammonia, not the penicillin and sulfa drugs made available in the late 1930s and early 1940s. Within this historical and political frame, Drigo's deployment of veneral disease as illness and metaphor voices dissent from the criminalization of the female sexual body inscribed in hegemonic discourses, as well as from the naturalization of the rural family and sexuality. The uncle's rape of his niece and the syphilitic disease with which he infects her signify the violation of "natural" sexual laws.

The knowledge that Mariutine gains about her mother from the woman healer, who reveals that, in fact, the mother suffered from the same disease and had therefore aborted several pregnancies with Zef's help, and the near certainty that her uncle would prey on Rosùte enable the girl to overcome her conditioning to submission.[25] Drigo's portrayal of Mariutine's discovery of what the mother's silence had repressed echoes the mother-daughter relation in Sibilla Aleramo's work *Una donna* (1906), in which the daughter must finally renounce her son in order to save herself and begin life anew, and alone. Yet thirty years later, Drigo can envision a future forged on preserving female ties, which are articulated throughout the story by Mariutine's nurturance of Rosùte's physical and emotional well-being and, moreover, by two highly symbolic actions. The girl teaches her younger sister to sing the traditional *villotte*, or folk songs, of their region, as well as new ones of her own creation. The language of songs, as Benedict Anderson (1983) suggests, creates "occasions for *unisonality*, for the echoed physical realization of the imagined community" (132). The images in the songs Mariutine sings have intratextual significance, resonating with the novel's themes concerning sexual oppression, as illustrated by the following stanza, which is repeated in the novel: "Oh lofty windows barred and shuttered / If you could only speak and witness bear! / But what I said to my little darling / No one else will ever hear" (10, 16). Yet the folk songs also possess intertextual meanings as part of a popular regional tradition that creates a sense of belonging to the female community. Passed from one generation to the next, such songs have a long-standing oral history among Italian women, which documents, through changes in the lyrics, different perceptions of oppressive female conditions (Passerini 1987, 129–30). This practice thus creates a gendered, cross-generational system of affiliation. Similarly, when Barbe Zef actually begins to play the pimp and delivers a necklace from Guerrino to Mariutine, she decides to divide the beads in half, to make a necklace for Rosùte, too. This act has several possible meanings. Literally, readers see the elder girl's devotion to her sister, her willingness to share what little she may have. But the division of the necklace, which marks Guerrino's claim on Mariutine, could mean that Rosùte will share a similar fate. Finally, the creation of the closed circle of the necklace may also symbolize the sisters' union and eternity.

Thus foregrounded, the steps that Mariutine takes when Barbe Zef threatens to separate the sisters, while shocking, fulfill the story's promise. After Barbe Zef informs Mariutine that, in fact, he plans to send her to Guerrino, who will find her a job in town as a "servant," she acts to protect Rosùte, an ethical imperative Mariutine learned from years of her mother's protection, whose signs she only now comes to understand. She offers Barbe Zef the grappa. Then, as he sleeps, the girl gazes on him, struck both by the power she now possesses and by pity for her uncle, "who from birth to death had also remained a beggar, a poor unhappy wretch born perhaps without guile, but whom poverty, promiscuity, solitude, absolute privation of all that can sweeten and elevate life, had brutalized and overwhelmed" (181). Nonetheless, with the thought of the seven-year-old Rosùte (likely Zef's own daughter) in mind, she aims at the man's neck and swiftly brings down the axe, with a strike whose symbolic meaning cannot escape the reader. It could be argued that this is the only course of action that Mariutine can take in the face of such an unbearable situation. We might think, for instance, of the concluding scene in Verga's powerful veristic short story "La lupa" (The shewolf). Though the roles are reversed, here a wave of passion draws Pina toward Nanni as he swears he will kill her. The fate of both characters, evoked through natural imagery, appears to be directed by forces beyond human control. But I wish to suggest a different reading along the lines theorized by Rita Felski (1989) for the feminist bildungsroman. This form, she proposes, "combines the exploration of subjectivity with a dimension of group solidarity which inspires activism and resistance rather than private resignation, and makes it possible to project a visionary hope of future change" (139). In contrast to the many Italian novels, as well as those in other national literatures, that craft the heroine's taking of her own life as the only act of self-assertion to gain freedom from impossible conditions, *Maria Zef* envisions a different ending, and beginning. First of all, the conclusion refuses the ideological imperative of the heterosexual plot. Moreover, the relationship between "sisters" may be read at both the literal and allegorical levels, representing the figuration of female family relations and affiliation based, in this case, on an ethic of care and responsibility as Mariutine claims the future for herself and her sister.

Rome: A City of Women and the Sexual Politics of Space

Like *country*, the word *city* has, over the centuries and especially during Fascism, evoked powerful associations in the social imaginary, founding and shaping ideas about community, a central issue problematized by De Céspedes in *Nessuno torna indietro*.[26] The novel, which relates in kaleidoscopic fashion life interludes as experienced and perceived by a heterogeneous group of young women living in a Roman boarding-house while attending the university, immediately put the author in the public eye. Reading communities across Italy and abroad made the book an international best-seller, going through eight editions in the first year alone (Giocondi 1990). Such important critics as Silvio Benco and Maria Borgese showered the "masterpiece" with praise, while commentators supporting the regime censured the book for its lack of Fascist ethics. A directive issued in 1941 by the Ministry of Popular Culture succinctly expressed the regime's position on De Céspedes, ordering the press, "Don't give any publicity to Alba De Céspedes."[27]

Despite the critical acclaim that *Nessuno torna indietro* earned, literary histories and anthologies written in the postwar years, as Bruce Merry (1990) points out, tend to give short thrift to De Céspedes, if not omit her literary contribution altogether. My reading explores this author's novelistic inventiveness as situated in the context of the interwar neo-realist aesthetic, though it is necessary to bear in mind how certain narrative features intersect with other generic conventions. Elisabetta Rasy (1984), for example, places *There's No Turning Back*, along with *Dalla parte di lei* (1949) and *Quaderno proibito* (1952) in the rubric of the female psychological novel. Bruce Merry (1990) and Carole C. Gallucci (1995) note how the atmosphere and metaphors also appear indebted to the gothic. Merry also suggests that the novel's pattern is typical of a "saga" or "romance," at the same time highlighting the author's accomplishments as "social historian," as evidenced by the veracious depictions of attitudes and dispositions in daily life. While recognizing these diversified components, I want to suggest that several features in De Céspedes's novel participate with interwar notions proposed for a new realism that, as in the postwar period, encompass a fluid variety of elements resisting codification. First, the author fashions a literary language that, while evocative, fabricates objects, habits, values, and ideas marking the characters' quotidian space. Accordingly, De Céspedes focuses her lens not on exceptional or spectacular events but on the preoccupations and hopes that the characters entertain from one day to the next in their commonplace lives. Diverging from realist variants of the 1800s, she privileges an interpretative narrative form over a clinical adherence to the verifiable appearance of things. Last, if a major aim of interwar neo-realism concerned depicting social problems and directions for change, as Carlo Bernari and Mario Pannunzio proposed, then the ways in which each of the women characters attempts to negotiate restrictive societal expectations and material conditions may be interpreted in this key. The contending feminine models embodied by the female boarders and the open-ended conclusion solicit reader engagement, also bringing to mind conventions of postwar cinematic neorealism.

The significance of De Céspedes's novelistic production as cultural critique has inspired renewed critical attention, primarily in feminist studies. Among the important analyses are, for example, *Femminile a confronto* (The female in comparison, 1984) by M. Assunta Parsani and Neria De Giovanni and "Il passaggio del ponte" (Crossing the bridge, 1991) by Maria Rosaria Vitti-Alexander, which reappraise the evolution of the author's representations of female gender roles. In "Donna pro-prio ... Proprio donna" (Such a woman ... really a woman, 1991) by Ellen Nerenberg and "Alba De Céspedes's *There's No Turning Back*" (1995) by Carole C. Gallucci, the authors examine the female cultural models cre-ated in the novel within the specific sociohistorical and political context of their production. In different ways, each reading posits questions about how the notions of gender and its construction, the female body and sexuality represented by De Céspedes may intersect, uphold, or chal-lenge the regime of the masculine and the feminine constituted by hege-monic relations during Fascism.

While expanding on this conceptual itinerary, I plan to focus my examination on the performative functions fulfilled by the ways that De Céspedes represents female practices of urban space, specifically, the female-gendered spaces founded as the characters stroll, inhabit, and transform the streets of Rome. Indeed, the novel takes us on a virtual tour of places in the Eternal City and makes abundant use of an urban and architectural lexicon to express the construction of female subjec-tivities. However, this study will not compose a travelogue, which would surely tire the reader. Instead, working through Michel de Certeau's (1988) theorization of the relations between the regulatory grammar of urban design and microspatial practices, the ways in which bodies write an urban text, I intend to analyze the "migrational" or "metaphorical" city of Rome envisioned by De Céspedes. I contend that her stylistic fashioning of the Roman metropolis creates a site for the production of an alternative discourse that subverts the panoptic, spectacular, and totalizing vision of Rome as a symbol of the Fascist nation erected in official discourse.[28] I am also interested in the interactions between the female body and the city that may enunciate transgressive politics of spatiality. "The politics of space," as Beatriz Colomina (1992) tells us, "are always sexual, even if space is central to the mechanisms of the erasure of sexuality" (n.p.). A reading of the forms of sexuality and subjectivity inscribed in the young women's appropriation and refashioning of Rome puts into question, I propose, normative notions of community and the affiliative ingredients traditionally constituting them—location, gender, and class, for example. Furthermore, the ways in which De Céspedes frames issues and questions concerning the relations that women may construct in the urban social environment offer a unique critical perspective on postwar neorealist representations of Rome in literature and cinema, which, though intended to create a new national identity founded on an inclusive notion of collective life, tended to cast women onto the margins of discourse.

For the purposes of evaluating the sexual politics of urban space enunciated by the paths women weave in De Céspedes's Rome, we must first look at the rhetoric of Rome created in Fascist discourse and urban design. In prescriptive writings and city plans, the Fascist vision of Rome would create what de Certeau (1988) calls the planned or geographical city, which establishes the "proper use" of space where power is distributed and regulated. From the March on Rome through the years of imperialist expansion, Mussolini and fellow party members played on the manifold symbolic meanings attached to Rome as the centuries-old seat of civic and spiritual communities, while overlaying new images and associations. The dream for Rome invoked by Mussolini in 1926, in his first speech to the Roman populace, exhibits a totalizing perception of the function that Rome would perform as the center of authority for the nation of Italy, as well as for the Latin world beyond. The duce proclaims that the capital of Fascist Italy "will have to be not . . . only the living, pulsating center of the renewed Nation, but also the wondrous Capital of the entire Latin world" (cited in Bottai 1992, 122). For this reason perhaps, Rome enjoyed a privileged status dispensing it from the pathology of the city as a site of moral and physical disease, constructed in Fascist commentary promoting the interconnected demographic and rural campaigns.[29] In the same speech, Mussolini presents some specific ideas for bringing to fruition *la terza Roma* (the third Rome) by resculpting the city's surface so that it will appear

> vast, ordered, potent, as it was at the time of the early empire of Augustus. You will continue to free the great oak of all that still encumbers it. You will make passages around the Theater of Marcellus, the Campidoglio, the Pantheon: all that grew around them in the centuries of decadence must disappear. You will also liberate the temples of Christian Rome from profane and parasitic constructions. The ancient museums of our history must loom in the necessary solitude. Hence, the third Rome will spread over other hills, along the banks of the sacred river as far as the beaches of the Tyrrhenian sea.[30]

This passage highlights the ideals underpinning the program for the panoptic administration of urban arrangements in Rome. Significantly, Mussolini employs the oak tree, a sacred, classical figure symbolizing strength, longevity, and a world axis (Cirlot 1971, 238), naturalizing an extensive range of projects. These involved not only renovation and new construction, but also the demolition of buildings that housed residences and businesses in order to open up spaces, thereby "freeing" monuments and the gazes beholding them from clutter, distractions. In his 1938 piece "The Renewal of Rome" (Il rinnovamento di Roma), Giuseppe Bottai furnishes an interesting report on the major changes to Rome's urban face, which have restored the grandeur of the Empire while attesting to the current greatness of the Fascist Nation issuing from it. Among the many design projects under way or already completed, we find the restoration of the Theater of Marcellus, begun in 1926 as Mussolini foresaw; the demolition of houses near the Vatican, to set off the beauty of Gian Lorenzo Bernini's colonnade and the symbol of papal Rome; likewise, the "liberating" of such sites as the Traiano Markets, the Mouth of Truth, and the Imperial Forums to spotlight the heroic, "monumental" past of the Empire; the enlargement of streets and the creation of arterial thoroughfares, as in the cases of Via del Tritone and the new Via Regina Elena; the construction of the Foro Italico; and, certainly, the development of EUR, the new, modern quarter at the southwest of Rome, planned for a 1942 international exposition, the Universal Exposition of Rome, which did not take place.

Such projects, according to Bottai's account, respond to aesthetic criteria as well as to such growing urban problems as the decay of architectural structures in the historical center, and increases in population and traffic. Yet as Diane Ghirardo (1990) concludes, Fascist urban design in ancient city centers and New Towns put "symbolic emphasis on the new power as only the most recent in a series of significant political forces which had given shape to Italy" (184). While constructing ties with selected historical epochs, the regime also asserted its dominance in the order of things as it territorialized the country with New Towns and redesigned the urban fabric in cities disposing of space. Philip Gibbs (1934) records the potentially shocking effects of Fascist renovation in accounts of his travels through Mussolini's Italy.[31] On entering Brescia, he nostalgically recalls its rich history, reaching back to the Romans, consoled by the fact that the city has not been entirely lost to Americanization and industry. Then, suddenly, Gibbs and his fellow travelers enter a piazza that horrifies the author:

> We were in a modern piazza—so modern that there was even a skyscraper in the American style, though not so high as the Americans make them. The banks and the postoffice were in the pure style of Fascist art—boxlike buildings without decoration, and with straight lines this way and that, most austere. The skyscraper was of yellow brick and, in my eyes, an atrocity. The shop fronts were of black marble. The whole square was brand new and in the modern spirit, which is good for those who like it. (162)

After commenting on a sculpture in the square that displays liberties with the "beauty of young manhood," whose details Gibbs leaves to our imagination, he observes the way that the space is set for Fascist spectacle, boasting a pulpit for speeches. Architecturally congested areas, like Rome, posed a different order of problem. Yet the state developed strategies to disperse the material signs of Fascism there, too. It appropriated famous or strategically located buildings for Fascist organizations and institutions such as the National Fascist Party (PNF) or the Fascist University Groups (GUF). Furthermore, the regime virtually littered the cityscape with Fascist iconography including the *fasci,* effigies of the duce, his name or slogans, for instance, "The duce is always right," appearing on banners, placards, and posters, if not carved onto the faces of buildings. Last, Mussolini himself—the sole architect and architecture of Fascism in the eyes of some avant-garde artists—staged appearances in Rome that made spectacular use of piazzas and ancient sites like the Colosseum and the Roman Forum (Ghirardo 1990).

Considering the breadth of Fascist projects altering the Roman cityscape when De Céspedes's story unfolds, from 1934 to 1935, the paucity of references to the regime's urban development may surprise the reader. Aside from an important scene in which a prospective employer informs Xenia, in Milan, that in order to be hired she must first obtain a membership card from the GUF, the architectural and iconographic symbols of Fascism do not appear in the itineraries designed by the female students in Rome. Instead, in realist fashion, the narration represents with descriptive detail the largely unpredictable paths that the characters weave together from the Villa Borghese to a cafe in Via dei Condotti, from the Trinità dei monti and the Piazza di Spagna to a market near the Tevere, from the Pincio to Monte Mario. The author's polyphonic, fragmentary, and episodic manner of representing the young women as they strike out each on their own way, walking purposefully or just strolling, creates a different urban text that refuses the unitary vision of the mapped city "colonizing" places. As the character Emanuela says, "Everybody knows a city in their own way, everybody cherishes a different image of it" (1972, 62).[32] De Certeau (1988) elucidates the significant effects achieved by the narrativization of trajectories and gestures of walking, asserting that

> their rhetorical transplantation carries away and displaces the analytical, coherent proper meanings of urbanism; it constitutes a "wandering of the semantic" produced by masses that make some parts of the city disappear and exaggerate others, distorting it, fragmenting it, and diverting it from its immobile order. (102)

Although the material signs of Fascism do not figure prominently in the mobile city created by De Céspedes, the "invisible" apparatuses designed to create disciplinary spaces for the administration of hierarchical power relations pervade the text. We encounter the first such space in the very opening of the novel, which pictures the various perceptions the young women have of the Grimaldi, formerly a convent that the nuns have converted into a boardinghouse for female university students. Neither monochromatic nor static, De Céspedes's depiction of this lived space incorporates both realistic physical description and a range of metaphors with ideological and allegorical force. Most important for this study, the boardinghouse represents a city within a city—a women's city in Rome. As Emanuela concludes, "The institute in itself was a city with its laws and tribunals" (1972, 282). Indeed, the establishment imposes rules to regulate those who reside there and the activities they conduct. These include such seemingly innocuous rules as not using lipstick or smoking cigarettes and obeying the curfew, which structures the girls' comings and goings. Hence, the Grimaldi initially appears to have the dour atmosphere and prohibitions of a prison.[33] For example, Xenia, a vivacious character determined "to get somewhere" in life, complains, "I'm caged up in this cloister of nuns, while life flies along outside, fortune is passing by" (12). This refrain echoes through the narrative, articulated primarily by Xenia and Vinca. Yet even Emanuela, a single mother, feels "imprisoned," though she has just arrived from her financially comfortable life in Florence so that she can visit her daughter at the school for girls in Monte Mario. Moreover, at the hour for lights out, Sister Prudenzina intrusively flings open the doors to the individual rooms in order to surveil the boarders' activities.

However, de Certeau's formulation of "micro practices of space" enables us to read this miniaturized city text not only in terms of oppression and discipline. "These procedures," he argues, "far from being regulated or eliminated by panoptic administration, have reinforced themselves in proliferating illegitimacy, developed and insinuated themselves into the networks of surveillance" (1988, 96). This concept finds literary expression in operations that evade or negotiate the nuns' administration of space and movement—in the literal and figurative senses of going from place to place and proceeding toward states of life. The most significant example concerns the nightly meetings conspiratorially set by members of the group of women studying literature, who form a community unto themselves within the institution. Alternating the places for their rendezvous, the female boarders migrate, even in the darkness that descends after the nuns turn out the lights; they make their way down hallways and staircases of the geographic city/structure, counting the number of steps separating one floor from another. When they converge on one member's room at the assigned time, the conspirators have books in hand, prepared to feign a study session for the nun's room check. The atmosphere of secrecy intensifies after lights out when, amid the long shadows cast by the candles, the girls commit minor infractions— smoking cigarettes or even breaking church laws and conducting a séance. The women create a space with these operations and, moreover, with their practices of sociability and talking.

In fact, a major topic of discussion among the young women concerns what constitutes lasting ties of affiliation and community. Through confessions and heated debates the characters voice highly differentiated ideas on religion, love, sex, marriage, friendship, work, and the nature of their relations to each other, which in a female community should ideally follow an ethic of honesty and sincerity. De Céspedes does not, however, create a utopian female space. Silvia perceives the lie that Xenia tells about the date of her exams as an unforgivable breach of confidence; Augusta and Valentina expel Emanuela from the dwindling circle when they discover she has deceived them by not telling the truth about having a daughter. Yet Valentina, like each of the other women, has something she keeps secretly to herself. Although Sister Lorenza and Augusta envision living among only women as a peaceful ideal, the author's depiction of daily life in the Grimaldi emphasizes the equivocal, tenuous ties formed and dissolved as the students negotiate the obstacles and possibilities of making their own way. Vinca, for example, in love with Luis, a fellow student from Spain who leaves Rome to defend his homeland as civil war ignites, abandons the Grimaldi and establishes a new community with Pilar and Ines, two women who share her cultural heritage, politics, and affective ties. Once Luis marries another woman, Vinca leaves this settlement of exiles to live on her own. She nostalgically recalls the space inside the Grimaldi as protective, defending the women "from love, from war. . . . From life" (1972, 217). Similarly, Augusta, the eldest member of the group, maintains that life in the boardinghouse is not part of reality at all. It merely creates the "illusion" that the women are not, she says, searching alone for "our true way of being" (1972, 261). The differences in national identity, ethnicity, regional origin, as well as personal beliefs and dispositions appear to make community formation impossible among the women. Nonetheless, in the following observations Emanuela perceives such diversity in productive terms as compared to the apparent cohesiveness of the younger students who have just arrived at the Grimaldi. Reflecting on her companions, she maintains that

> it was a group that seemed held compactly together by the diversity of the girls who composed it: all of them different, with unique intelligence and inspiration, and a lively taste for debate and different opinions. In the new students the taste for debating things had disappeared; their personalities seemed faced with stone and covered by the same varnish. They often talked about sports. (433–34)

This representation of the younger generation brings to mind the views of conformity during Fascism created by Elio Vittorini in *Conversaton in Sicily* (1973) and Alberto Moravia in *Il conformista* (The conformist, 1951). Yet the way that De Céspedes contrasts individuality and conformism puts into doubt the image of the unified Fascist collective as a constructive social value.

By highlighting the distinct, multiple terms of social identity that the characters attempt to incorporate, transcend, or invent, De Céspedes writes against an egalitarian politics of sisterhood, drawing out some profound differences among women. The strategies the author employs to mark out subjectivities deriving from diversity invite a variety of approaches. I will focus, however, on the fascinating way in which she represents the interrelations between sexuality and public space, where the female body is both the product and the producer of urban spatiality. Elizabeth Grosz (1992) theorizes such interactions as

> the ways the body is physically, socially, sexually and discursively or representationally produced, and the ways, in turn, bodies reinscribe and project themselves onto their sociocultural environment so that this environment both produces and reflects the form and interests of the body. (242)

In comparison with the other characters, Emanuela's peregrinations in the city, her style of walking, and the transformation of urban surroundings receive by far the most plentiful attention. She thoroughly enjoys

the streets of Rome as she sets out to visit her daughter, strolls nomadi-
cally, window-shops, or, while following her footsteps down the cobble-
stone streets, pauses in her mind's eye over paths she led in her native
Florence. Emanuela's itinerant walking along the cityscape brings to
mind the flaneur. But she does not blend into the crowd; she acts on the
surroundings in several ways. First, as Andrea notes, she walks in a striking manner, a harmoniously self-possessed style of women who "get
somewhere by strength of will, of control" (1972, 167).[34] She also uses the
city sites to her advantage. When Emanuela falls madly in love with
Stefano Mirovich, a young pilot from Portorose, she shows him around
Florence, choosing places that will frame and flatter her. Beautiful, styl-
ish in a way that cultivation and money make possible, Emanuela basks
in her eye-catching powers. The sense of agency and control she attributes to her ability to attract and distract the male gaze is exemplified by
a scene following a visit with Vinca. Feeling liberated from the weight
of Vinca's poor living conditions and the talk about the war in Spain,
Emanuela glories in the freedom of a walk punctuated by the admiring
attentions of a young man who follows her (324).

The figure of Emanuela exemplifies the distracting female presence,
which in the eyes of male cultural critics—whether Fascist or not—wreaks
havoc on the social, cultural, and economic order. No one expresses this
position better than the clerical Fascist Paolo Araldi, who writes in 1929:

> When woman brings her art of seduction through the public streets, she
> doesn't consider the effects on mature men who have the right to the peace
> of mind necessary for wielding a strong hand in business affairs, on which
> the happiness of an entire nation may depend.... and young men ... have
> the right to not have their will power exposed to the serious dangers of
> temptation, which is the beginning of weakness and decadence, since the
> first sin can be the start of an entire life of failure. (cited in Meldini 1975, 162)

For Araldi, among others, the anxiety about women's passion for going
out to cafes, shopping, and going to the movies concerned not only their
distracting presence in the city, but also their absence from the domestic
sphere. As Alfredo Panzini rhetorically asked in *Signorine* (1921), if the
women are out, who is minding the homefront?

While De Céspedes's portrayal of Emanuela's urban occupations re-
codes the modern city, transgressively threatening male authority, the

notion of female sexuality and social identity inscribed in these new spatial relations is not without problems. As the character recalls her second, fateful meeting with Stefano, who dies in a plane crash before marrying her, she entertains a perception that attributes their ensuing love affair, her pregnancy, and current predicaments to an accidental detour. As she walked along the Arno at dusk Emanuela "wanted to turn at Ponte Vecchio, to take the way back, but that time of day was so beautiful that, lingering, she decided to continue on and take the other bridge. A few steps later, there he was" (101). She later returns to this moment, thinking that "everything depended on an instant, that tragedy; all she would have had to do was turn at Ponte Vecchio, instead of walking on" (290). The character thus represents, though in a different cultural context, what Panivong Norindr (1993) calls "errance," a process of "swerving from the path and from truth—as deviation or perversion—and wandering from one place to another" (54). Emanuela's chance meandering alters the course of her life. She deviates from the mores and behaviors associated with her gender and class. It could be argued that this character represents an emancipated, feminist model. She refuses a fixed place or term of identity, which motherhood or marriage to Andrea would offer. Similarly, the frequent references to the character's desires to "remake herself" (442), and to staging moments of self-fashioning that, as she puts on new clothes (415), transform her perception of self might invite us to interpret her fluid position and performative play as an empowering strategy. Yet sadness colors her vapid preoccupations, as she is caught adrift in the possibilities of modernity. Expressing Joan Riviere's notion of female masquerade in provocative terms of spatial relations that collapse the boundaries between private and public and inside and outside, the author pictures Emanuela's life as

> a complete lie, an airy cathedral built on deception, a glass cathedral; soon it would collapse with a tremendous crash. The various characters inside her would find themselves face to face, each one unmasking itself before the other. She would lose everything: Andrea, her friends, and her daughter, too. (288)

The novel's conclusion, far from resolving the ambivalence surrounding Emanuela's notion of self, highlights the sense of uncertainty, as we shall see shortly.

The urban text that Silvia's paths write arises from her different desires—for she represents the cultural model of the intellectual woman—and from regional differences that resist metropolitan acculturation. Born and raised in Calabria, Silvia experiences the city streets with an almost paralyzing sense of fear, provoked not so much by the immediate effect of the crowds and shocks to the senses, but by a historically and culturally constructed perception conditioned by centuries of domination on the part of foreign powers and northern Italian politics. The anxiety arresting Silvia as she crosses a busy street in Rome comes from a fear that "some unexpected, yet everpresent danger might catch her alone, defenseless" because she and her fellow Calabrians

> have been defenseless for centuries: For centuries, someone stronger has always overtaken us, overwhelmed us, if we abandon some scrap of land or sidewalk, that shelters us for better or worse. To separate ourselves from what we have—a friendship, a place to live, even the small space of a room—is a form of daring that frightens us. (1972, 218)

Such conditioning, along with Silvia's determination to achieve intellectual success, partially explains the single-minded way in which she shuttles between the Grimaldi, the university, and the house of Professor Belluzzi, for whom she does research. She focuses on her destination, undeterred by the city's surroundings and charms. If nothing in the city spectacle can distract her vision, it is also true, as Silvia notes with shame, that she moves among the Roman streets without being seen, unlike Emanuela and Vinca. It could be said that the invisibility of this intellectual woman, or her erasure, symbolically suggests her situatedness beyond the traditional configurations of the masculine and the feminine organizing the vision of public space. Indeed, De Céspedes incorporates the idea, popularized in Fascist writings and some media, that intellectual labor defeminizes women. Andrea thinks she is ugly, and therefore, in his eyes "she doesn't even seem like a woman" (139). The comments voiced by Dora, Professor Belluzzi's wife, condemn Silvia for her "lack" of feminine beauty as well as her southern Italian origins marked, it seems, by a dark skin tone. Describing Silvia, Dora complains that "it's like having an animal in the house . . . an old dog. I don't question her intelligence, but she's so dark she always seems dirty" (155). While engaging with popular prejudices, De Céspedes's representation of Silvia as a woman intellectual also introduces alternative components for this social model.

The different perceptions of self and desires that Silvia exhibits and brings to the attention of her fellow women boarders articulate a process of (inter)mediation between dominant codings of female gender and her particular philosophy and practices of self-construction. De Céspedes employs a suggestive metaphor to convey the idea of identity formation represented by Silvia, as we see in one of the group's discussions. While criticizing Emanuela for the way she squanders time and money, Silvia attempts to convince the women of the satisfaction derived from "building day by day a path for yourself to follow" (293). The tension between the models represented by Silvia and Emanuela has significant implications. For although both young women deviate from the beaten path as they proceed toward different stages in the course of life, Emanuela wanders with no sense of purpose, whereas Silvia appears to make her own way based on the principles of committed action and the development of a consciousness of a value uniquely her own (1972, 177). Yet since Silvia's daily occupations and dreams are shaped by her passion for books and devotion to intellectual labor, her femininity is persistently put into question by the women companions and men, an issue that Ellen Nerenberg (1991) and Carole Gallucci (1995) explore. Therefore, I wish to focus on De Céspedes's representation of positions constructed by Silvia in relation to canonical forms of femininity, romantic love, and desire inscribed in urban and literary texts.

The scenes between Silvia and Professor Belluzzi propose both a form of female romantic desire arising from shared intellectual labors of love and its impossibility. For although Silvia appears to seek Belluzzi's attentions as an intelligent collaborator and as a woman, the professor represents normative, institutionalized vision; only traditional codes of "feminine" beauty, gestures, and occupations make woman legible. Indeed, De Céspedes makes ample use of double entendres in the dialogues between these characters and Silvia's reflections on them, many of which concern the unreadability of Silvia as woman. For example, as she thinks joyfully about Belluzzi's choosing her as his assistant out of all the other women students, and his statement that she "will go a long way," she fantasizes about hearing him say "I've never seen a woman like you" (93). Typically equivocal, this dream may voice Silvia's desire to be viewed as a different kind of woman, constructed on new terms of femininity, yet it is precisely this difference that situates her beyond the reaches of the gaze. Nonetheless, in a scene depicted in the later version of the novel, De Céspedes delicately insinuates Silvia's stirrings of romantic desire into the landscape of Rome and suggests that the development of mental faculties does not silence the longing to desire and to be desired. Having defended her thesis with outstanding success, Silvia finally contemplates the site before her eyes, significantly, Bernini's Fountain of the Four Rivers, where the figures of the Danube, the Ganges, the Nile, and the Plata stand planted around the obelisk, at the center of Piazza Navona. With the tumbling water resounding in her ears and sprinkling her body, as if baptizing her, Silvia thinks:

> That water . . . that roaring or whispering sound she found over again running from piazza to piazza, from neighborhood to neighborhood, was the secret voice of the city which, from the beginning, had seemed mute, indifferent. Instead, you had to know how to interpret the way it spoke. Perhaps she also had to interpret the professor's language.
> She went to the edge of the fountain. One of the statues stood still on the baroque rocks in a pose of fear and shock, an attitude that resembled her own attitude toward life, and that all men should, perhaps, have had. But instead, they went around sure of themselves—alone, or arm-in-arm with a woman—as if they weren't afraid of anything. As if to understand and to love were the easiest things to do. (1972, 242–43)

In this highly evocative passage, De Céspedes problematizes the interactions between sexuality and space. As the language of the water, fluid and, in general, associated with the feminine principle, solicits Silvia, her body is representationally produced by the city. She then links this language with a discourse of love that she hopes to discern in Belluzzi's words. At the same time, Silvia appears to project herself onto the urban text as she produces the vision of the Rio Plata statue in terms of her subjectivity; she associates the gesture of "fear and shock" inscribed on the male figure with her own position toward life. In the process Silvia feminizes the statue, for the disposition that she and the statue share is not the attitude exhibited by "all men," by implication one of fearlessness and mastery.[35] Although Belluzzi, Andrea, Dora, and Emanuela, for example, situate Silvia's body beyond the "feminine" sphere, this scene challenges the reading of the female intellectual purely as a model of the masculinized woman. Furthermore, if gender is performatively constituted through its expressions, as Judith Butler (1990) contends, then it could be argued that De Céspedes's representation of Silvia disrupts the codings of the male and female bodies as natural symbols of coherent, distinct roles in social and sexual relations.

It is interesting that in the 1938 version De Céspedes stages a different city scene following Silvia's defense of her dissertation. Though we see the same ambiguity shading the images of female social identity represented by Silvia, the scene conveys a stronger sense of how the path she carves diverges from common tendencies. Seated along with the women students outside the boardinghouse, Silvia laughs to herself about the label "ugly woman," while she "painfully peels off the possibility of being a woman like the others" (360). The choice of expressions is especially suggestive, for *staccarsi di dosso* implies agency to remove or take off something that is obviously not inextricable from the body. Second, the statement begs questions concerning the alterations of femininity. Is Silvia renouncing "womanliness" altogether? Or does the statement indicate that she proposes to craft a kind of woman different from the others? Although the questions remain open, her following comments sharpen Silvia's idea of self-formation. As she watches a group of boys playing soldiers, one of them, unlike the others, catches her eye. He insists on being the leader and not just part of the platoon. Engaging with this militaristic metaphor, Silvia thinks to herself,

> It is necessary to know how to be the person who walks in front of the others. I won't stay in the platoon, in the herd; women often let themselves be tamed by the senses or the little faith they have in themselves. Others distance themselves from love with disgust, effortlessly, like Augusta. But it is hard to distance oneself from something you like. (361–62)

Silvia's analysis of the rhetoric of walking—its rules and common patterns—has political, social, and sexual valences as her reflections move from general issues to gender-specific problems. Refining her subject position through her thoughts on the individual and the collective, leaders and followers, women and love, Silvia does not assume an alienated or strictly oppositional stance. Instead, De Céspedes situates Silvia in relation to other women, perhaps proposing her socially committed and self-assertive role as one to follow. The final images of Silvia enhance the inventive terms of the social identity she fashions, and its possible functions as a model for change.

Although few references to Fascist iconography and architectural projects appear in De Céspedes's representation of the geographical city of Rome and, as explained earlier, the mobile city texts composed by the women, the author explores the urban designs of Fascism and what they stand for as Silvia's story line comes to an open ending. Following her departure from the Grimaldi, Silvia embarks on the beginning of another path and stage of development when she takes up her teaching position in Littoria, a new city constructed by the regime. In a letter addressed to the women still boarding at the Grimaldi, Silvia describes her impressions and experience of the city space, which, she notes, alienates newcomers at first sight. Moving from the material to the phantasmic, she tells the readers there are

> few streets, wide, open, well lighted. Everything is clear, transparent, you see your reflection everywhere, your image comes at you in a thousand ways, you can never forget you exist. A new city lacks traditions, and so it seems as if everyone is waiting to know what they have to do. No one has an intimate life of their own; you still feel the need for an organizing community that could help to overcome the coldness of the buildings and streets. (430)

As an example of the regime's urban development projects, Littoria, we might expect, could emblematize a "totalitarian" organization of the body and space. In fact, by naming the city Littoria De Céspedes represents a common rhetorical strategy in Fascist discourse, which evokes the Roman Empire through figures of speech. Littoria derives from the word *lictor*, an officer of ancient Rome bearing the fasces as the insignia of his official position. In addition to its associations with the empire, state officialdom, and the juridical, *littorio* and *littoriale* appear frequently in Fascist speeches and writings, even in the name of youth organizations, creating a symbolic line of descent. Yet as Silvia notes, the new city by definition lacks traditions, just as it lacks a story of origins, legends, and lines of social history and community.

Indeed, the wide streets and new buildings emblematize a form of Fascist modernity that, surprisingly perhaps, does not appear to establish a regulatory grammar of urban space for the disposition of gender and social relations. The author's visualization of the body and public space merits particular attention. In contrast to Rome, where Silvia walked without being seen, the new city produces an optics of hypervisibility, her body appearing as both object and subject. But what might this exposure say about the body and social power in the architecture of Fascism? In one sense, as Silvia states, everything is clear, transparent, therefore knowable and subject to intervention. Does this imply the establishment of normative vision and control? At what point might transparency, enabling the observer to "see through" and be "see-through" make the body disappear? In her excellent analysis of advertising images produced during Fascism, Karen Pinkus (1995) examines what the phenomenon of bodily disappearance might mean in the regime. She proposes that it "could be understood as a strategy for escape from a political and moral arena of such overmanagement that the body cannot possibly suffer," or as a form of "disavowal" where "the body both adapts to control and, at the same time, absents itself" (238). In De Céspedes's text, the specular body, produced through the constant, myriad reflections and refractions of bodily images, would seem to dissolve boundaries and the sense of corporeality sustaining them. This state of visuality insistently brings the body to the observer's attention and, indeed, Silvia confesses, creates the need for a refuge.

While De Céspedes's representation of the new relations between the body and urban space emphasizes their distracting and troubling effects on Silvia, such conditions are not entirely disorienting. The author amplifies this character's role as a pioneer of new ground as she assumes her position in the classroom, which may be read as a micropolitical space within the institution. Underscoring the independent manner of thought and practice distinguishing Silvia's speaking position, she declares in her letter, "I am unable to pray, to believe, and I refuse to blindly accept everything others have already prepared for me: I always have that damned need to reason things out" (430). Although veiled by the reference to religion, the refusal "to believe" invokes a central element of the Fascist motto, "Believe, Obey, Fight." Silvia goes on to assert that, standing at her podium, a position of authority, she can voice "my words, my ideas" (431), leading the younger generation in her charge.

The relations that Augusta has with the geographic city and the metaphoric city offer the final, and perhaps most complex, example of the way in which De Céspedes's depictions of women's practices of space inscribe shifting configurations of subjectivity and sexuality. In a careful reading, Nerenberg examines how the ideas that Augusta expresses and silences demonstrate the inscription of the lesbian subject, as well as how the novel participates in filmic discourse on lesbianism in girls' schools of the time.[36] Here I want to pursue some of the additional questions that De Céspedes's representation of Augusta raises about the representability of a lesbian positionality in the context of the sexual and textual politics of space during Fascism. We could begin with the panoptic vision of the nation invented in Fascist discourses virulently defending the borders of a heterosexual regime, engendered also by punitive and incentive pronatalist policies intended to safeguard national integrity. How, if at all, does the narrative inscription of the lesbian body on Rome, which stands for the center of Fascist authority and the nation, alter the idea of what constitutes Italian nationhood? The Grimaldi represents a city within a city, in other words, a microcosm of Rome inhabited by differentiated communities of women. If, as I have argued, women's trajectories and practices of space write a mobile text on the geographical city, then what can Augusta's microspatial practices tell us about Rome, and about the women's metaphoric city in the Grimaldi? And what performative value might gender and sexuality have for the formation of affiliative communities?

In the twenties and thirties, the demographic campaign forms the matrix of Fascist discourse prescriptively equating nation and a heterosexual regime of the masculine and the feminine regulating citizenship. As Mussolini writes in 1928,

> In order to speak about national problems, first of all, the nation must exist. Now a Nation exists not only as history or territory, but as human masses that reproduce themselves from generation to generation. To do otherwise means servitude or the end. Italian Fascists: Hegel, the philoso-

pher of the State, said: He who is not a father is not a man! (in Meldini 1975, 150)

In the interests of the nation, writings by party exponents attempt to reverse the modern blurring of gender boundaries by reconstructing the male and the female as two "natural" types, whose coupling will fulfill the differentiated needs, abilities, desires, and destinies that biologically determine each of them. Thus, any disposition, attitude, or behavior that oversteps the borderlines separating male and female gender roles represents a form of deviance tantamount to a crime against the family, race, and nation. Ferdinando Loffredo typifies this position in 1939:

> Intellectualism, professional equality, sexual freedom, immodesty, promiscuity, and sports masculinize woman and therefore diminish her disposition for being a good ruler of the domestic government and a mother of numerous, healthy offspring. The state that doctors call intersexuality, which derives from men and women frequently living in promiscuity, reducing the healthy sexual impulse along with the desire for a home and children, is seriously harmful for the race and for the family. (in Meldini 1975, 269)

The Fascist rhetoric on "mixed sexual types" as a "criminal" sign of bisexuality expands on writings that medicalized female socialization and friendship in the late 1800s. Among the first of these studies in positivist anthropology and sexology is Le "amicizie" di collegio: Ricerche sulle prime manifestazioni dell'amore sessuale (Boarding school friendships: Research on the initial manifestations of sexual love, 1898), written by Giulio Obici and Giovanni Marchesini. The authors make the linkage between female attachments—companionate friendships, passionate infatuations, and lifelong intimacy—formed in girls' schools and their potential to become perversions. As Michela De Giorgio (1992) tells us, this study transformed attitudes about adolescent female relationships from an accepted expression of emotional bonds into a harbinger of danger, as "the latent risk of homosexuality—a sinful fruit of female socialization born from the 'parallel development of the emotions of social attraction and of emotions of a sexual origin'—takes the place of the 'impure sin' or 'solitary sin' in the preoccupations of moralists and scientists" (120). The representation of lesbianism as perversion, or disease, could avail itself of an existing discursive apparatus, shaped by doctors who treated prostitutes suffering from venereal disease in the 1880s. According to Mary Gibson (1986), doctors reported widespread lesbian relations in the clinics (194). Given the theorized potential for lesbian relations among female groups, it is interesting that Fascist youth organizations grouped members according to sex as well as age. In the case of women's sports, however, the call went out to supervise the players closely so that their feelings of friendship would not develop into lesbian relationships (De Grazia 1992, 220). Furthermore, the Rocco Code of 1930 forbade acts of homosexuality.

Within this discursive field, De Céspedes's construction of the lesbian positionality, though not unproblematic, challenges founding myths about Rome, the nation, and its constituencies. The subversive power of the lesbian body represented by Augusta derives in part from the importance of female iconography deployed to symbolize not only the Catholic world, but also the "motherland" and "mother Rome" as the heart of the Fascist nation. In fact, George L. Mosse (1985) contends that "lesbians threatened society . . . to an even greater degree than homosexuals, given women's roles as patron saints and mothers of the family and the nation. Motherhood was central to the image of women who, like the Madonna, were supposed to be chaste, yet mothers" (105–6). While we can say that the practices of daily living and ideas about communal life attributed to Augusta refuse the heterosexual logic organizing the symbolic and material situatedness of woman within the Fascist nation, the author's representation of the relations between lesbian sexuality and the city produces a highly equivocal view of the social constitution of the lesbian subject.

In relation to Emanuela, Silvia, and other members of the Grimaldi community, Augusta strikes me with her indifference to Rome's allures. In fact, she rarely ventures out into the city. The apparent absence of exchanges with the geography of Rome emphasizes the "closeted" nature of her lived space. Moreover, the author locates the configurations of Augusta's subjectivity through successive layerings of the city. Moving inward from one stratum to another, we pass from the Rome that De Céspedes creates to the city of the Grimaldi, and finally to the city of Augusta's own invention, authored in her latest novel. As she explains to

Emanuela what the novel is about, Augusta articulates a radical separatist politics. She begins with a rhetorical question, "What does woman have to do to free herself from man's tyranny?" (327). The answer, she explains, is to cast out all men, and woman

> must take his place. An autonomous life, freed even from the servitude of the senses: complete independence of spirit and body. . . . This way no woman among us will ever be afraid of old age again, the degeneration of one's beauty. It's like dying, you know? To see your body slowly withering, becoming flabby. And all this frightens us because of men. When each woman among us has her own independent life, we won't worry about all this anymore. Although a woman ages, the artist stays young forever; in fact, as the years pass, she reaps the greatest kinds of fulfillment, or, if she works in business, in industry, she'll have the highest positions. It's a kind of safety. Do you understand? (327, 328)

Augusta's imagined community does not merely substitute women for men within patriarchal structures but outlines an essentially different metaphysics, while creating a space for the articulation of lesbian desire. Although Augusta symbolically affirms her concept of identity within her own text, De Céspedes problematizes the performative value of sexuality and gender as defining principles of affiliation.

Augusta constructs woman as a homogeneous category and, in the process of doing so, brings out the very differences among women she apparently desires to erase. For example, she claims that her novel is "universal" and, as represented in the above quotation and in other passages where Augusta expresses "the instinctive repugnance woman feels toward man" (259), that it assumes to speak for all women. Indeed, as she describes her book to Emanuela, who represents a model of modern female heterosexual desire, the reader cannot help but wonder who will form her "women's" community. Emanuela fails to identify with Augusta's ideas about and reactions to men and begins to avoid her company. Yet Augusta's vision of autonomous female sociability momentarily seduces Emanuela, inspiring her to imagine Augusta traveling throughout the land, from town to town, spreading the word to women everywhere, and she speculates that

> maybe the women would have followed her, leaving their homes; they would have gone to encamp all together, who knows where, creating a new

city. In that place there wouldn't be any more suffering over Stefania and Andrea; she would peacefully listen to music, as Augusta always lectured her to do. (329)

But this utopian dream is just that. And meanwhile, Augusta seems to encamp in her room, the only accommodations in the Grimaldi that feel "like someone really lived there" (29). Hence, we might reasonably conclude that De Céspedes situates the lesbian positionality in a fixed position at the margins of women's culture and, of course, men's.

I want to offer a different interpretation, however, based on the author's evocative fashioning of the bridge, which recurs throughout the novel in the names of places, as part of Rome's urban design, and as metaphor. In an often-cited passage of the novel, Silvia employs the figure of the bridge to describe the Grimaldi and the young women's lives there:

> Not all of us will be here next year. You see, it's as if we were crossing a bridge. . . . We've already left one shore and we haven't arrived at the other side yet. What we left is behind us; we don't even turn to look back. The shore awaiting us is still behind the fog. We don't even know what we'll find when the fog disappears. One woman leans over to look at the river, falls in and drowns. Another one, tired, sits down and falls asleep on the bridge. The others, for better or worse, pass over to the other shore. (125)

To remain on a bridge, as to be a "boarder," means to lack a fixed place. At the novel's conclusion, three women from the original community remain on the bridge. Milly dies, Xenia flees to Milan after failing her exams and becomes a wealthy businessman's mistress, and Silvia, as we know, leaves to begin teaching in Littoria. Anna returns to Puglia where she'll marry her fiancé, and Vinca settles in Rome, giving private lessons. In contrast, Emanuela, with her daughter in tow, leaves Italian shores, with no destination in sight, when she embarks on a world cruise. Metaphorically, she leaves one bridge for another. Amid the hollow chatter onboard, a fellow itinerant traveler notes that, with so many journeys, their "real country" is the "ponte," which means deck in this context yet resonates also with the word's meaning of bridge (457). Only Augusta and Valentina remain at the Grimaldi, with no thought of leaving or crossing over to the shore. Yet to occupy the bridge has far-ranging implications for relations of power, limits, and subversion. Explaining potential meanings of the bridge, de Certeau (1988) states:

As a transgression of the limit, a disobedience of the law of place, it represents a departure, an attack on the state, the ambition of a conquering power, or the flight of an exile; in any case, the "betrayal" of an order. But at the same time as it offers the possibility of a bewildering exteriority, it allows or causes the re-emergence beyond frontiers of the alien element that was controlled in the interior, and gives objectivity (that is, expression and representation) to the alterity which was hidden inside the limits. (128)

Following this paradigm, the lesbian positionality Augusta represents is neither fixed at the borders in resigned alienation nor entirely shut out of the dominant culture. At the symbolic level we could interpret the mobile ambiguity of the lesbian subject as a transgression of the regulatory technologies engendering nation and narration during Fascism. This reading of the symbolic implications created by De Céspedes's representation of lesbian subjectivity raises more questions about the textual and social constitution of the body than can be satisfactorily answered here. For example, though the author avoids the stereotype of the lesbian subject as a woman who, rejected or jilted by men, then turns to relations with women, the portrait of Augusta increasingly incorporates markers of masculinity. Emanuela, for example, observes how Augusta, consumed by her writing, has begun to use masculine gestures and to smoke constantly. Therefore, it is unclear whether this ostensible "masculinization" derives from textual or sexual production. Similarly, the author's staging of scenes between Augusta and Valentina remains within the conventions of heterosexual romantic courtship. On occasions when Emanuela goes into Augusta's room, she "finds" the two women "reading poetry, holding hands, as if their fantasies and breath mingled" (433). Yet even in the later version of the novel, revised after the fall of Fascism, De Céspedes offers no elaboration of lesbian sexual desire, which, according to Teresa de Lauretis, among others, is perhaps the most important issue at stake (1994, especially chaps. 2 and 3). However, De Céspedes's representation of the lesbian subject illustrates the need for historiographic research on the ways in which lesbian women mediated apparatuses structuring the heterosexual Fascist regime.

The metaphorical cities of Rome arising from the texts that Emanuela, Silvia, and Augusta write in their particular styles furnish a different vantage point for questioning the postwar reconstructions of national identity and the body politic in, for example, the novels *La romana* (The woman of Rome, 1947) and *La ciociara* (Two women, 1957) by Alberto Moravia, *Cronache di poveri amanti* (Chronicles of poor lovers, 1947) by Vasco Pratolini, and in such films as *Open City* (1945) by Roberto Rossellini and *The Bicycle Thieves* (1948) by Vittorio De Sica.[37] Moreover, the novels by Alba De Céspedes and Paola Drigo demonstrate the need to interrogate the notion that the neorealist aesthetic theorized among male intellectuals in the postwar years somehow fostered the success of contemporary women authors by legitimating their use of realist conventions. These works specifically provide new terms for examining women's novelistic production during Fascism and how their literary practices figured in the constitution of the canon, as illustrated by *Natalia* (1930) by Fausta Cialente, *Pensione Flora* (The Flora boarding-house, 1936) by Giana Anguissola, and *Le catene* (The chains, 1930) by Lina Pietravalle, among numerous others. More generally, the narrative practices employed by De Céspedes and Drigo to construct female positionalities in the geography of Italy raise important questions concerning realist aesthetic politics and how national and continental boarders/borders are constituted.

FIVE

Generatrices of Poiesis: Registers of Women's Poetry, Modernism, and the Avant-garde

It is doubtful whether poetry can come out of an incubator. Poetry ought to have a mother as well as a father. The Fascist poem, one may fear, will be a horrid little abortion such as one sees in a glass jar in the museum of some country town. Such monsters never live long.

VIRGINIA WOOLF, *A Room of One's Own*

It seems as if the matrix of female strength can be lost with the passing of one generation.

THE MILAN WOMEN'S BOOKSTORE COLLECTIVE, *Sexual Difference*

What is a Fascist poem? Do certain motifs, such as nationalism, colonial aggression, virility, and antifeminism sound the measure of Fascist value by their mere presence? How might formal linguistic properties or generic modes figure into this equation? Given the discursive tendency toward heroic, totalizing vision exemplified by Mussolini, as well as fellow exponents of Fascism, is the epic poem more Fascist than the futurist words-in-freedom or the lyrical prose fragment? Working through these issues, Robert Casillo (1992) sets up cantos 72 and 73 in the standard edition of Ezra Pound's *The Cantos* (1987) as paradigms of Fascist poetry. The criteria that Casillo formulates include the way in which Pound, an outspoken sympathizer of Mussolini, celebrates heroes of Fascism, along with the values of violent action and antifeminism; his incorporation of the language and slogans produced by the regime; and the mode of address, which calls Italians to rally their support for the duce. In contrast, Andrew Hewitt (1993) focuses on the performativity of the text in his critical analysis of F. T. Marinetti as the "seminal figure" in the production of Fascist modernism.[1]

Sharing some of these concerns, Enrico Falqui's essay "Poesia e Fascismo" (Poetry and Fascism, 1970a), first published during Fascism in 1935, views the associations between poetry and Fascism from a somewhat different angle. Written as a review of poetry anthologies published in the 1930s, some of which directly link the poets with Fascism by boasting such titles as *Poeti in camicia nera* (Blackshirt poets, 1934) and *Antologia di poeti fascisti* (Anthology of Fascist poets, 1935), Falqui's essay notes the thematic concerns that recur in the poems: a passion for risk, the desire for glory, and a quest for truth. Yet he approaches the texts as a form of civic poetry, characterized by practical, not aesthetic, value. Although he speculates that such poems may herald "the birth of civic poetry," their topical, stereotypical subjects and celebratory design augur a swift decline. In the future, he predicts, the bellicose poems will "become pale, lose their shape and contours, until they completely disappear. Only archaeological material will be left" (404).

Keeping in consideration the interpretative models proposed for assessing the ways in which themes, forms, modes of address, and functions might make a poem Fascist, what criteria could we adopt to theorize the elements constituting an anti-Fascist poem? Should we set the micropolitical, the feminine, and the feminist against the nationalist, the virile, and the antifeminist? Falqui (1970b) turns to just this problem in an essay on the relation between poetic creation and "resistance," titled "Poesia e Resistenza" (Poetry and resistance), which was written in 1955, some ten years after the Resistance Movement and the liberation of Italy from Fascist rule and Nazi occupation. While performing a critique of the collection *Antologia poetica della Resistenza italiana* (Anthology of poetry on the Italian Resistance), Falqui presents two ideas that continue to shape how we think about poetry and politics during Fascism and the immediate postwar years. First, he argues that by changing the referent from "pistols to pens" (I need not supply the signifier that would complete the series of such a familiar phallic economy), hermetic poetry dating back to the 1930s was a resistance literature written against Fascism. In support of his position, Falqui quotes a 1944 article written by Pietro

Pancrazi, who contended that Italian poetry "could not have stood in greater contradiction to Fascism because it responded to the state's desire to have civic poetry with forms that were crepuscular, intimist, and hermetic" (410). Some forty years later, Umberto Eco (1995) holds the lines of this position as he re-presents the stylistic practices, language, and mood in poems by Eugenio Montale and fellow poets associated with hermeticism as a "literary protest" against the Fascist regime's "bombastic style" and "cult of optimism and heroism" (13). For those of you who may be unfamiliar with Italian hermeticism, I should note here that its canonical figures consisted of men poets.

The second thesis presented by Falqui has equally important implications for the canon of Italian poetry. Drawing exclusively on the terms of hermetic aesthetics, Falqui credits the Resistance movement with promoting "the transition from hermetic emotion to posthermetic emotion, from the taste for the absolute word to the need for the mediatory word, from a mute faith to a spoken solidarity, from guarded privacy to generous sociality, from poetry as negation and absence to poetry as affirmation and presence" (409). Thus, Falqui constructs a patrilineal system of affiliation between the hermetic poetics produced during Fascism and the "renewal" of poetry in the years following the liberation.

Critical theory and analysis produced in recent years have fostered a greater understanding of the complexity of hermetic practices of signification and how they may challenge Fascist ideology, myth, and rhetoric at the discursive level. Furthermore, the personal testimonies, aesthetic declarations, and poetry offered by men poets who practiced their vocation from the 1930s through the 1940s bear witness to the claims that Falqui, among others, makes about the key role that the Resistance played in the changing configurations of male poetic subjectivity. Salvatore Quasimodo provides an excellent example of the nearly seismic rift in the notion of what it meant to be a poet:

> The birth of a new poet is an act of violence, and therefore, a preexisting order cannot continue. . . . Today, after two wars in which countless dead became the hero, the poet's commitment is all the more serious because he must *remake* man. . . . To remake man—this is the fundamental problem. For those who believe poetry is a literary game and think the poet is still detached from life, a person who climbs up the stairs of his tower at

night to speculate about the cosmos, we say the time for speculations is
over. To remake man—this is the commitment. (in Esposito 1992, 26)

This passage powerfully underscores a personal and artistic transformation from hermetic poetics to a notion of poetry as social praxis, as
Quasimodo formulates the coming into being of a new poet, begotten by
the seeds of consciousness that World War II created.

I do not dispute the critical value of such declarations, which scholars
have privileged as representative of the major trends in Italian poetry of
the time. I would argue, however, that the resultant paradigm, tracing
the genealogy of poetry from the anti-Fascist hermetics through the Resistance to the socially committed posthermetics, virtually shuts women
poets out of discussions about the forms of interwar poetry and their
potential relations to Fascism and literary "resistance." By merit of this
exclusion, which construes the genre of poetry as a male-identified enterprise, the so-called anti-Fascist tradition of hermetic poetry approxi-
mates Virgina Woolf's notion of Fascist poetry—lacking a mother and
artificially gestated in a masculine textual body. I realize that Woolf is
never so literal and might have intuited the androgynous coupling of the
masculine and the feminine in hermetic texts. Yet it is not insignificant
that Quasimodo's new poet is born in "an act of violence" from the rub-
ble of war, fought for liberation but a war nonetheless, and proposes to
"remake" man, thereby addressing the universal, or male, social subject.
The birthing scene thus invokes the terms of masculinity that Woolf
amply critiques in her essays and fiction. At the very least, we can say that
the writings by Falqui, Pancrazi, and Quasimodo, among others, produce a gendered ideology of inter- and postwar poetry and the political
functions it is claimed to perform.

This critical model has served to create a lacuna around women's poetry of the 1920s and 1930s, thereby limiting the questions that we pose
about poetic subjectivities and the discursive field during Fascism.[2] Indeed, of all the genres where works by women participated in constituting the interwar canon, poetry is the field where the most research—
archival, theoretical, and critical—needs to be done. Ironically, the recent
boom of interest in contemporary Italian women poets has made this
gap more painfully obvious. For example, poems by such artists as Maria

Luisa Spaziani, Patrizia Cavalli, Amelia Rosselli, and Giulia Nicolai have begun to make their way, alongside those by male poets, into anthologies designed to represent the current panorama of Italian poetry. Both the bilingual volume *New Italian Poets* (1991), edited by Dana Gioia and Michael Palma, and *Twentieth-Century Italian Poetry* (1993), edited by John Picchione and Lawrence R. Smith, exemplify this promising trend. Furthermore, since the 1976 publication of Biancamaria Frabotta's edited collection *Donne in poesia* (Women in poetry), featuring poems by postwar female practitioners and the interwar poetry by Antonia Pozzi, several excellent anthologies dedicated exclusively to contemporary women poets have been published. These include, for example, Maria Pia Quintavalla's *Donne in poesia* (Women in poetry, 1992) and Domenico Cara's *Le donne della poesia* (Women of poetry, 1991).[3] As might be expected, recent years have also seen a corollary critical interest in the complex individual perspectives in the poetry by Italian women on such current topics of debate as aesthetics, myth, metaphysics, sexual difference, and the postmodern.[4]

However, where the early 1900s, and especially the interwar years are concerned, poetry anthologies and literary histories for general audiences tend to re-present a stable list of canonized male poets.[5] Beginning with poetry of the late nineteenth century, they generally introduce us to the markedly different symbolist redactions crafted by Giovanni Pascoli and Gabriele D'Annunzio, to the work of such crepuscular poets as Sergio Corazzini and Guido Gozzano, and, in the early twentieth century, to the avant-garde project proclaimed by F. T. Marinetti. To represent the interwar years, such new lyricists and hermeticists as Umberto Saba, Giuseppe Ungaretti, and Eugenio Montale hold center stage. Usually, however, sample selections of interwar poetry do not include modern women poets. It is perhaps true that the thematic interests and expressive forms in poetry by such established and lesser-known writers as Ada Negri, Sibilla Aleramo, Antonia Pozzi, Ofelia Mazzoni, and Giovanna Biasotti, who published some of their major works during Fascism, do not fit squarely into the mainstream of these canonized movements. But how do we explain the absence of Benedetta, Rosa Rosà, or Maria Goretti, each outspoken protagonists in the futurist movement? Since general anthologies presumably address novice readers, it would seem all the more reason to include samples by award-winning female poets as well. Instead, women artists frequently escape mention, promoting the all-too-familiar impression that women either did not write poetry during Fascism or that their works are of no consequence. By creating a gap in the history of poetry composed by women, such works imply that its lineage is perhaps discontinuous, frail, and vulnerable to the whims of history and artistic inspiration.

Moreover, the tendency to not re-present or examine women's lyrical production of the interwar years fosters erroneous assumptions about the diverse sites of women's cultural interventions and their contributions to genre formation. Michel Foucault's theoretical formulation of discursive *rémanence* highlights these interactive relations while elucidating one of the ways that women's poetry has been forced from literary history, and thus memory:

> To say that statements are residual (rémanent) is not to say that they remain in the field of memory, or that it is possible to rediscover what they meant; but it means that they are preserved by virtue of a number of supports and material techniques .., in accordance with certain types of institutions .., and with certain statutory modalities. . . . This also means that they are invested in techniques that put them into operation, in practices that derive from them, in the social relations they form, or, through those relations, modify. (1972a, 123–24)

Reviews and critical essays written in the twenties and thirties indicate that women's lyrical production was fully engaged in and by social and cultural apparatuses prior to and during Fascism. Such writings also suggest that poetry represented the most intensely embattled creative territory, where the politics of gender and genre exploded into outright sexual warfare. In the trenches, such major figures among the literary elite as Benedetto Croce, Giovanni Papini, and Camillo Pellizzi devoted significant attention to the work of women poets. While tracking the course of women's poetics, in the same gesture critics overtly or covertly employed the ideals of transcendence, universality, and linguistic refinement as ramparts to defend poetry as the bastion of male cultural authority. Undaunted, or perhaps incited by this position, scores of women recast or revolutionized both the figure of the female poet, which boasts a tradition virtually unbroken since Compiuta Donzella's poems of the

1200s, and poiesis, conceived as a process for the inscription of the female-gendered body, spirit, mind, and creative power.[6] In her book *Poetesse d'Italia* (Women poets of Italy, 1916), the critic and author Camilla Bisi presents what she sees as the new meanings of lyrical expression, adopted by women not to veil the body of desires, thoughts, and feelings, but to unveil their subcutaneous being in defiant acts that, as a consequence, expose the poets to "vivisections" performed by men critics. Nonetheless, she tells us, the genre of poetry had special, widespread appeal among women authors and, she prophetically suggests:

> Perhaps the time will come when someone will investigate the phenomenon that prompts women to write so much poetry; the causes will be discovered in customs, literature, and history. Perhaps some women poets who now triumph in ephemeral glory will disappear, overcome by oblivion. But not all of this steadfast troop—multiform yet solid, a beautiful phalanx rich with energy and exquisitely sensitive, which our times have managed to shape—will be disdained or fade entirely from memory. (7–8)

While vividly evoking the sexual battle over poetry as an expressive form for the creation of meaning, Bisi's study draws out the nuanced differences between the poetic voices, motifs, styles, and concerns fashioned by a full range of female poets, several of whom continued to publish poetry during the regime. Her book as well as both volumes on Italian women edited by Maria Bandini Buti, titled *Donne d'Italia: Poetesse e scrittrici* (Women of Italy: Women poets and writers, 1941/1942), are virtually teeming with the names of women who pursued the vocation of poet throughout the history of Italian literature, and especially during Fascism. These invaluable resources, which furnish information on the artists' lives, works, and critical reception, document the strength of women's contributions to the canon of poetry and graphically show the extent to which it has been eviscerated.

Women's claims to the authority of poetic discourse may explain, in part, the preoccupation with male-female relations manifested in interwar debates over the nature of lyrical creation, artistic beauty and truth, and sexual difference. In this study I want to reopen debate about modern and avant-garde women's poetry, which raised such heated controversy in the 1920s and 1930s, by exploring the positionings constructed by women artists in the hegemonic field of poetry from the 1920s to the early

1940s. My discussion aims at providing a more nuanced paradigm of the diverse registers of poetic discourse that may provoke different questions about poetry, Fascism, the avant-garde, and "literary resistance." The first part of the examination offers a brief overview of the critical reception of poetry written by women. It focuses on the poetic tenets propounded by such critics as Croce and Pellizzi, and their estimation of how women's poetry adheres to or breaks aesthetic rules. I then train attention on the deployment of the birthing metaphor in writings by men critics and artists, which, I argue, plays a major role in the production of a gendered ideology of poetry from the early 1900s through the 1930s. Performing a twofold function, this trope serves to rationalize both the concept of poetic creation as masculine and its "legitimate" cultural authority and, at the same time, to essentialize a concept of procreation as feminine, casting off women's artistic offspring as illegitimate.

Expanding on the lines of inquiry suggested by the tensions between the terms *creation* and *procreation,* and the symbolic, aesthetic, and political meanings attached to them, I then explore the ways in which women poets formulate and bring into poetic life the figure of the *generatrice* (generatrix).[7] I also employ this designation in the standard manner, denoting "a female that generates," in the multiple senses that she begets, causes, or produces. The diversified figurations of the *generatrice* invented by women poets expand on and redesign the meanings of *mother,* proclaiming women the rightful subjects of both procreation and creation. This reappropriation wrests the birthing metaphor from its male-laden tradition and, I propose, disrupts the ideology of poetry and woman produced by the dominant cultural and political elite during Fascism. I do not intend, however, to claim that this rhetorical strategy or the poets examined here are representative of unifying currents or the full range of women's poetry written in the interwar years. On the contrary, I have chosen to read texts by women of different generations who crafted highly differentiated voices and visions of female poetic identity formation. The artists include such figures as the avant-garde futurists Maria Goretti and Maria Ginanni, as well as poets known for their use of more or less mimetic lyrical conventions—Aleramo, Negri, and Pozzi. My examination will focus on the different redactions of the generatrix and aesthetics generated by these women in their poems and extrapoetic discourse, as well as how they represent the female body and eroticism, technology and notions of time and space, and mother-daughter relations. This method is designed in part to avoid the risk of producing "sameness," which would replicate the Fascist tendency toward an essential, naturalized vision of woman or, more generally, as Darcy Grimaldo Grigsby (1991) contends, "threatens not only to level diverse artistic projects but also to totalize the female body by some kind of (aesthetic) consensus" (83).

Although inflected toward the points of difference displayed by women's poetic subjectivities, the analyses also endeavor to suggest contiguities among female poets as well as male artists of the time. These respective contingents are frequently polarized on the basis of gender and aesthetics. However, might the forms of textuality fashioned by Goretti or Ginanni, for example, be somehow indebted to a feeling, thought, or problem culled from the lyrical production by more "traditional" women, like Negri or Aleramo? Likewise, did the experimental forms of verbal and visual poetry, breaking conventions of gender and genre, enable established women poets to pursue new aesthetic directions? And what specific features differentiate the positionalities adopted by individual women poets in the discursive field of poetry? Last, in addition to interrogating women's literary interventions as sites for the construction of discourses operating within and against prevailing artistic currents, an approach shaping the preceding studies, here I also want to examine the productive engagements that women poets may have forged with predominantly male movements, futurism in particular. Feminist scholarship in Italian studies has examined ways in which women negotiated the difficulties of constructing subject positions in the futurist movement. While building on this research, I intend to follow a line of thought suggested by Susan Rubin Suleiman (1990) and explore how male futurists, and not such fellow women poets as Negri or Aleramo, set the occasion for vanguard women to further their artistic and social projects. This undertaking may enable us to make important distinctions about the field of poetic discourses comprised within and beyond futurism. Moreover, it points to differences between futurism and such other avantgarde movements as Dada and surrealism, which Anglo-American critics have tended to overlook or collapse.[8]

The Poetic Body and Its Mis(sed)-conceptions

As noted in the preceding examination of realism, the aesthetic hegemony during Fascism comprised a pluralistic field of propositions for
artistic production in diverse genres. We could say, however, that the
chief paradigms formulated literature as either a site for sociocultural
change or a sphere of creative activity transcending social and political
interests. The avant-garde futurists, the *Novecentisti,* and the neorealists
articulate the former position in markedly different ways, and the latter
stance was represented by artists aspiring to pure poetry, the Rondisti,
and the hermetics. Thus, it should hardly surprise us that women's
poetry had both its champions and detractors. In general, however,
prominent critics voiced ambivalent responses. With almost unanimous
praise, such figures as Croce, Camillo Pellizzi, and Luigi Russo noted the
inspirited originality distinguishing the motifs and perspectives that
modern women endeavored to put into lyrical form, which is indebted,
they contend, largely to their keen attention to intellectual, psychic, and
affective nuances of "feminine" being in the world. Nonetheless, these
same critics claim that poems by such artists as Annie Vivanti, Ada
Negri, and Sibilla Aleramo fall short of "true poetry" because of the flaws
in their content and formal properties, described in terms of excess and
lack. When evaluated against the Crocean paradigm of pure poetry, in
the opinion of interwar scholars the poems produced by women display
excessive autobiographical materials and frankness, at times exposing
discomfortingly intimate details of personal experiences as women,
lovers, mothers, and artists. Furthermore, this poetics of experience
brims with effusions of emotions and, sometimes, as in the case of Negri,
aspires to an undue commitment to social critique. These general traits
hardly conform with the terms of pure poetry or those of hermetic poetry that Falqui proposed—"mute faith," "guarded privacy," and poetry
as negation or absence. The forms of poetic expression also appear to
contrast with the absolute value that hermeticism purportedly ascribed
to linguistic form. The expressive features crafted by female poets—
encompassing the elaboration of images, metaphors and analogies, the
lyrical rhythm, and musicality—reveal, Croce and Pellizzi maintained, a
lack of erudite preparation, a lack of poetic intuition, and a lack of lin-

guistic refinement. In short, they viewed women's poetry as stylistically lackluster.

These refrains in critical discourse, which predate Fascism yet persist among some today, may lead us to infer that women's literary works in poetry—perhaps the most symbolically powerful genre signifying artistic authority and creative synthesis—were inherently second-rate.[9] In fact, by employing ideas and metaphors associated with reproduction, in the senses of biological childbearing and of making a copy, some commentators create an unmistakable linkage between sexual difference and the construction of the "male poet" as original and the "female poet" as an essentially inferior copy. Rarely do critics reach the shrill extremism of Giovanni Boine (1914), who, among other Vociani, rejected the scientific claims of positivism to explain male being yet unabashedly made essentialist declarations, announcing that "Women lack the lyrical" (259).

In this respect, Croce provides more typical examples in his writings on women poets. The first essay I want to examine, though published in 1906, concerns us because it elucidates the principal ideas shaping Croce's evolving theory of aesthetics and pure poetry, as well as his evaluation of works by women poets, both of which exerted major influence on the gendered ideology of poetic creation during the interwar years. In his piece on Negri's poetry, titled "Ada Negri," Croce (1906) employs metaphors associated with human conception and birth to explain that the process of creating poetry encompasses two essential gestational phases, devoted respectively to "generation" and "regeneration."[10] During the initial lengthy period of incubation, a poem assumes its embryonic form of life. If the poem is to become artistically viable, it must, Croce argues, undergo a process that "renews the original inspiration," enabling the poet to perfect all of its parts. The body of women's poetry, however, appears to suffer neglect at the regenerative stage of stylistic elaboration. Shifting his attention from Negri's poetic tendencies to female poetry in general, in lapidary fashion Croce comments on a lack of stylistic refinement:

> It is, for the most part, a particularly female defect. It seems that women, who are able to develop a germ of life inside them for nine months, to deliver it through the painful labor of childbirth, to raise it with wise, almost infinite patience, may be incapable of normal poetic gestations; their artis-

tic deliveries are almost always premature. In fact, the moment of *déliver-ance* instantaneously follows conception, and the newborn child is tossed out on the street, deprived of all the help it needs. I'm not saying there might not be exceptions in the past or in the future. But this is the rule, and Ada Negri escapes the rule even less than other women poets. (362)

Croce's observations raise several points of interest. First, within the context of the essay, his arguments appear as much concerned with defending his own notion of artistic creation as with analyzing the themes and expressive practices of women poets. In fact, his introductory statements about the acclaim Negri won in some camps that praised her antiliterary, "sincere" poems for the way they made readers feel the pain and struggles of social injustices indicate that he is nettled by such an apparent lack of discerning taste. He then elucidates the distinction between art and life, poetry and nonpoetry, maintaining that "every attempt to make art a mission kills art. Poetry is an end, not a means" (352). Following this logic, to employ lyrical expression as a form of social praxis can only produce nonpoetry. Moreover, in order to achieve pure poetic style, elaborated in the regenerative phase of gestation, the poet, as Croce explains in a later essay published in 1940, "must find himself alone with the universal 'I' and not with the private self, with humanity, which is totality" (1940b, 292). From this perspective, authorized by the tenet of universality, any endeavor to fashion poetry as a site for the construction of female subjectivity would belong to the generative phase of creation in which emotions, psychic states, or insights that the poet has intuited or experienced inspire the germ of artistic creation.

Yet what concerns me most is the way in which Croce employs the process and terms of female birthing and maternal care, and not the pen-penis metaphor, to articulate his model of lyrical production in a pronatalist project for pure art that underwrites exclusively paternal lines of affiliation. If Croce's point is to show that women, with bodies and souls supposedly designed to bring flesh-and-blood offspring into the world and raise them to perfection, can only produce misbegotten fruits of artistic labor, then clearly the metaphor is anatomically correct. Furthermore, as Emily Braun (1995) explains, the appropriation of the birthing metaphor has a long-standing tradition among male artists and intellectuals who have adapted it to express both the anxieties and the fulfillment of their work. Unable to reproduce in fact, men reproduce in fiction, begetting immortality through art and usurping the procreative role for the furthering of humanity in an intellectual sense. Conversely, the metaphor underlines the traditional divisions of labor in society—men create, women procreate. (189)

But given the growing success of women writers in prose and poetry in the early 1900s, which legitimized their claims to the authority of artistic creation, could we not also read men's use of the birthing metaphor— invoked by other male poets, Croce tell us—as a marker of male poetic anxiety, and an attempt to phallicize the womb?

In typically polemical style, F. T. Marinetti conveys a similar sense as he describes the miraculous birth of the futurist subject in "The Founding and Manifesto of Futurism" (1909), and also in the fantasy of self-sufficient male procreation projected in *Mafarka le futuriste* (1909). This symbolic birth founds the futurist myth of self-creation, promising, as Rosalind E. Krauss (1986) notes, "the potential for continual acts of regeneration, a perpetuation of self-birth" (157). Futurist texts produced from 1909 to the early 1940s support this birthing technology, creating practices of art and life designed to bring into being rejuvenating models for cultural, social, and political production. Yet as Andrew Hewitt (1993) points out in his sharp analysis of the writings by Marinetti, "there is a privileging of (re-)production as an essentially masculine activity which by some biological freak has fallen to the lot of women" (151). Likewise, perhaps the preoccupation with the myth of Orpheus in hermetic poetry of the 1930s, though radically different from an aesthetic standpoint, may also be read as symptomatic of a similar form of womb envy. In her insightful examination of mythic revisionism as a potentially feminine aesthetic project, Lucia Re (1993) highlights the particularly significant figuration of Orpheus to denote allegorically the functions of poet and poetry conceptualized by hermeticism, "a poetic tendency," she states, "coupling rarefied, evocative but almost impenetrable lyrical diction with an elegiac tone, and celebrating the 'secrets' of self-made, small-scale and unassuming personal mythologies" (81). Thus, though the male poet is incapable of creating life, the Orphic tale may compensate him, as it authorizes his power to revive life, to rescue it from the dark underworld of death.[11] Such a reading offers a different perspective on hermeticism and the convulsive nascency of Quasimodo's new poet and provides as well an important dimension to the critical context for analyzing the conceptualization and poetic fashionings of the birth metaphor in women's writings.

Biotechnic Poetics: The Birth of Female Futurist Subjectivities

I want to begin to explore the ways that women poets conceive the figure of the *generatrice* by looking at the model invented by the futurist artist Maria Goretti in her suggestive work *La donna e il futurismo* (Woman and futurism), published in 1941. Including critical assessments of works by men futurists, theories of artistic production, poetry, and autobiographical passages re-creating the author's own rebirth as a futurist subject, this text offers invaluable materials for examining the thought and discursive practices elaborated in the late years of the avant-garde movement when futurism, according to critics like Matei Calinescu (1986), was irreparably tainted by Fascism. In fact, Goretti problematizes this very issue on the title page of her book, where we find two epigraphs that put the prevailing Fascist construction of "mother" and a model authored by the futurist Benedetta in dialogic relation. The first epigraph reproduces Mussolini's infamous declaration, "War is to man as maternity is to woman," followed by his patronymic name written in longhand, as if signed personally. The second epigraph, drawn from Benedetta, whose name appears in authoritative block letters, reads, "The Italian woman is a mother. When we say the word *mother,* we must give the word its great meaning of generatrix; generatrix of men, of emotions, of passions, of ideas." Goretti's invocation of the notion of generatrix proposed by Benedetta neither totally rejects nor accepts the normative maternal role. Rather, her deployment of the term appears to expand the meanings of the maternal to claim authority for women as the subjects of both procreation and creation. This discursive strategy and the meanings that Goretti attaches to the *generatrice* mark one of the shifts in the positions elaborated by avant-garde women on the notion of the maternal and its relations to life, culture, futurity, and tradition.

In order to evaluate the significance of Goretti's formulation of woman as a producer of life and art, we should review how she situates her theory and practice of poetry in the field of poetic discourses. Indeed, from women's first engagements with Italian futurism, as exemplified by Valentine de Saint Point's "Manifeste de la femme futuriste" (Manifesto of the futurist woman, 1912, cited in Salaris 1982), to their final writings of the early 1940s, women's discourses exhibit consistent attention to inventing their own subject positions in the field of cultural production and to problematizing their individual relations to fellow artists within futurism and beyond. So let us look first at Goretti's assessment of women poets. In 1941 the value of women's poetry in the Italian literary tradition seems a foregone conclusion to Goretti. Thus she opens her "Manifesto of Aeroic Female Poetry in Futurism" by stating:

> It's fruitless to still ask whether female poetry worthy of
> singing in the immortal skies exists
> We only need to recall the names of Sappho the Beautiful
> Gaspara Stampa and Ada Negri limiting ourselves to the
> consecrated classical Italian world
> (141, punctuation, or lack thereof, is Goretti's)

This representation of recognized women poets as constituting the canon is hardly anomalous. In 1916, for instance, the futurist Marietta Angelini composed an open letter, published in *Vela latina* (Latin sail), challenging such writers as Grazia Deledda, Amalia Guglielminetti, Ada Negri, and Annie Vivanti to break their bonds with the outmoded tradition of high literary culture and become futurists.[12] Thus, Angelini and Goretti highlight the difference they perceive between their speaking positions and those of their female contemporaries. Goretti's rejection of the iconography and expressive forms constituting the classical tradition of Italian poetry is enacted in the following poem, titled "Rose" (Roses, 1941):

> Roses
> meritorious
> all the poets have kissed
> your perfumed flesh
> old bad cheap essence
> on all the beds
> of eternal illusions
>
> Roses
> unrepenting sinners
> pray on some

> solitary country altar
> but diabolic to laugh to laugh
> your insane impure perfume
> You see I don't sing
> your secular beauty
> rotted in the well
> of my adolescent literary loves
>
> But
> to hang
> to crush
> to massacre
> your putrid beauty
> in this morning's horrible verses
> And free free free
> to forget
> I my body my soul.
> (1941, 114–15)

At the level of syntax and grammar, this playful critique revels in destroying the logic of the rose, and the infinite associations expressed by this timeworn metaphor of woman in the history of poetic and secular discourses. When situated in the hegemonic field of Fascist and Catholic writings on woman, this text performs several functions of note. The organic metaphor of the rose participates in the iconography of the Virgin Mother, romantic love, and traditional notions of femininity engendered by the humanist paradigm of presence and nature, which grounded Fascist models of the family and state. Goretti deconstructs the rose and the normative ideas it stands for, thereby denaturalizing woman. Indeed, the speaking subject is liberated by forgetting the body, which makes the body immaterial. This feature of Goretti's thought and poetic practice also stands in clear contrast to the forms of corporeality we will see in poems by Negri and Aleramo.

In Goretti's critical evaluation of the field of women's poetry, she also notes that not all women poets reach the heights of creativity attained by Stampa and Negri. In fact, she identifies specific traits that make some female poetry of her time mediocre. These include forms of autobiographism that fail to attain universal significance; a monotonous focus on affective life; overly meticulous attention to formalistic concerns that prevent the creative transfiguration of inspirational materials into art; and nostalgia and pessimism. Although some of these weaknesses recall the "defects" identified by Croce and fellow exponents of pure art, Goretti does not explain them in essentialist terms. Instead, she executes a strategic move that first links characteristics she perceives as flaws in women's poetry—rationalistic analysis, emotionalism, patient attention to infinite details—to the social construction of gender. She then proposes a project for the social and symbolic "remaking" of woman. In life and art, woman may overcome traditional "feminine" flaws, for, she declares in revisionary definitions, "Woman is intuition"—conceived as power of synthesis—"Woman is moral fortitude," and "Woman is imagination" (143). In conclusion, Goretti situates her artistic development and aesthetic within the current of female aeropoetry, which was formed by Benedetta, Dina Cucini, and Immacolata Corona and, she adds significantly, was prompted by "Italian futurism created in Milan in 1909 by the poet Marinetti" (144). Thus contextualized, her manifesto proposes seven properties that women's aeropoems should combat, which include those weaknesses indicated above.

The positions that Angelini and Goretti, among other women futurists, adopt toward major and minor female poets imply that futurism afforded a new space and tools enabling the construction of a different revolutionary female subject position. However, the specific ways in which futurism solicited avant-garde women to execute a project of social and cultural revolution, prompting female artists to carve out a space in a male-dominated movement as opposed to assuming a revolutionary position located in relation to the modern tradition of women's poetry, remain paradoxical. The current difficulties in assessing the progressive and/or regressive strains constituting women's speaking positions in the futurist movement derive largely from the undecidability of the pronouncements made by F. T. Marinetti on art, society, feminism, and woman as a cultural construction. Yet the problem has been exacerbated by the tendency in discussions about modernism, the avant-garde, and F/fascism to oversimplify futurist theories and practices.[13] Focusing attention almost exclusively on F. T. Marinetti, some discussions depict the "Father" of futurism as assuming the function of Other, a deviant strain isolated to maintain the integrity of modernism and its national borders against the taint of Fascism. In more thoughtful analyses of modernist forms of textuality, Marinetti is invoked to exemplify the misogynist tendencies shared by major artists of modernism and the historical avant-garde alike. In his perceptive chapter "Mass Culture as Woman," Andreas Huyssen (1986) skillfully develops this point. He argues first that the "masculine mystique" articulated by Marinetti and Wyndham Lewis, along with many others, is linked in some way to the manner in which mass culture becomes gendered as feminine. He then concludes that "in relation to gender and sexuality . . . the historical avant-garde was by and large as patriarchal, misogynist, and masculinist as the major trends of modernism. One need only to look at the metaphors in Marinetti's 'Futurist Manifesto'" (60-61) or, he continues, at writings by Marie Luise Fleisser about Bertolt Brecht, or those by members of the Russian avant-garde and French surrealists. Admittedly, the inflammatory, riotous rhetoric Marinetti employed in his manifestos enacts a dualistic scheme that disparages woman and associative notions of femininity, decadence, and the past, while exalting man as a signifier of virility, production, and futurity. From this standpoint, it supports Huyssen's reading.

Yet such representations of Marinetti, however warranted within the specific context of the arguments advanced, tend to collapse historical and cultural distinctions between futurism and other avant-garde movements. More important, in the process they serve to repress the voices of women poets shaping futurism and other aesthetic projects, thereby replicating the tendency they endeavor to critique. Read at face value, representations of woman created by Marinetti, Fillìa (Luigi Colombo), and Umberto Boccioni, among others, reproduce the call for "contempt for woman" proclaimed in the founding manifesto. However, on closer scrutiny, we see that Marinetti's writings offer shifting positions on female gender roles as cultural and social formations, which create an indeterminate field. Lucia Re (1989) and Clara Orban (1995) have amply charted and examined the resultant paradoxes and their implications for women undertaking a critical writing of traditional feminine models and the invention of new forms and expressions of modern female subjectivity.[14] Therefore, I intend to offer a brief profile of some of the relations between futurist men and women that distinguish the historical avant-garde in Italy. I then turn to the conceptual and theoretical opportunities that futurism afforded for reconceiving women's production of self, life, and art.

Although the birth and infancy of the futurist movement inscribe exclusively masculine forms of subjectivity, soon Marinetti and fellow male futurists appear to have admitted, if not invited, women artists into their circles, as indicated by publishing practices, coauthored writings, musical recordings, and photographs of group gatherings.[15] In contrast to the surrealist movement, which, as outlined by Suleiman (1990), largely resisted female participation from its founding in 1924 until the midthirties, futurism developed more permeable frontiers. In fact, as Salaris notes, prior to launching the futurist movement, Marinetti's publication *Poesia* (Poetry, 1905–1909) diffused works by women writers esteemed in Italy and in other European countries, including, for instance, writings by Vittoria Aganoor Pompilj, Ada Negri, Amalia Guglielminetti, Valentine de Saint Point, and Hélène Picard. Moreover, from the sporadic interventions of the early teens, following de Saint Point's pointed response to Marinetti's avowed "contempt for woman" as a founding principle of futurism, notable circles of avant-garde women formed around the influential publications *L'Italia futurista* (Futurist Italy), active in Florence from 1916 to 1918, and *Roma futurista* (Futurist Rome), published from 1918 to 1920. Among the merits of these journals and the many less-renowned futurist publications is the venue they created for open, frequently heated intellectual exchanges over notions of woman posited by male and female artists alike.[16] Last, the original, prolific textual production achieved by women artists engaging with futurism, which for the most part still awaits critical assessment, testifies to the movement's appeal. While such women as the painter Leandra Angelucci Cominazzini, the photographer Wanda Wulz, and the aerodancer Giannina Censi contributed to shaping these areas of futurist culture through exhibitions and performances, primarily in the thirties, the ranks of women generating experimental literary forms that pushed the verbal and visual imagination into new horizons grew steadily, publishing novels, short stories, poetry, and diaries.[17]

The construction of female subject positions within the futurist discursive field and the movement's apparent solicitation of women artists provide a different perspective on the sexual politics of the historical avant-garde in Italy. By so doing, this partial vision shows the need to reevaluate the tendency to either collapse differences between futurism, surrealism, and dadaism, or to invoke Italian futurism as merely the regressive visage of vanguardism. This field of inquiry would benefit from the kind of critical model elaborated by Rita Felski (1995) in *The Gender of Modernity,* which recognizes the dialogic tensions between masculine and feminine sociocultural models. Lest I leave you with an all-too-utopian picture of the Italian avant-garde, I should clarify that my examination is intended to suggest that futurism is less misogynist than many critical representations would have us believe. This is not to say that the writings by Marinetti and such other founding members of the movement as Boccioni, Carlo Carrà, Luigi Russolo, and Balilla Pratela merit a revisionary reading as purely progressive exponents of egalitarian relations between the sexes in life and art. In fact, as in the case of surrealism, the signatories of the major futurist manifestos produced from 1909 to the late teens, which initially defined the movements's aesthetics for painting, music, photography, sculpture, words-in-freedom, cinema, and fashion, represent a male speaking position. Thus the importance of de Saint Point's manifestos on the futurist woman and lust should not be underestimated; she carves out a female-gendered positionality that may function prototypically in the early stages of the movement. But as Barbara Spackman (1995) argues, de Saint Point's line of reasoning binds progressive and conservative elements in the manner of male futurist discourse, and later, Fascist rhetoric. Interesting here is the founding manifesto of the futurist student "fascio" (Fascist group), signed by young men and such women as Elda Norchi and Iole Calzavaro and published on 22 June 1919 in *Roma futurista.* Although this document implies a collaborative effort among the younger generation, the manifestos written in the twenties and thirties tend to maintain gender boundaries, as they are authored either by men or by women. Some noteworthy exceptions include the manifestos "Aeropittura" (Aeropainting, 1929) and "La plastica murale futurista" (The plastic futurist mural, 1934), each signed by Benedetta along with male artists.

Clearly, futurism constructed sites for the staging and dissemination of a broad variety of works in performance art, photography, painting, and poetry. Equally important is the conceptual space fostering, among other theories, the paradigm of infinite possibilities for rebirth, announced first in the founding manifesto. With good reason, scholars generally read this text of origins as the foundational example of misogyny embedded in futurist subjectivity.[18] I suggest, however, that the idea of self-generation had particular implications for women and may help us to theorize the sexual politics of the futurist paradigm of generatrix created by Benedetta and Goretti. Marinetti's representation of the "maternal ditch" and the birthing of the avant-garde futurist in the founding manifesto (1909) offers a stellar example of the male appropriation of the birth metaphor. The artist invites us to witness the miraculous event as he appears to make his way through the birth canal:

> O maternal ditch, almost full of muddy water! Fair factory drain! I gulped down your nourishing sludge; and I remembered the blessed black breast of my Sudanese nurse. . . . When I came up—torn, filthy, and stinking—from under the capsized car, I felt the white-hot iron of joy deliciously pass through my heart! (cited in Apollonio 1973, 21)

In its immediate sense, the mise-en-scène signifies the nascency of the Italian male futurist subject, yet it also generated formative myths for the historical avant-garde. As Rosalind Krauss (1986) explains, the description of futurist parturition shapes the vanguardist notion of originality, "conceived as a literal origin, a beginning from ground zero, a birth. . . . This parable of absolute self-creation that begins the first *Futurist Manifesto* functions as a model for what is meant by originality among the early twentieth-century avant-garde" (157). Yet the birthing metaphor also creates an inviting space for feminist intervention in the social and symbolic spheres. As women slough off the remnants of tradition, they emerge in but the first of infinite rebirths that constitute an ongoing process of self-generation in experimental forms of life and art.

The creative and analytical writings produced by futurist women during the interwar years and into the early 1940s show both the consistent importance that the notion of rebirth exerted on the concept of female artistic identity, as well as shifts in thought. For example, the meanings that Fulvia Giuliani attaches to her birth into futurism are structured according to familiar dualisms problematized by de Saint Point before

World War I and by the debates that again erupted in its wake due, in part, to the socioeconomic mobility achieved by increasing numbers of women. In an article published in *Roma futurista* in 1919, Giuliani describes her transformation, claiming freedom from the maternal role: "I feel futurist. I became this way almost without being aware of it! . . . I'm not an incubator, one of those women whom She—like professor Labriola—calls females. I belong to the ELECT women."[19] Putting everyone on notice, Giuliani announces a project of social regeneration, spearheaded by women: "We will remake, form, mold, clean up; we will organize" (41). In conclusion, she defiantly challenges those who deride such a female undertaking as the misguided ways of youth and promises, "We will know how to make youth yield for the victory of our cause, of our right, which is to be at your side, and not to proliferate like bitches!!!" (41). Giuliani's frontal attack on the model of woman as mother—reproducer of the race—maintains the binary opposition between procreation and creation, past and future, tradition and innovation. In a delightfully playful yet critical manner, Giuliani's creative works take up these themes, often expressing irreverence toward the "sacred" symbols of Western culture. Thus, in "Autoritratto" (Self-portrait) she "tells the beads of daily boredom as if they were a rosary polished by profanities" and concludes that she and the organ-grinder's monkey are in the same cage. As in Goretti's poem "Rose," Giuliani's "Protesta" (Protest), written, the text says, against the author herself, the poet aims her barbs at the female icons of high culture; Berenice has a set of squeaky dentures while Margherita wears a wig, and Isabeau becomes a model.

The representation of futurist rebirth created by Goretti in 1941 shares the sense of liberation that Giuliani accentuates yet, through its form and thought, locates the means of female self-creation specifically in the act of producing art. Goretti opens *La donna e il futurismo* (1941) with the first aeropoem she wrote, "Colloquio col motore" (Conversation with the engine), which enacts the original moment when she, a young woman who used to write sonnets and had degrees in philosophy and law to her credit, regenerates herself, fabricating a "new soul and new poetry," liberated from nostalgia, pessimism, and bourgeois concerns. The poet plays on the tradition of women's love poetry addressed to the male object of desire while claiming the full force of the futurist aesthetic for new forms of modern female being. Not a mere infatuation, the declaration of passionate love for the engine, which supplants the chivalrous knights-errant of old, produces an excess of dynamism, energy, desires, and opportunities fueled as the hearts of woman and machine beat as one. This coupling with the engine, as the speaker declares, enables her to cross "the multiform paths / of my instantly new world / up high, high, high!" and urges her onward to ever new horizons, unbound by barriers of time and space. Goretti's figuration of the engine in the final lines is particularly significant for the way in which she employs the futurist aesthetic to project female subjectivity:

> I love you
> ardent mechanical soul
> mechanic metallic electric:
> the reflections all the reflections
> of my iridescent dreams
> dreams of impossible conquests
> and of impossible victories
> all the reflections of my most audacious dreams
> are all lit up by the sun
> shining on your steel coverings
> exquisite body of solid shimmer!
> (14–15)

As a site for the generation of meaning, this poem privileges the machine, not the inner self, as a matrix for the creation of never-ending occasions for female self-invention. Furthermore, Goretti's elaboration of the "aeroperspective"—a mode of vision for the technological age—represents different forms of temporality and spaciality that challenge the traditional oppositions between past and future, life and art. She claims, in fact, that the most innovative aspect of futurism is the way that

> it resolved the need for an antithesis to the past with the positive glorification of the present—a present that eternally becomes the future. As a consequence, it fully reintegrated the coupling of art with life, audaciously declaring the new beauty of simultaneous synthesis provided by the velocitizing machine. (37)

Here we see how the experimental practices of art and daily living designed by futurism to explode passé models and generate revolutionized cultural, social, and political production in the new age of technology synchronized, in part, with avant-garde women's two-pronged endeavor to critique the outmoded ideology of femininity and to reinvent female subjectivity in the imbricating social and artistic spheres.

However, Goretti does not uncritically reproduce the masculine terms afforded by futurism. In the following passage, we see how Goretti constructs a provocative model of the female futurist subject as she fashions a Janus-like figure inscribing the markers of sexual difference on the anatomy of futurism. Picturing the avant-garde body, she states:

> Futurism displays two faces to me: one is universal, giving the meaning of life and art; it is mystical. The other face answers a particular social and artistic problem: the position of woman in life and art. Therefore, I am right to speak about "my" form of futurism, not only in the sense that I give "my" philosophical interpretation of futurism, which is "mystical," but also in the sense that, besides the fact that my words-in-freedom are different from the ones written by all the highly original futurist poets, my futurism is futurism lived and thought by a woman. (20–21)

Here the two visages, which in the Roman tradition of the Janus symbolized oppositional pairs while evoking associations with destiny, time, and war, may stand for the simultaneous occupation of disparate parts constituting Goretti's position of enunciation. She appears to claim two locations at once, one being mystical, universal (read male) and the other specific, female gendered. This model helps us to understand the potentially contending drifts of Goretti's own discourse. Her representation of this complex positionality shows an affinity with the model of "double-voicedness" elaborated by Suleiman (1990) in her examination of the situatedness of women in other vanguard movements. Attending to both the obstacles and possibilities represented by the male avant-garde, she states:

> A double allegiance characterizes much of the best contemporary work by women: on the one hand, an allegiance to the formal experiments and some of the cultural aspirations of the historical male avant-gardes; on the other hand, an allegiance to the feminist critique of dominant sexual ideologies, including the sexual ideology of those same avant-gardes. (xvii)

Although we must keep in consideration the heterogeneity and fluidity characterizing the field of poetry by futurist women, Goretti's formulation has useful applications for theorizing futurism's appeal to artists who identified with the avant-garde project yet also reelaborated components of the founding aesthetic for the inscription of female sexual difference. Briefly, as Peter Nicholls (1987) and Andrew Hewitt (1993) have shown in their respective works on Marinetti, the metaphor of the machine functions as the matrix for the futurist aesthetic, whose experimental forms performatively enact dynamic, ultramodern modes of life, politics, and art, while exteriorizing subjectivity in the process. Such poems as Maria D'Arezzo's "Volata" (Flight, 1920), Maria Ginanni's "I ponti delle cose" (Bridges of things, 1917), Benedetta's words-in-freedom "Benedetta fra le donne" (Benedetta among women, 1919), and Goretti's "Colloquio col motore" (Conversation with the engine, 1941) exemplify how the artists project the female body and subjectivity onto graphic signs and such recurrent topoi as the city, cars, the skies, and airplanes. They thus create female representations of spaciality and futurity that overthrow ideas conventionally associated with woman, for example, passivity, inertia, and nostalgia. These performative functions are typified in Goretti's poem about aerial acrobatics on the letter A.[20] As we see in the first lines of the Italian version, which should suffice here, Goretti produces a sense of verticality graphically through the repetition of the capitalized letter A, and through the sensations and affective states she evokes. And as is typical of futurist texts, she produces a suggestively eroticized engine rhythm with the repetition of the a sound.

> Abbrividire
> Ansia
> Ansia che Affoca Avvampa Abbrucia
> Ansia d'Azzurro nell'Abbacinante cielo di stamani
> Ansia d'Azzurro nel folgorante Acciaio
> Angelici Augurali Adoranti i miei occhi seguirti
> Appassionatamente
> Abolite Ah potere
> Abolire distanza Astronomica che ci divide
> Arrivare A te
> Accostare pianissimo
> Aleggiare nuvola soffio Alito
> Allacciare Anche sì Anche Attimo solo
> Ansia mia trepida Alla tua intrepida Audacia
> (1941, 111–12)

> To shiver
> Anxiety
> Anxiety that sets Afire flares up burns
> Anxiety for Azure in this morning's dazzling sky
> Anxiety for Azure in the lightning steel
> Angelic welcoming Adoring my eyes following you
> Passionately
> Abolish Ah power
> To Abolish Astronomic distance that divides us
> To Arrive at you
> To Approach you so slowly
> To hover cloud whiff breath
> To even connect too even for only an instant
> My trembling Anxiety to your intrepid daring

The later lines of the poem enact the fulfillment of the speaker's desire, as she flies around the chimeric hope signified by the airborne machine and consummates their passion with a kiss. In the act of aerocoupling, indicated also by a play on the word *Anche,* which can mean "hips" (as well as "too" or "also"), the woman masters the machine as she "softens its will." This poet thus claims the technology of aviation and the horizons as sites for female agency and self-generation.

In relation to the narratives on modern technology provided, for example, in Andreas Huyssen's (1986) excellent reading of Fritz Lang's *Metropolis* in "The Vamp and the Machine" or Hewitt's (1993) analysis of Marinetti's writings, Goretti's projection of the airborne woman-machine offers a markedly different perspective, raising questions about women's relations to technology and woman as cultural construction. In order to theorize the functions that this female-encoded body technology may perform in the broader discursive field of futurism, the mass media, and Fascism, I find Anne Balsamo's (1996) analysis of the conjoining of the biological and technological body highly useful. This merger, she explains,

> relies on a reconceptualization of the human body as a "techno-body,"
> a boundary figure belonging simultaneously to at least two previously
> incompatible systems of meaning—"the organic/natural" and "the
> technological/cultural." At the point at which the body is reconceptualized
> not as a fixed part of nature, but as a boundary concept, we witness an

ideological tug-of-war between competing systems of meaning, which include and in part define the material struggles of physical bodies. (5)

In the specific field of futurist aerial discourse, Goretti's figuration of the female aerobody diverges from the system of production in such works as the aerial performances conceived in 1918 by the aviator Fedele Azari, Marinetti's 1935 "Aeropoem of the Gulf of La Spezia," and Mario Scaparro's 1920 drama *A Birth*. Scaparro's performance piece is particularly interesting for the way in which he anthropomorphizes two airplanes, one a sleek, "masculine" Albatross and the other a more shapely "feminine" seaplane, which, as Michael Kirby (1971) tells us, perform aerosex under the cover of a cloud. The seaplane then lands to expel four aviators from her pregnant belly. This staging appears to appropriate the birth metaphor to naturalize the technological production of futurist subjects. In contrast, Goretti's merging of woman and airplane as a textual generation of art, ideas, and futurist subjectivity may work as a denaturalizing strategy, uprooting woman from the earthbound construction signifying the organic, traditional maternal body. As such, the female techno-body may be read as a progressive project whose symbol, the airplane, also had a strong purchase on the mass female imagination, as discussed in relation to Liala's romance novel *Signorsì*. Likewise, read in relation to Mussolini's pronouncements on Italian women pilots (see page 112 above), the conjoining of woman and airplane appears to challenge traditional gender boundaries projected by the duce onto the aviational horizon. Yet the emancipatory implications engendered as woman-machines invade the sexually embattled skies are not unproblematic. By 1941, the airplane, a symbol of a modern, technologized, imperialist Fascist Italy, comes to stand for the pursuit of national victory in the arena of World War II. Goretti's work incorporates an unmistakable nationalistic invocation of Fascist Italy in her model of the "aesthetic of war," as well as such poems as "Vincere" (Victory, loosely translated) and "Aeroinvocazione all'Italia" (Aeroinvocation to Italy). Moreover, she claims to write her aeropoetics under the sign of Fascism, directly linking her futurist paradigm of art-life with activist Fascist praxis. As discussed here, however, to claim artistic modes for political functions hardly controls the production of meaning in the process of signification.

The conceptual reinvention of temporal and spacial categories anchors Goretti's potentially subversive resolution of the dichotomy between female procreation and male creation with the figure of the *Donna generatrice,* which, in an interesting way, anticipates Julia Kristeva's theory of the woman poet's relation to the semiotic and the symbolic (1980, esp. 240–42). To generate, Goretti states, drawing freely on Benedetta's ideas, means "to give to radiate to offer: men ideas passions" (1941, 102):

> Here lies the constructive, unitary value of Benedetta's thought, a long way from Valentine de Saint Point's dualistic conceptions, in which woman struggled between flesh and spirit and was divided fatally into lover and mother, and the mother was considered in a naturalistic sense, as the generatrix of the body and the protectress of the infant. In Benedetta woman becomes Maternity, in which sense and spirit are both overcome in the reality of a creation that is the creation of spirits.
>
> Thus matter becomes spiritualized: the meaning of life coincides with the scope of art. (103)

Read in relation to Marinetti's claims to (pro)creation as a masculine sphere, Goretti's proposition reappropriates the birth metaphor as a signifier of multiple forms of feminine creation. As such, it represents what I call a biotechnic poetics, whose lexicon and practices inscribe female sexual difference on the art-life paradigm and authorize the speaking position of the mother-poet. Cast in this manner, Goretti's model challenges the movement's antifeminist elements. But is Goretti's *generatrice* a total redefinition, or an instance of binding regressive and progressive elements that adheres to the proto-Fascist strategy of Valentine de Saint Point, whom she critiques? When examined within the ideological frame of Italian Fascism, which addressed specific sectors of women as the mothers of and for the nation, how might the mother-poet disrupt the law of the father underwriting both the symbolic order and conventions associated with woman in art and daily living?

Goretti's reconception of the maternal and the multiple meanings it bears stakes a claim on simultaneous positionings in the semiotic and symbolic for the generation of ideas, art, life. Therefore, the *generatrice* contends with the normative terms of male authority at the level of signification. Alice E. Adams (1994) elucidates this transgressive potentiality in her reading of Julia Kristeva's essay "I Who Want Not To Be," as she theorizes the speaking position of the mother-poet. As Adams charts Kristeva's own use of the birthing metaphor, intended to formulate the (impossible) position of the mother in relation to the symbolic, she argues that "the contradiction inherent in Kristeva's theory, its simultaneous assertion of antiessentialism and dependence on sexed principles, presents a gap, an unattended space which the mother-poet might occupy" (49). Within this space, Adams continues, "the mother-poet doubles herself, existing at the 'threshold' and the 'intersection' of the symbolic and the semiotic" (49). Herein lies her power to disrupt, since the mother-poet threatens "to dissolve dualisms and oppositions that are essential to our symbolic order" (49). We could say, then, that Goretti's figuration of the mother-poet disrupts the ideology of gender and genre, conceptualizing poetry as the site for women's creation of meaning and life.

Sibilla Aleramo: The Poetics of Embodiment

While keeping in mind the figure of the *generatrice* conceived by Goretti and the sociocultural functions it is designed to perform in an avant-garde aesthetic, let us turn to some of the more readerly fashionings of the womb and birthing to see how, if at all, they breach the borders maintaining the traditional division between female procreation and male creation, proposing notions and images of the female body as a site of multiple forms of generation—self-creation, procreation, and artistic creation. Since the great debate of the thirties on the politics of aesthetics, such diverse critics as Theodor Adorno, Roland Barthes, Kristeva, and Hélène Cixous have questioned the oppositional power of texts that incorporate practices of mimetic representation and linguistic conventions, which, they argue, would compromise potential critiques of phallocentrism. It is clear that poems by Aleramo, Negri, and Pozzi do not call attention to poetry as a signifying practice by undertaking the kind of formal experimentation with syntactical constructions, punctuation, graphic signs, and images that jolt sense and senses in such words-in-freedom as Mina Della Pergola's "IL TRIONFO DELL'F" (The triumph of the *F*, 1919) or Goretti's composition of acrobatics on the letter *A* (1941). But what of other forms of experimentation that may exploit the gendered ideology of genre, the meanings that poetry and its conventions bear within the cultural tradition, to produce different connotations?[21]

Specifically, if cultural discourses from Croce to Marinetti to Montale encode birthing as a category for the creative genius of the male artist—a gesture that masks male lack by attempting to phallicize the womb—then what can we say about women's crafting of the female body as an organicist metaphor expressing the identity of the mother-poet and, naturally, her mediation of the relations between life and art?

The poetry written by Sibilla Aleramo during the interwar years, collected along with pieces of other periods in *Selva d'amore* (Woods of love, 1947), superbly illustrates the embodiment of the mother-poet, or generatrix, as a subject of enunciation engendering different meanings, in part, by working poetic conventions. This does not mean that she wrote in isolation from the avant-garde, impervious to its propositions. Indeed, in the early 1900s Aleramo took an active interest in futurism. For example, at Aleramo's request, in 1913 Marinetti sent her samples of futurist manifestos and art, including words-in-freedom poetry and photographs of paintings, for an article on futurism she intended to write for a Russian publication (see Conti and Morino 1981, 87). Shortly thereafter, Conti and Morino write, Aleramo declared her support for the avant-garde project (87). Yet Aleramo's literary writings do not seem to bear out some of the declarations she made in her personal correspondence from 1913 to 1916, when she cultivated relationships with men and women of the vanguard. Most notably, as the brief, passionate affair between Aleramo and Umberto Boccioni—an influential futurist theoretician, painter, and sculptor—ignited heated exchanges, in a letter of 1914 Aleramo answered Boccioni's charge that she tended to dramatize, volleying, "Get off it! I'm more of a futurist than you, in substance and form, and I always told you so. I'm the barbarian, as Mr. Mortier called me last night, seating me across from the 'extrêmement civilisée' Madame Mendès" (in Conti and Morino 1981, 102). In fact, Aleramo earned the regard of Marinetti, who praised the strange "virility" of her creativity, and Aurel (A. M. Mortier), whose writings appeared in *Poesia*. In a letter to Boccioni dated February 1914, Aurel acclaims the Italian artist's singularity: "Sibilla isn't one of the great women, she is *the great woman* in your country. She is the first female consciousness" (101).

Although Aleramo shared esteem, friendship, and commitment to artistic life with the avant-garde, her poetry does not visibly shift toward the aesthetics and topoi proposed by the futurists. Instead, as Fiora Bassanese (1995) convincingly argues, Aleramo's practices of daily living and poetry show "the willed construction of an exceptional personal identity, the convergence of biography and art, and the tendency to self-exaltation and titanism," which constitute the artist's textual body as a "living poetic myth" (137). Thus, Bassanese continues, Friedrich Nietzsche and Gabriele D'Annunzio serve as more fitting prototypes for the designs of Aleramo's poetry, which bring into being a mythic, exceptional self, written however under the sign of female sexual difference. This aspect of her poetic subjectivity is amply demonstrated in *Selva d'amore*. The collection includes lyrical poems that voice a full range of female desires— artistic, erotic, amatory, and maternal. As Rachel Blau DuPlessis (1994) contends, the lyric "activates notable master plots, ideologies, and moves fundamentally inflected with gender relations" (71). In order to assess how Aleramo's lyrical production is situated in relation to the gendered ideology of the lyric, we must look at the tradition in Italian literature. As critics note, Aleramo's lyrical poems participate in the prominent tradition of the Italian *canzoniere*, originating with Petrarch's famous "songs" of love exalting Laura. The formative influence of Petrarch's model on subsequent genre formation and the encoding of the male as speaking subject and of the female as object provide a crucial interpretative context for theorizing the subversive potential of Aleramo's poetry. In her analysis of the significant role played by Petrarch's *Canzoniere*, Juliana Schiesari (1990–91) maintains that his

> poetics could be said to be the institutionalized eros of the Italian Renaissance. Petrarch's glorification of Laura became the means through which Petrarch attained glory and through which woman as the specular object for erotic self-recuperation became institutionalized. The ecstasy and despair of Petrarch's lyric eroticized *lack* in terms of a lost object. (12, emphasis added)

The decidedly female-gendered speaking position that Aleramo creates, as Bassanese (1995) tells us, contradicts this configuration of the poetic subject and desire. Furthermore, as we see in such poems as "Fiamme" (Flames), "Ancora ascolto una rosa" (I listen to a rose again), "Castità" (Chastity), and "Turbamento" (Disquiet), the poet does not perform a mere reversal of positions, which would retain the traditional economy of lack. Although a current of yearning, even unfulfillment, runs through these poems, it contrasts with self-celebratory bursts of plenitude and excess articulating the embodied nature of multiple female desires. The imagery in the following poem, titled "Tempo, che irridi al numero!" (Time, you mock the number!),[22] illustrates the general importance of corporeality in Aleramo's poetry, as well as how her evocation of the body overcomes the dualism between body and mind, flesh and art:

> Time, you mock the number!
> Dazzling smile
> of innumerable moments
> beating to the heart!
> Poems I did not write
> but lived.
> Stirrings I left unnoted,
> and today, it's been ten, twenty years,
> it's an unmeasured theory of time,
> return flashing to illuminate glimpses of themselves
> a page a line a tone
> of the sole volume of mine!
> Unexpected,
> as, unexpected, they first created themselves,
> return the causes
> that seemed to isolate life,
> they slip in softly,
> they were destiny
> they were blood,
> they return rhythmic true,
> musical flashes. . . .
> (35)

Here, as in poems by women futurists, the poet conflates life and art. However, in contrast to the futurist paradigm, which privileges art as the originary site for the creation of modes of living, Aleramo invokes the experiential, affective dimensions of being as the life's blood of her lyrical production. The imagery and words she uses articulate the inter-relations between bodies of flesh and words. Aleramo's manner of situating the body as the site of artistic enunciation may be read in terms of the feminist notion of embodiment. In this model of subjectivity, as Rosi Braidotti (1991) explains, the body is seen as an inter-face, a threshold, a field of intersection of material and symbolic forces; it is a surface where multiple codes of power and knowledge are inscribed; it is a construction that transforms and capitalizes on energies of a heterogeneous and discontinuous nature. (219)

As seen in the following diary entry (5 December 1940), Aleramo's way of thinking her body, "poetry incarnate," incorporates the (inter)relations that Braidotti outlines, while articulating the transformative female power exercised through the generation of self and art:

> All that was life in me, all that, through time, was inscribed in my essence and made me a living symbol, a living poetic myth. All that I've barely expressed in words, quite possibly because I've gone on and on creating myself lyrically with that living material into a unique, almost demonic, work, every day, every instant. . . . Something in me has remained eternally unsatisfied: the yearning for a child of love, a being that was all together a masterpiece of my flesh, of my heart, of my spirit. And I loved, or thought to love, many men, waiting unawares. . . . my poetry was generated this way. And the thousands of pages I've written to narrate myself, to explain myself. Even to this [page] today. A rage of self-creation, incessant. (in Bassanese 1995, 137, 152)[23]

Not unlike the notion of text theorized by Goretti, Aleramo's elaboration of the written word, a kind of *tableau vivant,* functions performatively not as a process intended to discover a stable, unified "self," but as a dynamic mode exploiting the regenerative possibilities presented by each new moment. Moreover, this passage highlights Aleramo's sexualization of poetic practice, written in the language of the mother-poet. In a cogent analysis, Bassanese (1995) charts this writer's circular logic between female procreation and creation, stating that "the *creatura* (child/being) is the masterpiece achieved in flesh, not words; poetry is generated, like children; writing is equal to self-creation, words made flesh" (152). If, from one standpoint, lyrical production assumes a compensatory meaning for Aleramo, from the other, her lyrical evocation of the maternal body and creative labor challenges the patriarchal control of maternity. Resonating with the idea of maternity advanced by Benedetta and Goretti, meaning "to give" ideas and passions (as well as children), Aleramo offers her poetry as offspring, an endowment bearing part of herself, as we see in the poem "Miei versi" (My verses):[24]

My verses,
my nobility,
you alone,
out of everything,
immense sums,
I gave to life,
you alone remain,
slight in a slight volume,
shining,
everything turned into a gem,
tears smiles nocturnal yearnings
wind and roses,
the thought of human squalors
and the faces of loves,
oh my verses,
my nobility,
you alone remain,
shining . . .
(49–50)

With the repetition of "nobility" and "shining," Aleramo underscores the positive value of female poetic generation, which bestows everlasting life on a range of ideas, feelings, and perceptions. Her use of the word *gemmeo* has special significance because it denotes the precious, illustrious qualities that life's vicissitudes assume in her verses, as well as meanings associated with nascent life. The root word *gemma* also means "bud," thus embodying the promise of new life and growth.

Antonia Pozzi: Poetics of the Verge

As in the cases of Aleramo and Goretti, whose fashionings of the maternal as a paradigm for poetic theories and practices bring into being highly differentiated works of poetry, the images, perceptions, and feelings that Antonia Pozzi crafts in poems that express her notion of artistic creation in terms of maternity yield another, contrasting redaction of the mother-poet. We find none of the irreverence or sense of jouissance and discord exhibited in futurist poems. Quite the contrary! Pozzi, who was born in 1912, perceived poetry as fulfilling a sacred function from the time she began secretly writing verses in notebooks, discovered only after she committed suicide in 1938. In a letter to Tullio Gadenz, dated

29 January 1933, Pozzi elucidates the spiritual meanings she attached to poetry:

> I believe our duty, while we wait to return to God, is precisely to discover as much of God in this life as we can, to create Him, to make Him leap forth, shining from the friction between our souls with things (poetry and pain), from the contact between our souls (charity and fraternity). This is why, Tullio, poetry is sacred to me. This is why the sacrifices that robbed so much of my youth are sacred. This is why the souls I feel, beyond earthly guises, in communion with my soul are sacred. (1943, 143)

The youngest of the poets examined here, Pozzi pursued her university education during Fascism and received her degree in literature from the State University of Milan in 1935. Although she admired works by such modernists and hermetics as T. S. Eliot, Ezra Pound, Quasimodo, and Montale, the notion of poetry and its performative functions developed by Pozzi align more closely with the poetics conceived by the *linea lombarda* (Lombard line), primarily made up of a group of students who attended the University of Milan between 1930 and 1936. Including Pozzi and such cultural figures as the philosopher and aesthetician Antonio Banfi, then a professor, Enzo Paci, and the poet Vittorio Sereni, the *linea lombarda* posited a form of poetry that responded "most of all to the solicitations of objects of the time; it is born from a realm of faithful, quotidian images in an air of retiring emotion," as Luciano Anceschi explains (cited in Baffoni-Licata 1991, 358). Similarly, Pozzi fashions objects, commonplaces, and ideas drawn from daily living, investing them with a sense, feeling, and power of their own that may weigh on the soul as an almost unbearable consciousness of being in its joys and discontents. Her poetry thus stands in contrast to the spectacular, epic rhetoric of Fascism and to the cryptic micromythologies of some hermetic poetry.

The differences between the poetics elaborated by Pozzi and the practices of hermetic poets are not coincidental. In her dissertation on Flaubert, Pozzi critiqued the negative stance of hermeticism, stating that it represented

> a form of intuitive arbitrariness that no longer has a measure of comparison in the objectivity of expression (and thus today poetry seems to have turned away from the fullness of human reality and only has the character

of evasion and inner refuge, not the sense of understanding and the resolution of life in its entirety). (1989, 10)

In contrast, such poems as "Preghiera all poesia" (Prayer to poetry), "Pudore" (Modesty), and "La porta che si chiude" (The closing door) exemplify this poet's exceptional talent for crafting the ordinary—sights of a
landscape, a lark, a mother's smile—into an extraordinary symbolic system that invites readings at different levels of interpretation. The seemingly natural eloquence, purity of sound, and precision of imagery in her
poems earned Pozzi the admiration of, among others, Negri, Alfredo
Galletti, and Montale, who applauded her work in an essay first published in 1945. Among the important issues that Montale introduces in
his critical assessment is the way in which he positions this artist's poetics in relation to pure poetry and to women's poetry of her time. Montale speculates about the directions Pozzi might have pursued:

> Antonia probably would never have set out toward the banks of fog and
> dangers of pure poetry. But one notices her desire to reduce the weight of
> words to the bare minimum, and that desire already enabled her to escape
> from generic female gratuitousness, which is the dream of so many male
> critics. (1948, 10)

As Montale claims elsewhere in the essay, Pozzi's stylistic prowess illustrates her exceptional talent and, to his mind, her exception to the rule of
female poetry, which, he argues, fails to overcome spontaneity. Betraying
the bias of his stance, Montale concludes with an ostensible compliment,
proposing that Antonia Pozzi "was a woman to the extent necessary to
describe herself without losing control" (13–14). Despite its limitations,
Montale's commentary enables us to appreciate particularizing features
that Pozzi's lyrical practices exhibit. Yet I want to suggest that these distinct traits represent not an exception to women's poetry, but a different
register. Furthermore, as I intend to show, this artist's conception of poetic identity and of poetry as a generative site of meaning intersects with
some of the same concerns of fellow women poets of her time.

Conflicting with notions of poetic production in works by Aleramo
and Goretti, in such poems as "Pudore" (Modesty), "Lamentazione"
(Lament), "Maternità" (Maternity), and "La porta che si chiude" (The
closing door) the analogic relations that Pozzi draws between bearing a

child and a word of love, and the symbolic representations of the womb
and parturition fail to produce an enabling synthesis of life and art.
Rather, this poet's use of dialogue structures, the appositions of antithetical images—the air and water, mountains and valleys, inside and
outside, dream and reality—as well as imagery enhancing dualisms between the material body and soul articulate the experience of the cleavage
between daily living and poetry, and the resultant dialectical relations.
These features constitute what I call a poetics of the verge, indicating
both a limit or border, and the potential transgression of it. The following poem, "Preghiera alla poesia" (Prayer to poetry, 23 August 1934), exemplifies these features, while offering an illustration of how Pozzi envisions the relations between the generation of self and poetry:

> Oh, blessing you weigh on me
> soul, poetry:
> you know if I falter and get lost,
> you then deny yourself
> and become silent.
>
> Poetry, I confess to you
> you are my voice deep within:
> you know,
> you know I was unfaithful
> I walked on the meadow of gold
> that was my heart,
> I trampled the grass,
> ruined the land—
> poetry—that land
> where you told me the sweetest
> of all your songs,
> where one morning for the first time
> I saw the lark flying in the calm
> and tried to ascend with my eyes—
> Poetry, poetry you remain
> my deep remorse,
> Oh help me to find again
> my abandoned lofty land—
>
> Poetry you give yourself only
> to those who with tearful eyes
> search for themselves—

> Oh make me worthy of you again,
> poetry you look at me.
> (1989, 224–25)[25]

Although Pozzi represents poetic creation as the expression of her most intimate self, the forms of address to poetry in this prayer—both a confession and entreaty—foreground a process of doubling that has fundamental importance in her construction of a figural poetic identity and her lyrical production. The quotidian imagery, cast to evoke the inner landscape of the poetic persona, draws out polarities, such as the fixity of the land versus the mobility of the air and the lark, whose flight in the calm sky and melodious song parallel poetry's transcendent potential.[26] Furthermore, the invocation to poetry in the final stanza suggests that artistic production can bring about meaningful transformation of self in psychic space, as indicated by the final image of poetry gazing at the speaker, which conjures the specular body.

Nonetheless, Pozzi's way of thinking the relations between life and art, flesh and spirit differs substantially from the notions of textuality proposed in the writings by Goretti and Aleramo. For these poets, the act of creating poetry affords seemingly limitless opportunities for exhilarated, furious female self-fashioning. The different ways that Goretti and Pozzi employ the "path" as trope elucidate this point. From the aeroperspective that Goretti articulates in "Conversation with the engine," multiple new paths unfold before the female speaker's eye. Her desires take flight, projected onto the expanding horizons she traverses. The vantage point constructed in the text alters the vision of self and relations to others in the world. In contrast, in the poem "Il sentiero" (The path, 30 January 1935), Pozzi pictures how life's passing dissipates girlhood hopes: "You dreamt wide avenues for your life— / A narrow path / Is all that remains."[27] Investing the mountain with maternal meanings, as it recalls holding the little girl in its lap, Pozzi employs such contrasting symbols as the skies and valleys, "lost banks," the wall and gate, to bring out the sense of loss as dreams pale in the light of days gone by yet never quite disappear. Indeed, the regenerative signs of spring in the seasonal cycle and the voices of children singing, evoked in the concluding stanza, stand as a sorrowful reminder that denies the woman peace of forgetfulness.

The poems "Un destino" (A destiny, 13 February 1935) and "Pudore"

(Modesty, 1 February 1933) exemplify the particular commingling of the trials and gratifications coloring Pozzi's perception of being a woman poet. They point as well to features that intersect with and diverge from those in poetry by fellow women of her time. As in "Prayer to poetry," the poetic voice in "A destiny" speaks directly to the addressee, here a woman. In two brief, three-line stanzas (the first and third), Pozzi evokes the communal life of society, signified by lights and shelters shared in the camps where the woman's companions have gone, each one, however, having an individual life. In contrast, the second stanza, comprising eight lines, deftly pictures the poet alone on a faint road where the elements of nature satisfy basic needs. The fourth and longest stanza discloses the conditions, insights, and feelings that constitute the solitary calling of being a woman poet, as expressed in the two short, strong lines closing the poem:

> But over your slow
> going like a river that finds no outlet,
> the silvery light of infinite
> lives—of free stars
> now quivers:
> and if no door
> opens from your labors
> if at each step
> the weight of your being returns to you
> if it is yours
> this thing that is more than pain
> the joy to continue on, a woman alone
> in the limpid desert of your mountains,
>
> then accept
> being a poet.
> (1989, 261)

In the Italian, Pozzi uses only the word *sola* in the female-gendered form (without the word *woman*) to denote the sex of the person alone, an important element generally lost in English translation, which carries the sign of sexual difference. By so doing, this poem invites different readings, for it may inscribe the kind of doubling we saw in "Prayer to poetry" or create a system of address to the female reader. In the poem "Modesty," Pozzi overtly calls the reader's attention to sexual difference as she likens

the affective relations between the woman poet and her poem to those a
mother may harbor toward her child:

> If some of my humble words
> please you
> and you tell me
> even if only with your eyes
> I break out
> in a blissful smile
> but tremble
> like a slight young mother
> who even blushes
> if a passerby tells her
> that her baby is beautiful.
> (1989, 113)

The analogy that Pozzi develops between bearing a word and a child recalls
Goretti and Aleramo, though the sense of pride she intimates certainly appears more retiring than the futurist invocation of the mother-poet.

A more complex example of how Pozzi crafts metaphors of motherhood to represent the problematic functions that lyrical creation may
assume appears in "Lamentazione" (Lament, 6 May 1933). For the way in
which Pozzi delineates the fabrication of poetry as a counterpoint to unfulfilled maternal desire, employing the word *creatura* for both child and
a creation of art, her thought and language show more than a passing
similarity with some of Aleramo's writings, as we see in this poem, a sup-
plicating lament addressed to God:

> What did you give me
> Lord
> in return
> for what I offered you?
> for my heart, open
> like a piece of fruit—
> emptied
> of its purest seed—
> tossed
> on the reefs
> like a useless shell
> after its pearl has been
> stolen—

what did you give me
in return
for my perfect beloved
pearl?
The pearl I chose
from the most sparkling necklace
as shepherds of old
chose the wooliest, the strongest, the whitest lamb
from the thick flock
and sacrificed it
on the hard altar?

What did you do
if not bind me
to this altar
as to eternal
torture?—

And I gave you
my only
being
my unsatisfied maternal
anxiety
the dream
of my uncreated being
its little face without
features
its little hand without
weight—
On the ruins of my unborn home
I scattered ashes and salt—

And you
what did you give me
in return
for my sweet immaculate
home?
if not this desert
Lord
and this sand that weighs heavily
on my hands of flesh
and clouds my eyes
and soils my wounds

and bores through
my soul—

Oh are there no longer clouds
in your sky
Lord
so that a bursting shower
might wash away
all this
misery?
(1989, 137–39)

Speaking through the female body, a place of enunciation inscribed in the imagery Pozzi crafts, the figural identity of the mother-poet embodies an unbridgeable gulf between the creative and biological bearing of life. The metaphors, drawn from the sights, objects, and language of daily living, generate a complex system of symbolic meanings, where rich female plenitude gradually gives way to an arid site of ambivalence. Thus, in the first two stanzas Pozzi expresses the nature and worth of the poet's gift with organic symbols of the womb and fertility, which evoke the sense of both creation and loss. The fruit and shell strongly represent female principles of fecundity, water, and generational ties. The shell may also raise associations with Aphrodite, the Greek goddess of love and beauty, who was born from a shell. However, the giving, or taking, of the poem—like the seed or pearl—leaves the site of generation empty. The pearl, described as *diletta,* an adjective often applied to literary works, has special significance here. While associated with shell symbolism, the pearl also conjures bonds between generations and eroticism, since it appears as part of a string forming a necklace, broken, however, once the pearl is offered. Likewise, as the poet further elaborates on the motif of sacrifice, delineated with the image of the white lamb, symbolizing purity and innocence, she explicity employs the enclosed space of the "sweet immaculate home" to evoke the womb. The choice of such adjectives imbues the verses with religious undercurrents that bring to mind the body of Mary, the Virgin Mother. Yet in this text the creation of poetic being fails to fulfill the body, as the figural persona mourns its ruins, a home become barren dust.

The poem "Lament" represents an important, intensely moving visage of the mother-poet that illuminates Pozzi's appreciation of the conflict between lived and created life, as well as a recurrent topos in notions of female creativity. Indeed, in the series of ten poems united in Pozzi's notebooks with the title "La vita sognata" (Dreamed life), no less than four pieces, located at the center of the collection, thematize motherhood, as the poet envisions what the child of her dreams might have been, might have meant. It was composed in 1933, after Pozzi's father prohibited her from continuing a relationship with Antonio Maria Cervi, her high school teacher of Latin and Greek with whom she apparently shared humanistic ideals, a strong sense of social responsibility, and sensitivity of spirit (Cenni and Dino 1989, 363). Thus, perhaps, the poems "Maternità" (Maternity), "Saresti stato" (You would have been), "Il bimbo nel viale" (The little boy in the avenue), and "Gli occhi del sogno" (The eyes of the dream) so effectively voice the kind of mournful loss that arises when the apparent possibility of making hopes into reality tempts the dreamer to the brink of belief, only to give way under the weight of real, yet contingent, circumstances. More specifically, these poems, like "Lament," work through the maternal, as potential corporeality and symbol of poeisis, to problematize female sexual difference and creativity. Noting the general pertinence of this issue in works by women poets—Sylvia Plath, for instance—Cenni (1989) states, "On one side the unrealized desire for motherhood can lead to the loss of identity; on the other, it opposes the risk of compensation in poetry" (17). However, she convincingly proposes, an alternative mediation of this bind emerges in Pozzi's elaboration of a "poetics of the threshold," whereby words represent "nascent thought."

Pozzi's particular notion of poetry as a site for the bringing to life of meaning, powerfully evinced in the poem "La porta che si chiude" (The closing door, 10 February 1931), displays yet another facet of generatrix as poetic agent. Read by Cenni as a "mimesis of childbirth,"[28] this exceptionally provocative poem represents the sensations and meanings of the gestation of words, their birthing, and the postpartum stage, as enunciated from the female body. The first verse, which opens a dialogue with a fellow woman addressed as "sister," introduces the motif of the threshold, as the poet employs images of "a gate post" and "barrier" likened to the "I," worn down by an onrush from within, an "erupting flight" of "prisoner words," we soon discover. In the second stanza, as in the following two, the repetition of phrases, words, and sounds, for example, the hard *b* and *p*, conveys a cumulative beating rhythm until finally, the "unborn words" move from the darkness to the light of the sun, letting out a mortal cry. Here the repetition of the *u* in *unica, luce, urto, urlo*, and *ultimo*, paired with day in the first line and dream in the last, might be interpreted as sounds of pain or breathing during the climactic moments of labor. The subsequent change in tone, introduced in the penultimate stanza as the door closes, bringing to mind vaginal closure, reaches particularly suggestive metaphoric dimensions in the concluding lines:

> And then, with locked lips,
> with open eyes
> under the shadow's mysterious sky,
> will be
> —as you know—
> peace.
> (in Allen et al. 1986, 57)

In contrast to the space behind the door—pitch dark, cold, and silent—the shadowy space beyond offers calm and vision. Thus, this poem performatively enacts Pozzi's notion of the functions poetry should fulfill. As the poet tells us in the following passage from a letter to Tullio Gadenz, dated 29 January 1933, poetry has a

> sublime task: to take all the pain that foams up and thunders in our soul, and to appease it, to transform it in the supreme calm of art, just as rivers flow into the sky-blue expanse of the sea. Poetry is a catharsis of pain, as the enormity of death is a catharsis of life. (Pozzi 1943, 140)

"The Closing Door" offers an especially powerful evocation of the generative poetic force of the female body, inscribed in the poem's rhythms and imagery. Associated with this stance is the perception of poetry as a productive gift, an idea that intersects with the discourses on poetry by Aleramo and Goretti. The poem "Lieve offerta" (Tenuous offering, 5 December 1934) best illustrates this aspect of this artist's poetics. Giving lyrical expression to what the poet wants her verses to accomplish for the reader, the concluding stanza reads:

I would like my soul to rest lightly
upon you,
and my poems to be a bridge for you,
slender and strong,
white—
over the dark chasm
of the world.
(1989, 237)

Pozzi's figuration of poetry with the architecture of the bridge suggests that poetic creation may mediate, though not reconcile, the dialectic between life and art, reality and dream.

Ada Negri: Maternal Genealogies of Poetic Life

For my last example of women's reappropriations of the maternal as a category for conceptualizing and authorizing notions of female poetic identity, I want to examine Ada Negri's discourse on birthing, and the relations among women she symbolically engenders. This dimension of Negri's lyrical production merits a reassessment, which has perhaps been forestalled by the negative reception of her poetry among some ranks, and by her sympathies for Mussolini and Fascism.[29] For example, seconding Croce's assessment, Renato Serra claimed that Negri's poems "reproduced" the worst elements of lyrical writings by D'Annunzio, Guido Gozzano, and Giovanni Pascoli, as Vittoriano Esposito (1992) points out. While Luigi Russo (1923) bemoaned what he interpreted as Negri's "self-idealization," Camillo Pellizzi (1929) took an elitist stance and charged her with "an inborn lack of taste for balance and proportion, almost a hereditary poverty" (75). However, other critics such as Francesco Flora and Attilio Momigliano have intuited instances of poetic originality and greatness, especially in the range of her love poems appearing in *Il libro di Mara* (1966c) and *Il dono* (1966b), the latter of which received the Firenze Prize. I want to concentrate however, on how the speaking position that Negri fashions as the mother-poet differs from models crafted by the women artists examined thus far, and also how it contends with normative codes (universality and transcendence) that serve to defend patrilineal authority over the poetic imagination as a site for the inscription of male subjectivity.

The poems by Negri that appear in collections published during the interwar years enable us to frame different questions regarding the relations between creativity and motherhood, as well as aging. Nearing her fiftieth birthday when *Il libro di Mara* was published in 1919, Negri subsequently produced four poetry collections, in addition to her autobiography and five works of prose fiction. She died in 1945, as Milan suffered increasing aerial attacks during World War II. Although Negri trained her lens on the material conditions and institutions limiting the terms of women's social identities, her later works in prose and poetry exhibit an expanding variety of related subjects, angles of vision, and aesthetic experimentation, which belies the association of old age and the ebbing of creativity. While the love songs in *Il libro di Mara* pose issues related to the female erotic body in midlife, as both the object and subject of passion,[30] Negri expands the depth and complexity of her field of vision in later works, thematizing, for instance, the nature of artistic creation, spiritual rebirth, death and the yearning for a homeland, and war. More important for the scope of this examination, Negri devotes numerous poems to the articulation of the phenomenological and psychic aspects of birthing, of being a poet and, simultaneously, a daughter, mother, and grandmother. Poems such as "Lettera a Bianca" (Letter to Bianca), "Donata" (the name of Negri's granddaughter), "I capelli" (Her hair), and "Parole a mia figlia" (Words to my daughter) represent valuable lyrical examples of what Leigh Gilmore (1994) terms "autobiographics." Among other interpretative possibilities, Gilmore's critical concept enables us to see the ways in which "the *I* is multiply coded in a range of discourses: it is a site of multiple solicitations, multiple markings of 'identity,' multiple figurations of agency" (42). By reading these poems, among others, against each other, the multiple, shifting positionalities of the mother-poet emerge within a genealogy of female affiliation.

The endeavors Negri undertook late in life to symbolize the mother-daughter relation, represented from the perspective of being both a mother and a daughter, should not be dismissed under the sway of the assumption that to write about motherhood in a serious, sometimes exalting, passionate manner during Fascism necessarily means to reproduce the regime's ideology of woman and pronatalism. In fact, since the poems examined here thematize filiative relations between women (their biological ties reaching across generations) and their forms of affiliation (associations constructed in society and culture) they afford a unique opportunity to explore how the experiences and meanings that Negri represents relate to prevailing notions of the maternal. As contemporary feminist philosophers and scholars have argued, mother-daughter relations tend to be underrepresented in culture. For example, Luce Irigaray, among other intellectuals who have developed salient theories on this problematic,[31] has critiqued the way in which canons of art repress the relationship between mother and daughter. Scarcer still are literary texts by women explicating diversified perspectives on being biological mothers and writers. In a meticulous reading of works by Freud, Helene Deutsch, and Melanie Klein examining female development, motherhood, and creativity, Susan Rubin Suleiman (1985) demonstrates the virtual absence of attention to maternal thought on motherhood and artistic creation. In psychoanalytic theories, she argues, "just as motherhood is ultimately the child's drama, so is artistic creation" (357). Exposing the biases—sexual and generational—structuring conventional paradigms, Suleiman pushes Roland Barthes's infamous definition of the writer as "someone who plays with the body of his mother" (1973) into places he may not have foreseen and speculates about the implications created when the writer "*is* 'the body of the mother'" (358). This theoretical frame outlines useful directions of inquiry for a critical reevaluation of Negri's poetic discourses on motherhood and artistic production. As Negri puts the body of poet, mother, and even the daughter within her into poetic forms for all to see, she raises some profound questions. For instance, how do biological filiation and the material relations between the mother-poet and daughter figure in the fashioning of Negri's creative identity? In the samples discussed, the mother crafts the position of enunciation and the daughter forms the source of lyrical inspiration. By so doing, Negri attributes literary value to the mother-daughter relation. But which symbolic functions do the images of the daughter perform? Last, as proposed earlier, men poets and critics tend to conceive poetry as a system for male forms of affiliation. Therefore, what does Negri's cultivation of poetic discourse for the symbolization of a maternal genealogy suggest about the sexual politics of gender and genre?

Beginning with Negri's first collection of poetry, *Fatalità* (Fate, 1892), she showed a propensity to fashion figures, events, emotions, and hopes from her life's experiences into poetic creation. Maternal bonds, as formed first with her own mother (rendered in *Morning Star*), and then with her daughter Bianca, born in 1898, provided an apparently inexhaustible source of inspiration, constantly in the process of transformation. The themes and tone of poems relating to motherhood and creativity exhibit changes that could be attributed, in part, to the differing kinds and intensity of demands associated with phases in the maternal life course and literary production. For instance, in the collection *Dal profondo* (From the depth, 1910), such pieces as "Il segno della croce" (The sign of the cross) and "Passione" (Passion) express a conflictual pull of desires, for freedom and independence, intensified by a loveless marriage, and the love and responsibility that the poet feels toward her young daughter. In "The Sign of the Cross," Negri delicately evokes this crosscurrent with the image of a nightly ritual performed between mother and daughter:

> (There is a way to escape the terrible anguish.
> But you hold me back with your sweet snare,
> you who cannot sleep if I don't make
> the sign of the cross on your forehead in the evening.)
> (Costa-Zalessow 1992, 162)

Understandably, later figurations of the mother-poet and relations with her daughter and art voice problems of a different order as other forms of filial bonds are constituted, transformed, and severed. The following piece, "Lettera a Bianca" (Letter to Bianca), is one of two poems with this title published in 1925, when Negri's daughter was twenty-seven years old and herself a mother to a daughter named Donata. Here we see the poet's consuming delectation of being on her own during a sojourn at Capri, which provided the inspiration for the collection of poems *I canti dell'isola* (Island songs). The poetic persona asserts her own desire for what appears to be a regeneration of self, a springtime in midlife, against the call of her daughter's home. The poem is worth quoting in its entirety for the way that it unites several themes and images that recur in Negri's other verses of the interwar years. The poem opens as if the mother-poet were reassuring her daughter of their reunion:

I'll return, don't fear, when the elation has fallen.
Everything falls: flowers and fruit, the berry and acorn.
Everything returns: the wing to land, the boat to shore.
I'll reappear at the home where Donata is trying out her
    first trills,
where Mikika purrs, rubbing her arched back against the
    tiles out in the sun.
Let me live, now—for my time is short—in the gardens of gold.
Maybe I wasn't alive until now, not even when
you broke my belly, being born, and you were my springtime.
Another May, that I didn't know could shine in the world, is
    here.
God led me to high places so in them I might glory
in myself, so I might reach the summits, so I might drink
    from sky-blue fountains.
So I might dress up all in roses and give the blood of love
    to the thorns.
One day, who knows? . . . my soul may be pierced by the
    desire
for a ploughed Lombard field, fresh with furrows, smoking
    and brown
in the fog as sunlight filters through. Then I'll come to
    that land,
I'll come to see you again, dark skinned and fertile like
    that field.
(1966a, 676)

In the first section of this poem, organic metaphors predominate as Negri invokes origins, and seasonal cycles of birth, growth, aging, and change to situate the maternal persona in relation to self, life, and family, represented by her daughter and granddaughter. As if following a law of nature and society, she will return home when her journey, like those of the bird and boat, is completed. As in other poems that speak of the relation between mother and daughter, the poet constructs the maternal body as the place of enunciation to re-create the birth of her baby girl as experience and symbol. Although the daughter's birth heralds a season of new life for the mother, too, the aging poet seems to attach greater meaning to the "springtime," or intense growth, experienced late in life. The references to God, the summits, and fountains suggest a form of rebirth and spiritual as well as creative development in the woman poet's construction of self. Negri's articulation of the mother-poet may thus authorize interrelations between motherhood, self-re-creation, and artistic creation—evoked by the Orphic image of drinking from the fountains. Nonetheless, the vision of dressing herself up in roses—a flower Negri frequently crafts to symbolize a range of different meanings—creates a sensual image of blood and passion that can infuse even thorns with love, partly confirming Goretti's view of Negri's links with the classical tradition. In addition to associations with the Virgin Mother, the rose may also function as a symbol of regeneration (Cirlot 1971, 275).

The closing vision of the Lombard landscape emerging in the poet's temporal and geographic horizon again takes up themes of origins, home, and death. Lombardy, a site in Negri's imaginary that recurs in such poems as "Nel paese di mia madre" (In my mother's land) and "Corale notturno" (Nocturnal choral), forms a rich matrix of meanings. It is the place where Negri was born and raised, and where she wished to be buried, alongside her own mother. This region is also renowned for the rich, fertile soil and fruitful abundance gracing its lands. Thus, Negri's poetic figuration of Lombardy conjures the motherland, the originary site of generational ties extending from mothers to daughters in a perennial cycle. The figure of the daughter, however, is not unproblematic. As we see in the final image of Bianca, Negri draws a simile between the daughter and the Lombard field. Such a focus on the organic "fertile" body, lacking other socially meaningful contours, creates a limited view of the daughter and, moreover, anchors the figure as part of the fertile landscape. Thus, although Negri invests the mother-poet with sociocultural mobility, the younger woman stands for nature, presence, and immobility, a familiar humanist paradigm. While it is true that the poem offers two contending figurations of the maternal, highlighting their differences, the "nature" of the differences and the structure of power they represent may prompt us to ask whether the mother artist's self-articulation necessarily silences the daughter.

Written some ten years after "Lettera a Bianca," the poem "Parole a mia figlia" (Words to my daughter) also draws out distinctions between the mother and daughter yet shifts attention from the pleasure that the poet derives from her solitary, replenishing life to maternal pain, prompted by the daughter's individuation. Structured as a dialogue, the

poem can be read as an attempt to create a language for the symbolization of the mother-daughter relationship in terms that valorize the diversity of women's subjectivities. Speaking through the maternal body,
the poet articulates female-embodied knowledge as she again remem-
bers the womb and birthing. As we see in the following passage, the poet
envisions matrilineal relations in terms of both similarity and difference,
continuity and separation:

> Daughter, you laugh at your children: if I think
> about the time when you broke every part of me
> so you could be born, and the pain was so strong that perhaps
> death might be better, and the joy was so great
> that nothing can be a greater joy,
> that time seems so far away now,
> more of a dream than truth.
> If I think that you are the life's being
> of my life's being, and that I deceived myself
> to see signs of me in your soul,
> I know the vain error.
> I know that I am me, you are you—we are different.
> And I bend before this human law, as old
> as the earth that nourishes us.
> Even so, never did I stop having you to hold
> in my arms, in spite of the years
> flying by, to rock you on my knees,
> to take you by your hand. You'll do the
> same thing with your children, and one day
> you'll suffer as I suffer, holding back
> the suffering within you, telling yourself: "It's right."
> (1966b, 818)

Symbolizing the perspective of the mother, Negri employs a form of
body politics that undermines masculine attempts to colonize the womb
and birthing for the expression of male poiesis. The mimetic re-creation
of the laboring body, as the baby girl—life of the mother's life yet already
separate—fights to pass the threshold, articulates an experience that the
male body cannot replicate biologically. The changing dynamics of filial
relations emerge through the delineation of telescoped phases in the female life course from birth to old age, and of generational cycles. Negri's
construction of female collectivity, however, serves not to define women

exclusively in terms of sameness. Instead, much of the poem's force derives precisely from the tensions between the consciousness of maternal communalities and the integrity of selfhood, which receive further elaboration in the following section of the poem.

With great economy, Negri moves from memories of her little girl's face, voice, and unique charm to her passage into womanhood, indicated by signs the mother reads in the daughter's eyes. The new configurations of the mother-daughter relation appear to expand ties of body and knowledge, symbolized by the recurrent image of blood, signifying both the blood the women share and their desire. Recognizing the daughter as sexual subject, the poet claims they can now each speak of "the supreme truths of life," one woman to another. However, employing the metaphor of the door to convey the limits between the daughter's intimate self, which she does not expose, and the mother's desire to know, Negri expresses an appreciation of the necessary yet heartrending autonomy between the lives they lead. The following lines graphically represent the severing of ties between mother and daughter, referred to in Italian with the female-gendered words *genitrice* and *generata:*

> The cord of pulsing flesh
> between mother and daughter is broken:
> tenderness is strong, but the bond
> we all make with our destiny is stronger; a bitter
> sentence of maternal solitude
> that will strike you too.

This passage highlights the pain of loneliness without, however, shades of nostalgia. Negri seems to refuse a language of control and domination, while creating expressive forms of affect that are not unlike Irigaray's notion of a female language aspiring "to reintroduce the values of desire, pain, joy, the body. Living values. Not discourses of mastery" (cited in Whitford 1989, 120). Furthermore, Negri's coupling of the words *genitrice e generata* (as opposed to *madre e figlia* or *creatrice e creatura*) produces a sense of connectedness in a genealogy of women's filiative and affiliative ties. She proclaims the value of this relation for the production of meaning that derives from sexual difference, exemplified in the concluding verse:

But the suffering
is not important, oh child born
by the labor of creating. It is important
to be a mother, to make out of our blood
new blood, new strength, new thought
that may pass us down, pass itself down: women eternal
in the unity of beings and time,
even if we might go to our tomb women alone. (819)

One could argue that Negri's language and tone, verging on a call to arms for motherhood, come alarmingly close to the Fascist rhetoric on women as reproducers of the race. Another problem concerns the way in which the poem seems to exclude women with interests, accomplishments, and dreams disassociated from motherhood. To state the obvious, the desire to become a biological mother cannot be upheld as an essential unifying principle of female collectivity, an issue problematized by Alba De Céspedes. But we may also interpret this figuration of the mother-daughter relationship as a construction that gives symbolic placement to women in a matrilineal system.[32] Negri, like Goretti and fellow women poets examined here, endeavors to expand the meaning of the maternal to encompass corporeal and conceptual forms of generation. In fact, the forms of production that she writes under the sign of the maternal—to make "new blood, new strength, new thought"— resonate with Benedetta's conception of the mother as generating "men, emotions, passion, ideas." However, Negri encodes this generative process as a system transmitted from one woman to another. Similarly, the image that Negri fashions of the daughter brought into the world by "the labor of creating" blurs the boundaries between bodies and texts, procreation and creation. The daughter represented in this poem stands for the flesh-and-blood child but is the creative construction of the mother-poet.

The way that Negri privileges the "mother" as an originary source of both life and meaning in a female-sexed system of reference suggests a metaphysics that potentially challenges phallocentric foundations of society and the symbolic order. The recent work by Luisa Muraro provides a useful theoretical model for assessing this component of Negri's poetic discourse. In her book *L'ordine simbolico della madre* (The symbolic order of the mother, 1991), Muraro critiques, among other philosophical constructions, the repression of the mother. Proposing an alternative to both Kristeva's view of the thetic break as indispensable for the passage from the semiotic to the symbolic order and to the poststructuralist dismantling of the metaphysics of origin, Muraro elaborates a model on the symbolic authority of the mother.[33] Thinking beyond the parameters of theological discourse, Muraro's notion of the symbolic mother does not function as a substitute for God but affords a means of mediation in the symbolic:

> The maternal greatness of which I speak is of a symbolic, not of an ontological order. . . . I do not see greatness in the fact of putting children into the world. . . . The woman who put me into the world is great because of her precedence, for her being upstream of every one of my choices and my greatness, which gives her a unique and unmatchable greatness, not substantial in itself but for the position she definitively occupies. (cited in Re 1993, 92)

This notion enables us to see the challenges and risks posed by the multiple forms of self-signification that Negri constructs, as the daughter of the mother before her, a mother herself, and grandmother in a line of descent. The poem "Donata," addressed to Negri's granddaughter, epitomizes the poet's manner of thinking herself in relation to the maternal:

> Little girl, as you entered the world you unveiled
>   living-life to your mother
> as she did to me, at the time when I was more flesh than
>   soul.
> Your eyes, the color of shadowy pools, don't resemble ours,
> the arch of your forehead is different, the sign of your
>   future is different.
> Even so, I know that one day the smile I had at twenty will
>   shine on your mouth,
> and in a gesture, a kiss, a surge of pure hate, of pure
>   love,
> in the burst of a song you'll again be the girl I was.
> Maybe, by the wisdom of our Lord, in the sunlight you'll
>   complete
> the beautiful work that remained closed within me, hapless
>   in life, hapless in death.

As my joyous mother passed into your mother's veins
so I am prolonged in you, and you, when the time is right,
in your children and in your children's children. No seed
   will be neglected
and no strength will be dispersed. Those who die will live
   on. I love you
in this certainty of love that goes from the beginning to
   the last descent.
(1966a, 682)

Upstream, in fact, the originary source of life and the meanings Negri attaches to it, the mother functions as a symbol of women's power and the knowledge they can reveal to each other. This particular celebration of a matrilineal genealogy, which constructs a sense of verticality for women, poses a serious danger, however, of merging women's identities in the maternal, a problem that concerns Irigaray, among others working on a rethinking of the maternal. Furthermore, Negri's use of organic metaphors to represent the maternal body and generational ties may tend to fix her models in a perennial cycle, resistant to change. Nonetheless, her attempts to create a language and forms to symbolize the mother-daughter relation offer a provocative window onto this field of inquiry, enriched by many of her other poems that represent different kinds of female sociality and pay tribute to women friends and historical figures. In such texts, Negri attends to social, cultural, and generational differences brought to bear on women's mediations of the body and sociocultural institutions.

This exploratory examination of how some of the major women poets working within and beyond avant-garde movements in the interwar years each formulated the notion of the maternal and produced highly differentiated paradigms of female artistic identity construction and poetics highlights the significant role that sexual politics play in the production of poetry and the ideology structuring the Italian canon of interwar literature. By broadening the field of vision to explore women's poetics, we can see that sociocultural debates of the time appear in a different cast. The redactions of the *generatrice* articulated by Aleramo, Goretti, Negri, and Pozzi engage specifically with the controversial issue of women's positions in life and art and represent attempts to bridge the split between mind and body, creation and procreation, a construct that was mass-mediated during Fascism but that has structured elite discourses of philosophy since Aristotle. Illustrating the central importance of motherhood in this metaphysical and material problem, Jane Gallop (1988) argues that "the mind-body split makes the mother into an inhuman monster by dividing the human realm of culture, history, and politics from the realm of love and the body where mother carries, bears, and tends her children" (2). It is significant that in the specific context of Italian Fascism such diverse figures as Benedetto Croce, anti-Fascist philosopher and critic, and Giovanni Gentile (1934), idealist philosopher and the foremost theoretician of the regime, deploy traditional maternal metaphors to exploit the mind-body split in defense of male cultural production.[34] Thus, the interventions performed by women writers to reconceptualize the mother as an agent of culture, bearing new forms and meanings for female generation, create a site and codes for an alternative ideology of gender and poetry.

However, the conflicts between the notions of the mother-poet posited by the artists examined and the metaphors and linguistic practices constituting them raise further questions about referentiality and how avant-garde as well as mimetic literary forms may restructure hierarchies of gender and genre. As Gallop (1988) cautions:

> A poetics of experience is no poetics at all if we understand poetry to be that effect which finds a loophole in the law of the symbolic. But if the poetics of experience is one that aims for a poiesis of experience, that attempts to re-construct experience itself, to produce a re-metaphorization, then although we cannot embrace simple unquestioned referentiality, neither can we unproblematically deny referentiality. (99)

We must ask whether the models of the *generatrice*, as products of women's thought and artistic practices, become caught in the threads of humanism binding the logic of the maternal or manage to produce a referential system enabling the transformation of the social, cultural, and political body. More important, by employing the mother-poet as the figure to symbolize women's relations to art and daily living, do these authors maintain the lines of the heterosexist regime? Does this symbolic economy exclude the lesbian poetic subject?[35] Or, by virtue of the different articulations of the mother-poet and the sociosymbolic meanings becoming her, might women's poetic discourses serve to highlight the maternal as a performative construction in culture and society, therefore inviting future interventions?

Such questions make it obvious that much more archival research and critical reading must be done if we are to explore the issues posed by the paradigm of *generatrice* as theory and practice, as well as the conflicting positions developed on female eroticism, nationalism, technology, and war, among other topics. Indeed, the study of literary works written by women during Fascism has barely begun. The examination of women's writings within the particular context of their production and reception enables us to explore the aesthetic, social, and political functions they may have performed as contingent signifying practices. Systematic studies of the corpographies that women generated in diverse genres through their structures, images, and linguistic practices would have far-ranging implications for the ways we think about Italian culture during the regime and in the postwar democracy. Moreover, reviewing this phase in literary genealogies constituted by women and the ways in which their texts intersect with, challenge, or restructure the broader dynamics shaping the discursive field forces us to reconsider normative paradigms of the feminine, Fascism, high literature, mass culture, and the avant-garde, as well as the sexual and national politics of vision authorizing their boundaries.

Notes

Introduction

Unless otherwise noted, all translations from Italian to English are my own.

1. The above epigraph is drawn from the *PrimeTime Live* interview that was aired by ABC on 2 April 1992 (transcript no. 239). I have made some revisions to the translation. For readers interested in historical treatments of the subjects that Judd Rose lapidarily presents, Alexander De Grand (1989) provides a concise history of Italian Fascism and how the Ethiopian campaign fit in the regime's foreign policy and colonial enterprises in his book *Italian Fascism*. Recent studies on the complex, changing relationships between the Italian Jews and the Fascist state in the early years of the regime, after the adoption of the racial laws in 1938, and during World War II and the Nazi Occupation include Leon Poliakov's *Jews under the Italian Occupation* (1983), Susan Zuccotti's *The Italians and the Holocaust* (1987), Alexander Stille's *Benevolence and Betrayal* (1993), and Philip V. Cannistraro and Brian Sullivan's *Il Duce's Other Woman* (1993).

2. In one sense, the irony that the virile, macho duce is re-presented through the feminine figure of his granddaughter cannot escape us. On the other hand, this logic in some ways replicates the deployment of woman as symbol in the Fascist dictatorship, as examined by Mariolina Graziosi (1995). For a similar treatment of Alessandra Mussolini see Eric Alterman, "The New Face of Fascism" (1994). Luciano Cheles (1991) conducts an important analysis of the images of women constructed in graphic propaganda by the Movimento sociale italiano (MSI) party from the 1970s to the 1990s.

3. The events and policies currently selected to define Benito Mussolini and Fascism clearly bear out the claim advanced by Walter Benjamin and Michel Foucault, among others, that present concerns shape the ways in which history is reconstructed and interpreted. Although the media now tend to focus on what they see as the violent and thus defining moments of the Fascist regime, as John P. Diggins (1972) points out in his analysis of American responses to Fascism, *Mussolini and Fascism*, in the 1920s and early 1930s Mussolini was not lacking supporters, ranging

from diplomats to news correspondents and jazz singers, who thought he would finally discipline those "unruly Italians."

4. I thank Giovanna Miceli Jeffries for alerting me to this essay by Eco.

5. Giving a broad idea about the numbers of women active in writing professions during Fascism, Stanis Ruinas (1930) sites more than five hundred female authors in *Scrittrici e scribacchine d'oggi,* whereas Maria Castellani, director of the Fascist Professional Women's Association, estimated there were some 391 Italian women writers and journalists in 1936, as noted in Alexander De Grand (1976, 960). However, much more archival research needs to be done to document biographical and bibliographical information on women authors and the works they published during the interwar period. For example, the two volumes of Maria Bandini Buti's landmark work *Donne d'Italia: Poetesse e scrittrici,* the first volume published in 1941 and the second in 1942, are virtually brimming with the names of literary women writing in diverse periods and genres. It is an invaluable resource for identifying authors who published during the twenties and thirties, in some cases achieving critical and popular success, yet who were not included in postwar literary histories. Similarly, in *Poetesse d'Italia* Camilla Bisi (1916) analyzes emergent trends in women's poetry, providing the names of many new poets still active in the interwar period. Based on these materials and my own archival research, it would be premature to speculate about the numbers of publications by women authors during Fascism, or which genres, if any, were more popular among literary women. Indeed, among the writers examined here, some figures show artful versatility in multiple genres. For example, Amalia Guglielminetti, who made her debut in poetry, wrote novels and short fiction. Ada Negri won critical acclaim for her autobiography, poetry, and short stories. Similarly, Grazia Deledda and Alba De Céspedes excelled in short fiction and the novel.

6. To their merit, such critics as Croce, Ravegnani, Camillo Pellizzi, and Borgese devoted sustained, serious attention to the issues raised by women's poetry and fiction about gender and literary production. For a discussion of the potential reasons why major works by women authors, widely reviewed and applauded during the 1920s and 1930s, were subsequently written out of the canon, see my afterword in *Unspeakable Women* (1993).

7. These essays, along with others by Bottai, provocatively articulate the political relations between Fascism and culture, and the undecidability of the regime's aesthetic designs. They appear in the collection *La politica delle arti* (1992).

8. Samples of these visual discourses are available in Laura Malvano, *Fascismo e politica dell'immagine* (1988) and Steven Heller and Louise Fili, *Italian Art Deco* (1993).

9. Significant exceptions that open this area of inquiry include *La nuova italiana* by Elisabetta Mondello (1987), *La corporazione delle donne,* edited by Marina Addis Saba (1988), and the individually authored essays in my edited collection *Mothers of Invention* (1995), which explore diversified forms of cultural production, including cinema, poetry, sculpture and painting, fashion, and avant-garde texts.

10. For detailed, thoughtful examinations of the diversified female models constituted in the Fascist state, see Elisabetta Mondello (1987), Marina Addis Saba (1988), Luisa Passerini (1987), and Victoria De Grazia (1992).

11. Barbara Spackman's (1995) brilliant essay on Fascist women's deployment of the rhetoric of virility expands on this notion, proposed in works by Alice Yaeger

Kaplan (1986) and Zeev Sternhell (1986), and forces us to see the heterogeneity of Fascist ideology in its complexity.

12. This passage is drawn from an interview in Sandra Petrignani's *Le signore della scrittura* (1984, 40).

13. This approach is indebted to Rita Felski (1989), who calls for critical assessments that address both the aesthetic and social value of artifacts. On the central ways in which the material and symbolic/social imbricate, Mary Douglas (1982) contends, "The social body constrains the way the physical body is perceived. The physical experience of the body, always modified by the social categories through which it is known, sustains a particular view of society. There is a continual exchange of meanings between the two kinds of bodily experience so that each reinforces the categories of the other" (65).

14. See *From Margins to Mainstream* by Carol Lazzaro-Weis (1993) for a splendid examination of this debate and the positions that Italian feminist critics have developed.

15. Here I have in mind insightful, foundational texts that have shaped debates on modernism in the American academy, though in some cases the authors work in foreign language departments. These include, for instance, *After the Great Divide* by Andreas Huyssen (1986), *Modernism,* edited by Monique Chefdor et al. (1986), and certainly the paradigms proposed by Ihab Hassan for understanding the modern and the postmodern, advanced in *The Postmodern Turn* (1987).

One. Unseduced Mothers: Female Subjectivities and the Transgression of Fascistized Femininity

1. Among the most important works adopting consent as the primary interpretative category are *Mussolini il duce: Gli anni del consenso, 1929–1936* (1974) by Renzo De Felice, *La fabbrica del consenso* (1975) by Philip V. Cannistraro, *The Culture of Consent* (1981) by Victoria De Grazia, and *La donna "nera"* (1976) by Maria Antonietta Macciocchi. De Grazia's contributions to "Alle origini della cultura di massa" and "Culture popolari negli anni del fascismo" clearly signal the shift from the consent paradigm to critical methods enabling analyses of contradictions among and within female subjectivities. Since the writing of this essay, the publication in 1992 of De Grazia's *How Fascism Ruled Women,* which documents a plurality of female models with extensive archival research while analyzing the shifting positions that women adopted in relation to the regime's sexual politics, stands as a landmark for as-yet-unexplored directions in the study of women as writing and reading subjects during the dictatorship.

2. Macciocchi's analysis of women's relations to Italian Fascism, from which she draws conclusions regarding women's complicity with current forms of fascist ideology, continues to be cited by scholars from Italy and elsewhere and thus merits a critical rereading. See, for example, Elaine Marks and Isabelle de Courtivron, eds., *New French Feminisms* (1980), and an earlier, though important article by Jane Caplan, "Introduction to Female Sexuality in Fascist Ideology" (1979), which contextualizes Macciocchi's theoretical concerns in her article "Female Sexuality in Fascist Ideology," appearing in the same volume of *Feminist Review.* (I thank Thomas Piontek for re-

ferring me to Caplan's article.) What concerns me here, however, is how Macciocchi's interrogation of female consent to the Fascist ideology of femininity has structured the thinking of literary critics who equate the inferior political status of women with inferior literary production and, as a consequence, represent this twenty-year period as a gap in the tradition of Italian women's writing. Important works, however, that work through this model include Augustus Pallotta, "Dacia Maraini" (1984), Paola Blelloch, *Quel mondo dei guanti e delle stoffe* (1987), and Maryse Jeuland-Meynaud, "Le identificazioni della donna nella narrativa di Elsa Morante" (1989). Sharon Wood (1995) presents a different view in *Italian Women's Writing 1860–1994*, which contextualizes women's texts in a sociohistorical frame.

3. For a provocatively engaging analysis of Mussolini's forms of address and antecedents, see Barbara Spackman, "The Fascist Rhetoric of Virility" (1990).

4. It is beyond the scope of this essay to examine either the convergence of Fascist and Catholic ideologies of woman and the family or the regional, socioeconomic, and political differences shaping both the popular reconstitution of Catholicism in different areas of Italy and women's different relations to Catholic systems of belief. For a salient analysis of this topic and a rich bibliography, see Stefania Portaccio, "La donna nella stampa popolare cattolica" (1981) and De Grazia, *How Fascism Ruled Women* (1992).

5. In *La voce che è in lei* (1980), Giuliana Morandini states that in the 1870s "besides opposing their oppression, [Italian] women, and therefore women writers, request work and autonomy, they want to participate in public life, and to have a political voice. Precisely in the 1870s, the request for women's suffrage is presented several times in parliament, and is strongly opposed. The same irritations and fears over 'the dissolution of the family and morality' cause the first battles for divorce" (15). In addition to considering the roots of positivist anthropology anchoring the claims made about woman in the 1920s and 1930s, we must also give serious thought to the components distinguishing elaborations of Fascist theories of sexual difference, as Lucia Re forcefully argues in "Fascist Theories of 'Woman' and the Construction of Gender" (1995).

6. Cinzia Blum's reappraisal of Marinetti was first presented in the paper "'L'uomo metallizzato e il cuore a compartimenti stagni': Defense Strategies in Marinetti's Discourse on Love," given at the 1989 American Association of Teachers of Italian conference. See also her article "Rhetorical Strategies and Gender in Marinetti's Futurist Manifesto" (1990), and Lucia Re's "Futurism and Feminism" (1989), which maps the contradictory drifts in Marinetti's positions on woman, women, and feminism. Marinetti's writings and the relations between futurism, Italian Fascism, and modernity have recently become a hot topic of debate, as seen, for example, in Russell A. Berman, "The Aestheticization of Politics" (1990), Jeffrey Schnapp, "Forwarding Address" (1990), and "Epic Demonstrations" (1992) and Andrew Hewitt, *Fascist Modernism* (1993).

7. Meldini's study of how woman figures in Italian Fascist ideology includes an extensive collection of articles written by Fascist exponents and ideologues, published primarily in Fascist journals. Unless otherwise noted, my examples in this section are taken from this collection of individually authored articles.

8. Meldini notes that in the 1934–35 academic year females comprised 88 percent

of the students in elementary school, 69 percent of those in middle school, and only 16 percent of those in high school.

9. According to the statistics provided by Meldini (1975, 73), the numbers of women employed in several sectors (domestic services, commerce, finance, administration, teaching, and health care) increased, sometimes markedly, between 1921 and 1931, while female employment in agriculture, the sector that Mussolini attempted to strengthen, sustained a notable decline. Increased mechanization in farming and population shifts from rural to urban areas may, in part, explain the decline in agriculture.

10. For a detailed examination of fashion as an expression of identity, desires, and ideas, see also Elizabeth Wilson, *Adorned in Dreams* (1985). More specifically, in *Bodily Regimes* (1995) Karen Pinkus offers a wealth of information and analysis of fashion, consumer culture, and advertising in the Fascist regime. Furthermore, as she points out, in view of the long history of anorexia, today we cannot uncritically read the slender female body as a form of resistance. My reading is intended to propose how Fascist commentators responded to models of the female body, as based on their writings. I agree that this issue merits further thought with respect to the complex relations of power during the interwar years.

11. See Leslie Caldwell, "Reproducers of the Nation" (1986), Passerini, *Fascism in Popular Memory* (1987), and De Grazia, *How Fascism Ruled Women* (1992) for studies of women's mediations of Fascist demographic policies.

12. In *Fascist Modernism*, Andrew Hewitt (1993) thoughtfully maps the points of convergence and divergence in the positions developed by Marinetti and Mussolini, respectively, on the nation, empire, and colonialism. See also Jeffrey Schnapp, "Forwarding Address" (1990).

13. This translation is drawn from Sergio Pacifici's *The Modern Italian Novel from Capuana to Tozzi* (1973, 49). I have revised some antiquated terminology and restored some images.

14. The short fiction on the cultural page originally replaced serialized novels and provided entertainment for "popular readers lacking the means to buy novels" (letter to the author from *Il resto del Carlino*, 19 March 1984).

15. We must keep in mind that illiteracy rates in Italy were still relatively high and were influenced by class, sex, and geographic location. According to Elisabetta Mondello (1987), in 1921 female illiteracy stood at 30.4 percent as compared to 24.4 percent among men, with higher rates of illiteracy among inhabitants of rural areas and southern Italy. An important point to be made about the short fiction published on the third page is that it generated social practices of reading, whereby stories were read aloud at home and in public places. See Enrico Falqui (1965).

16. Here we must also keep in mind that, as Edward R. Tannenbaum (1972) notes, it was not uncommon practice for newspapers to violate press orders.

17. Letter to the author from *Il resto del Carlino*, 19 March 1984.

18. For a comprehensive analysis of linguistic practices elaborated in popular literature by women writers, see Daniela Curti, "Il linguaggio del racconto rosa" (1987a).

19. Many of the short stories to which I refer appear in my collection *Unspeakable Women* (1993). For a closer analysis of some of these texts, which lies beyond the scope of this essay, see my "Poetics of Discovery" (1988).

20. See Beverly Allen's introduction to *The Defiant Muse* (1986).

Two. Pathologies of Autobiography and Outlaw Discourses

1. Camillo Pellizzi represents this tendency and exerted significant influence as both a literary critic and Fascist ideologue. Among his important works of this time are *Problemi e realtà del fascismo* (1924) and *Fascismo-aristocrazia* (1925).

2. In his introduction to *Studies in Autobiography* (1988), James Olney provides a useful overview of autobiography's changing status in literary studies. To give some idea of the situation in Italian studies, out of 177 entries under "Autobiography and Italy" in the MLA *Bibliography* (1981–92), there are ten article-length studies on women writers, four of which are dedicated to Sibilla Aleramo. Making allowances for some oversights, this picture is still dismal. Critical volumes on autobiography also show the scant attention that female writers have received thus far. For instance, in *Annali d'Italianistica* 4 (1986), an indispensable collection of theoretical and critical essays on autobiography, only one study out of fifteen, "Ecce Foemina" by Maurizio Viano, tests current theories of the genre against the writing of a female autobiographer. Since the writing of this essay in 1993, Graziella Parati has made an important new contribution to this field of study with her book *Public History, Private Stories* (1996).

3. In *Le pacte autobiographique* (1975, 14), Lejeune defines autobiography as a "récit rétrospectif en prose qu'une personne réelle fait de sa propre existence, lorsqu'elle met l'accent sur sa vie individuelle, en particulier sur l'histoire de sa personnalité" (a retrospective account in prose that a real person writes about his [or her] existence when the emphasis is put on one's individual life, in particular, on the history of one's personality).

4. "Autobiografia e romanzo" (1985) by Arrigo Stara, "Per una storia dell'autobiografismo metafisico vociano" (1984) by Clelia Martignoni, and "La cerchia infuocata" (1986) by Paolo Briganti are representative of this general approach. For a detailed treatment of the Vociani, see Romano Luperini, *Letteratura e ideologia nel primo Novecento italiano* (1973).

5. I am thinking here of Boine's autobiographical criticism in *Il peccato e altre cose* (1914), Papini's lyrical autobiography *Un uomo finito* (1913), Ardengo Soffici's realistic autobiographical work *Giornale di bordo* (1915), and Piero Jahier's lyric fragments portraying his early artistic development in *Ragazzo* (1919).

6. See, for instance, Ravegnani's characterization of Aleramo's *Amo, dunque sono* in *Contemporanei* (1930, 62), and Pellizzi's assessment of Maria Luisa Fiumi and Ada Negri in *Le lettere italiane del nostro secolo* (1929, 74–79). However, as Elizabeth Schultz argues in "To Be Black and Blue" (1981), personal history has traditionally been an important form of writing among oppressed groups, employed to represent and resist their relationship to the dominant society and culture (109).

7. See Salvatore Comes, *Ada Negri da un tempo all'altro* (1970) for the text of the letter that Mussolini wrote to Negri on reading her autobiography and for subsequent correspondence between the two figures (117).

8. Bruce Merry explores some of these difficult issues in "Ada Negri" (1988).

9. Page numbers of all subsequent references to this work will appear parenthetically in the text.

10. See Sidonie Smith, *A Poetics of Women's Autobiography* (1987, 46–51).

11. Mariolina Graziosi's study "Gender Struggle and the Social Manipulation and Ideological Use of Gender Identity in the Interwar Years" (1995) re-presents and examines the gender warfare that took place immediately following World War I and during Fascism. See also Perry Wilson's well-documented work *The Clockwork Factory* (1993), which focuses specifically on women's labor during Fascism, and David Forgacs's *Italian Culture in the Industrial Era, 1880–1980* (1990).

12. Two particularly insightful studies on mother-daughter relationships in women's life writing are Lynn Z. Bloom, "Heritages" (1980), and Stephanie A. Demetrakopoulos, "The Metaphysics of Matrilinearism in Women's Autobiography" (1980).

13. The relationships between Negri, her mother, and her brother, who is sent to live with an uncle living nearby, represent another source of ambivalence for the autobiographer yet is beyond the scope of this study.

14. In "Signore e signorine fra Otto e Novecento" (1988), Michela De Giorgio conducts a comprehensive study of female cultural models in Italian society of this period.

15. In "Leggere per scrivere" (1989), a comparative analysis of the thematic correspondences between autobiographies by Neera, Negri, Deledda, and Aleramo, Patrizia Zambon notes the fashioning of nature as a metaphor of women's literary experience and a site for symbolic expression.

16. For a more detailed account of the campaign against the intellectual woman conducted in Fascist publications, see Victoria De Grazia, *How Fascism Ruled Women* (1992).

17. All subsequent page references to this work will appear parenthetically in the text.

18. Bruce Merry represents this position in *Women in Modern Italian Literature* (1990).

19. Maria Marotti conducts an excellent examination of the thematic concerns and stylistic practices in postwar autobiographies by women authors in "Filial Discourses" (1994).

Three. Aeroromance: Reconfiguring Femininity, Fantasy, and Fascism

1. The nucleus of the theory Macciocchi presents in this book appears in her "Female Sexuality in Fascist Ideology" (1979) and is foregrounded by Jane Caplan's thoughtful assessment, "Introduction to Female Sexuality in Fascist Ideology" (1979). In "The Fascist Rhetoric of Virility" (1990), Barbara Spackman examines the complex, shifting valences of the signifier *virility* and its rhetorical effects in Mussolini's public address, showing how, at the metaphoric level, the rhetoric of virility actually seduces men as well as women, feminizing "all but the speaker himself" (84).

2. Among the recent studies on Mussolini's forms of self-display, see especially Luisa Passerini, *Mussolini immaginario* (1991), and Italo Calvino, "The Dictator's Hats" (1990).

3. This position in Italian scholarship on the romance genre is represented by Maria Pia Pozzato, *Il romanzo rosa* (1982), Antonia Arslan, "Vivere in rosa per vivere in casa" (1987), and Silvana Ghiazza, "La letteratura rosa negli anni venti-quaranta"

(1991). However, as Kay Mussell argues in *Fantasy and Reconciliation* (1984), romance texts engage a heterogeneous audience for diversified reasons and may confirm or challenge their experiences, beliefs, and hopes.

4. In her introduction to *Studies in Entertainment*, Tania Modleski (1986b) profiles the debates over mass culture as developed by the Frankfurt and Birmingham Schools of thought and proposes important new critical directions for theories of mass entertainment and their potential functions. For a more comprehensive idea of Adorno's positions on high and mass culture, which lie beyond the parameters of this study, see the letters and essays included in *Aesthetics and Politics* (1977).

5. In "The Androgynous Reader" (1992), Laura Kinsale advances a similar proposition, stating that "within the dynamic of reading a romance, the female reader *is* the hero, and also is the heroine-as-object-of-the-hero's-interest" (32). For a different perspective on the problematic of female identification, see Mary Ann Doane, *The Desire to Desire* (1987). Giuliana Bruno's *Streetwalking on a Ruined Map* (1993) examines problems associated with female spectatorship and identification within the specific context of Italy.

6. Among the extensive research conducted on the evolution of the romance genre in Italy and its relation to other forms of popular literature, especially useful are *Intorno al rosa* (1987), *La paraletteratura* (1977), Antonia Arslan Veronese, ed., *Dame, droga e galline* (1977), Umberto Eco, Marina Federzoni, Isabella Pezzini, and Maria Pia Pozzato, *Carolina Invernizio, Matilde Serao, Liala* (1979), and Angela Bianchini, *Il romanzo d'appendice* (1969).

7. In "Il romanzo rosa" (1987b) and "Il linguaggio del racconto rosa" (1987a), Curti conducts insightful analyses of the linguistic practices elaborated by women writers in romance fiction and the novel.

8. Fascist cultural politics in the mass media receive extensive analysis in Victoria De Grazia, *How Fascism Ruled Women* (1992), James Hay, *Popular Film Culture in Fascist Italy* (1987), and Adrian Lyttelton, *The Seizure of Power* (1973).

9. For the appeals made to female youth by Fascist organizations, the Catholic Church, and mass culture, see in particular De Grazia, *How Fascism Ruled Women* (1992) and Michela De Giorgio, *Le italiane dall'unità a oggi* (1992). Stefania Portaccio's essay "La donna nella stampa popolare cattolica" (1981) examines the contradictory messages on female beauty diffused by Catholic female models.

10. This conceptualization of mass culture, and of romance novels in particular, as a manipulative force engineering passive consent is also adopted by Lino Pertile in "Fascism and Literature" (1986), Maria Pia Pozzato, *Il romanzo rosa* (1982), and Antonia Arslan, "Vivere in rosa per vivere in casa" (1987).

11. The ads to which I specifically refer appeared in *La stampa*, 19 January 1931, 3 April 1931, and 17 April 1931. See also Elisabetta Mondello, *La nuova italiana* (1987) for historiographic information on the Italian fashion industry and advertisements published in the women's press during Fascism.

12. My analysis of Italian women's accomplishments in aviation is indebted to the archival information made available by De Giorgio in *Le italiane dall'unità a oggi* (1992), especially 254–59. For testimonies supplied by Italian male aviators about their feats during the interwar years, see the interesting collection *Cieli del mondo* (1994), edited by Gianni Guadalupi. The work *Italian Art Deco* (1993), edited by

Steven Heller and Louise Fili, furnishes a rich assortment of visual materials, documenting the use of airplane iconography on postcards, stamps, posters, and consumer products during the regime.

13. Claudia Salaris provides a useful analysis of the aeropoetics elaborated by women futurist poets and painters, as well as a varied selection of their works in *Le futuriste* (1982). Also interesting for the perspective it provides on futurist women and technology is Benedetta Cappa Marinetti's lyric novel *Astra e il sottomarino: Vita trasognata*, first published in 1935 and republished in 1991 by Editori del Grifo. In contrast to aeropoetics, here the avant-garde author draws on the technology of the submarine and feminine symbols of water and the sea.

Four. Continental Drift: The Politics of Realist Aesthetics and the Novel

1. This quotation is drawn from Ruth Ben-Ghiat, "The Politics of Realism" (1990, 153).

2. Interesting here is the ongoing commentary in news shows and the popular press about the "faces" of Fascism represented by Benito Mussolini and by current figures in the Italian Social Movement (MSI) party, now called the National Alliance. Representing Italian politics as more spectacle than substance, a *PrimeTime Live* interview with Alessandra Mussolini (2 April 1992) conducted during her campaign and a more recent article by Eric Alterman (1994), titled "The New Face of Fascism," faciley dismiss the ideas and policies that she claims to stand for. Furthermore, such sources doggedly attempt to give a crystal-clear idea of what Fascism "looks like" for the general public. As Alterman writes, "Benito Mussolini looked the way Fascists are supposed to. The egomaniacal Duce was a strutting peacock of a man, with big bulging pectorals, a shiny bald dome, and a jutting, muscular face that belonged on Hulk Hogan. Not so his granddaughter Alessandra Mussolini, who is poutily privileged and expensively groomed" (114). Thus, focusing on her beauty regime, he concludes, in a manner that would make Fascist ideologues of the twenties and thirties proud, that Gianfranco Fini "is clearly the brains" and Mussolini "is the alluring new visage of Fascism" (114). For a more informative, if general treatment of the coalition government and its participating members, see Niccolò d'Aquino, "Italy's Political Future" (1994).

3. In "The Aestheticization of Politics," Berman (1990) discusses the reasons why Benjamin cites Marinetti, which include Italy's paradigmatic importance as a case of the institutionalization of Fascism in the thirties and the figuration of Italy as a privileged site of aesthetic experience. Nonetheless, as Berman argues, the quotation from Marinetti's bombastic text catches the reader off-guard "because it breaks with the abstraction of the preceding argument" (49).

4. Among the growing number of recent studies that interrogate the notion and functions of aesthetics are Rita Felski, *Beyond Feminist Aesthetics* (1989), Richard J. Golsan, ed., *Fascism, Aesthetics, and Culture* (1992), Fredric Jameson, "Reflections on the Brecht-Lukács Debate" (in *The Ideologies of Theory* [1988]), Stephen Regan, ed., *The Politics of Pleasure* (1992), Bruce Robbins, ed., *Intellectuals* (1990), and Martha Woodmansee, *The Author, Art, and the Market* (1994).

5. The tendency to either overlook Italian modernism and the problems it raises for dominant paradigms in the American academy or to invoke F. T. Marinetti as the straw man rationalizing the dismissal of more than twenty years of Italian cultural production is by no means limited to *Modernism: Challenges and Perspectives,* edited by Monique Chefdor et al. (1986). Geoff Wade (1992), in "Marxism and Modernist Aesthetics," characterizes modernism of the East as "the progressive arm of Futurism (as opposed to Italian Futurism)," providing the main reference to Italian art in *The Politics of Pleasure.* In a similar gesture, Andreas Huyssen deploys Marinetti to illustrate the misogynist, masculinist trends of modernism in *After the Great Divide* (1986). Although his thesis, with which I agree, problematizes one male version of modernism presented by the Italian case, it does so by overshadowing other redactions fashioned by men and women writers in the avant-garde movement and beyond, issues that I take up in my study of poetry (chap. 5). If the anthology *Modernism: A Guide to European Literature 1890–1930,* edited by Malcolm Bradbury and James McFarlane (1991), merits attention for including among its forty-four selections an essay on Italian futurism, and two comparative studies that take into consideration Italo Svevo and Luigi Pirandello, the gaps and errors also deserve noting. Turning to the Chronology of Events, which lists major publications in the different communities of letters constructed by the editors, we find that conspicuous blank spaces follow the designation "Lat," which includes Spain, Italy, and Latin Europe, on no less than sixteen pages. (The politics of these categories, though intriguing, go beyond the immediate scope of my analysis.) Furthermore, in the entry for 1926 we see a glaring error in the name of Grazia Deledda (recipient of the Nobel Prize for Literature that year), here spelled "Deladda." For a thoughtful examination of where Italy fits in the current economy of art and theory, see Renate Holub, "Weak Thought and Strong Ethics" (1991).

6. In his controversial essay "Expressionism: Its Significance and Decline" (1981), Lukács concludes that, based on the German experience, "It is not accidental that fascism has accepted expressionism as part of its inheritance. Even in the field of literature, fascism has failed to produce anything genuinely new." However, he notes, fascism has produced a new "radicalism with which all knowledge of objective reality is rejected, and the irrational and mystical tendencies of the imperialist epoch are intensified to the point of nonsense" (111–12). Adorno (1973) voices a similar idea, though he focuses on the relations between mass culture and contemporary fascism.

7. According to Michele Giocondi (1990), *Nessuno torna indietro* has sold more than a million copies and continues to attract a large audience of contemporary readers. All of the translations from this novel are mine and are based on the 1938 edition, unless otherwise noted.

8. All of my quotations from *Maria Zef* are drawn from the English translation by Blossom Steinberg Kirschenbaum (1989).

9. The subject of the Italian novel, realism, and neorealism has generated an overwhelming amount of scholarship. Among the more recent studies on neorealism and the Italian novel that bear on my arguments are Giorgio Bàrberi Squarotti, *La forma e la vita* (1987), Salvatore Battaglia, *I facsimile della realtà* (1991), Alberto Cadioli, *Tra prosa d'arte e romanzo del Novecento (1920–1960)* (1989), Bruno Falcetto, *Storia della narrativa neorealista* (1992), and the still pertinent work by Romano

Luperini and Eduardo Melfi, *Neorealismo, neodecadentismo, avanguardie* (1981). See also Lucia Re's (1990) examination of debates about neorealism and Italo Calvino's aesthetics in *Calvino and the Age of Neorealism.*

10. For important examples from this debate, see the excellent translations provided by Jeffrey Schnapp and Barbara Spackman in "Selections from the Great Debate on Fascism and Culture: *Critica Fascista* 1926–1927" (1990).

11. As De Grazia (1992) notes in *How Fascism Ruled Women,* Sarfatti wielded tremendous power in the cultural undertakings of the regime and bestowed her patronage on the *Novecentisti* (229–30).

12. In "Epic Demonstrations" Jeffrey Schnapp (1992) maintains that Fascism did not merely "aestheticize" politics; instead, he states, "putting forward the first Modern(ist) politics of spectacle, it placed the conventional polarities of Marxist and Liberal theory under constant pressure, confusing superstructure with structure, private with public, the state with civil society. . . . Neither monolithic nor homogeneous, fascism's aesthetic overproduction relied on the ability of images to sustain contradiction and to make of paradox a productive principle" (3).

13. See Alberto Asor Rosa, "Lo stato democratico e i partiti politici" in *Storia della letteratura italiana,* vol. 1 (1982, 560–61, 604), and Romano Luperini, *Il Novecento,* vol. 2 (1981, 368).

14. In addition to Ben-Ghiat's "The Politics of Realism" (1990), see also her "Neorealism in Italy, 1930–1950" (1991).

15. See Falcetto, *Storia della narrativa neorealista* (1992) and Pasquale Voza, "Il problema del realismo negli anni Trenta" (1981).

16. Daniela Curti (1987a) examines the literary language fashioned by Italian women writers in the twenties in "Il linguaggio del racconto rosa."

17. In *Una donna* (1906), Sibilla Aleramo talks about writing "the book" that would cast off forever the trappings of femininity designed for women by male authors, and too often reproduced in women's literature. Likewise, Amalia Guglielminetti called for fellow female authors to interrogate, as no man could, the conditions of their own existences and to give the resultant ideas and feelings the particular literary voices suited to them, thus creating a sincere, truthful women's art. See "Aridità sentimentale" (1911).

18. Matilde Serao has become the subject of several important revisionist readings. Among them are "The Early Matilde Serao" by Lucienne Kroha, in her *The Woman Writer in Late-Nineteenth-Century Italy* (1992) and, by the same author, "Matilde Serao" (1991), and "Angel v. Monster" by Ursula Fanning (1991).

19. See Liliana Scalero, "Le donne che scrivono" (1937, 211–16).

20. Beverly Allen (1992) provides an important critique of the relations among gender, nation, and narration in the specific context of Italy in "Terrorism Tales." See especially 168–69.

21. Paola Drigo made her literary debut with the volume of short stories *La fortuna* (1913), followed by prose fiction published in literary journals, the collection of poetry *Col mio infinito* (1921), the book *La signorina Anna* (1932), and the memoirs *Fine d'anno,* published along with *Maria Zef* in 1936.

22. Foucault's theory of tactical polyvalence is also pertinent here. He states that "we must make allowance for the complex and unstable process whereby discourse

can be both an instrument and an effect of power, but also a hindrance, a stumbling block, a point of resistance and a starting point for an opposing strategy" (1980, 100–1).

23. The 1930 study *Indagine sulle condizioni di vita dei contadini italiani,* edited by Alfonso Ciuffolini, clearly shows the concern over the status and changing behaviors of countrywomen. In all of the chapters, which provide evaluations of the living conditions, socioeconomic structure, customs, and emigration trends in the different rural zones throughout the regions of Italy, there is a special section dedicated to women—their work habits, behaviors, and even style of dress—in an attempt to document the possible effects of modern urban mores.

24. *Maria Zef* also represents an important antecedent to the overnight best-seller *Volevo i pantaloni* by Lara Cardella (1989), which won acclaim for its treatment of incest in a Sicilian town.

25. Drigo leaves no room for doubt that Mariutine's submissive obedience is socially and economically conditioned. Following the girl's initial rebellion against Zef, in which she showers him with blows, the narrator states: "As a dog is able to break loose from the chain to which he is accustomed and can even bite the hand that feeds him, but quickly returns of his own free will with lowered tail and full of fear to the collar of slavery, so she bent her shoulders and lowered her head, gripped by terror and remorse over what she had dared" (167–68).

26. For an examination of the rich range of meanings created and attached to the words *city* and *country,* see Raymond Williams (1973), *The Country and the City.*

27. See Francesco Flora (1945), *Note di servizio,* 84. In an interview with Sandra Petrignani (1984, 40), De Céspedes recalls how the Fascist state attempted to silence her.

28. Important here is Giancarlo Lombardi's (1994) excellent study on the panoptical in *Quaderno proibito* and *Il rimorso,* which offers a different view of De Céspedes's novelistic production.

29. In 1928, Mussolini links the city, disease, and infertility, stating, "At a certain moment, the city grows in an unhealthy way, pathologically, not by its own virtue, but because of the contribution made by other people. The more the city grows and swells into a metropolis, the more infertile it becomes" (in Meldini 1975, 144.)

30. I have drawn this translation from Millicent Marcus (1986), *Italian Film in the Light of Neorealism,* 47–48.

31. I thank Andrè Iazzi for his keen eye, which lit on this interesting work of cultural criticism during one of his many travels.

32. As noted earlier, this novel went through several editions during Fascism and thereafter. Differences in the two editions I have used for this study raise some interesting questions about revisions that De Céspedes made after Fascism. For example, the 1938 version includes a lengthy passage describing the new city, Littoria, which is later revised. In addition, the author changed the sequencing of some passages and eliminated certain details from descriptive passages, which makes the style more evocative in the latter version. These revisions deserve future study but for the most part go beyond the scope of this essay. Unless otherwise indicated, the quotations are taken from the 1938 edition.

33. For more detailed analyses of the Grimaldi as a prison, see Nerenberg (1991) and Gallucci (1995).

34. The 1938 edition includes a lengthier passage on Emanuela's walking style. Andrea notes that Emanuela's walk was the first thing that struck his eye, exhibiting an unaffected, effortless harmony that distinguished her from other women. He also implies that her walk is a product of economic privilege, as well as her "challenging" femininity (275, 276).

35. I want to thank Barbara Spackman for this insight.

36. As Nerenberg tells us in *Habeas Corpus*, the representation of the lesbian subject is not without precedent in discursive formations of this time. Indeed, in the field of women's literary discourses, Aleramo's *Amo, dunque sono* (1927) includes fleeting references to her lesbian relations. With regard to the importance of the girls' boarding school in film, also important is Jacqueline Reich's (1995) "Reading, Writing, and Rebellion," which provides a detailed analysis of the schoolgirl comedy genre, mapping therein the plurality of female positionalities constructed and the trajectory of ideological subversion.

37. Among the many recent studies that include examinations of the diverse figurations of Rome in neorealist cinema are Millicent Marcus, *Italian Film in the Light of Neorealism* (1986), Pierre Sorlin, *European Cinemas, European Societies 1939–1990* (1991), especially 117–26, Angela Dalle Vacche, *The Body in the Mirror* (1992), and James Hay, "Invisible Cities/Visible Geographies" (1993). Giuliana Bruno (1993) offers a provocative analysis of women, urban space, and female spectatorship, among other issues, in her study on Elvira Notari's city films, *Streetwalking on a Ruined Map*.

Five. Generatrices of Poiesis: Registers of Women's Poetry, Modernism, and the Avant-garde

1. Numerous studies have been dedicated to the relations between futurism and Fascism. Among the most recent are Renzo De Felice, ed., *Futurismo, cultura e politica* (1988); Emilio Gentile, "The Conquest of Modernity" (1994); Clara Orban, "Women, Futurism, and Fascism" (1995); Claudia Salaris, *Artecrazia* (1992); Alberto Schiavo, ed., *Futurismo e fascismo* (1981); Jeffrey Schnapp, "Forwarding Address" (1990); and Barbara Spackman, "The Fascist Rhetoric of Virility" (1990). Cinzia Sartini Blum's excellent study *The Other Modernism* (1996) was published as this work went to press, so I was unable to incorporate her arguments into my discussions.

2. Certainly there are other important reasons for the underrepresentation of modern women poets, including periodization, how thematic interests and expressive innovations relate to what scholars construct as primary sociohistorical and artistic concerns of their age, and sometimes, as in the example of "hermetic emotion" provided by Falqui, even the forms of affect imbuing the worldview, read by commentators as typifying the spirit of the times. These issues deserve further analysis, which, however, goes beyond the parameters of this study.

3. Cara's anthology provides useful bibliographic information for some seventeen collections of Italian women's poetry published primarily in the 1980s.

4. See, in particular, Lucia Re's engaging discussion of these issues in "Mythic Revisionism" (1993).

5. For a recent example, see John Picchione and Lawrence R. Smith, *Twentieth-*

Century Italian Poetry (1993), an excellent anthology that, however, also represents this general tendency. Likewise, in the field of criticism, overviews of twentieth-century Italian poetry have overlooked how women's lyrical production figured in the currents shaping canon formation during the interwar years. Among recently published works, *The Modern Italian Lyric* (1986) by F. J. Jones and *Poesia non-poesia anti-poesia del '900 italiano* (Poetry, nonpoetry, antipoetry of the Italian twentieth century) by Vittoriano Esposito (1992) illustrate the tendency to give scant attention to the issues raised by women's poetry. In his salient, detailed analysis of individual poets and currents, Jones mentions that the potential connections between such postwar women poets as Ada Merini and Margherita Guidacci and their predecessors, Aleramo and Pozzi, for instance, merit notice. Yet he does not pursue the topic further.

Esposito, on the other hand, neither entirely excludes the production and reception of women's poetry of the twenties and thirties nor glosses over the subject. Instead, his substantive work, which offers a broad variety of topics and is impeccably documented, features an essay on the conflictual assessments that Ada Negri's poetry generated among Italian critics. As the sole example, Negri thus stands for the pluralistic cast of women poets writing in the first half of the century, which boasted such diverse figures as Antonia Pozzi and Enif Robert, for example. The structure of Esposito's work, comprising four major sections, further compounds the complexity of problems associated with representing women's contributions to the genre of poetry. Whereas three of the sections examine questions and issues shaping the canon of poetic discourses, the third section, titled "Le donne nel parnaso italiano" (Women in Italian poetry) actually contradicts its heading. Here we find biographical and bibliographical information on more than fifty postwar female poets. This representation of gifted women who have distinguished themselves in the art of poetry unquestionably marks a welcome development. The internal organization Esposito adopts for his book, however, suggests that these literary women are not really "in" the circle of Italian poetry; they appear in a section unto themselves, visually and conceptually isolated. We cannot overlook the effects that this fashion of bracketing contemporary women poets has on how we think about their art and its relation to the canon and to the lyrical projects undertaken by interwar progenitrices. Esposito misses the opportunity to contextualize this section with a brief outline of the contours shaping women's poems written during Fascism and their authors, who might have symbolic or literary significance as forerunners. Thus, the ways in which Rosa Barbieri, Daria Menicanti, Milena Milani, and Elia Malagò, for example, fabricate the female body and erotics in verse, rewrite Western mythologies, or attack the patriarchal order of the symbolic and daily life seem to represent a new phenomenon.

6. The introduction to Costa-Zalessow's (1982) anthology documents the venerable tradition of Italian women's poetry and the history of publishing collections dedicated to female poets, the latter of which dates back to the Renaissance. To its credit, the selection of poems translated in *The Defiant Muse*, edited by Beverly Allen et al. (1986), underscores the strong, continuous production of poetry by Italian women through the ages. The editors also include sample poems by women who made their literary debuts in the late-nineteenth and early-twentieth centuries and continued to publish their work during Fascism.

7. Although contemporary recommendations for nonsexist writing suggest avoiding the suffix -*trix,* the term *generatrix* is essential for understanding how the women poets examined here *recast* the figure of the generatrix as a gendered model denoting both artistic creativity and procreativity. From a poetic and conceptual perspective, the model of the generatrix is equally important for the critical positions and notions I examine, the nuances of which would be weakened if I were to use the term *female generator.*

8. In "The Modern and the Postmodern," Dino S. Cervigni (1991) analyzes the specific meanings of the term *modernismo* in Italian culture and history, pointing to some of the problems this designation presents. Because of the religious connotations of the word *modernismo* in Italian, as he explains, the terms *il moderno* (the modern) and *il postmoderno* (the postmodern) are used in debates on modernism and postmodernism in Italian studies. The volume of *Annali d'Italianistica* on "The Modern and the Postmodern" (1991) makes an important contribution to understanding how these issues are framed among Italian scholars. See also *Modernismo/ Modernismi* (1991), edited by Giovanni Cenci, which unites essays on an engaging range of subjects, such as imagism and vorticism, the modernist novel in Britain and Russia, futurism, myth, and the modern metropolis.

9. See Frabotta (1976) and Re (1993) on the reluctance of some women poets to identify with the nomenclature of *woman poet.*

10. Croce also elaborates this paradigm of poetic generation and regeneration in his essay "La contessa Lara-Annie Vivanti" (1948b, 340), where he notes a lack of attention to the regenerative phase in women's poetry.

11. F. J. Jones (1986) offers an insightful analysis of how Orphic myth structured much Italian men's poetry, arguing that "during the period between the two wars . . . this particular outlook gave rise to a modern religion of art, a modern orphism" (33).

12. As Salaris points out, Angelini is recognized as the first documented Italian words-in-freedom woman futurist, though Flora Bonheur, author of *Diario d'una giovane donna futurista* (ca. 1914) was likely a precursor. For samples of Angelini's words-in-freedom, see Salaris (1982, 51–52). The ways in which words-in-freedom texts by Angelini and Benedetta, for example, challenge the dualistic conceptions of the relations between visual and verbal forms of art merit further study. As Marina Perez de Mendiola (1995) suggests, in the hegemonic relations between the arts during modernism, poetry asserts dominance, a form of "tyranny of the pen over the paintbrush," constituting a binary regime: "Reading versus seeing, the verbal expressivity versus the speechless image" (73). The use of graphic and verbal signs in such poems as Benedetta's "Benedetta fra le donne," which describes a female positionality visually and verbally, raises provocative questions regarding sexual and artistic hierarchies.

13. For a more comprehensive analysis of this debate, see pages 128–29 above in my chapter on realism. The most important point for this discussion of women and men in the futurist movement is the way that the positions on futurism taken by such diverse critics as Lukács, Benjamin, and Adorno in cultural commentary of the 1930s have, for the most part, been recycled in the American academy. Indeed, within the pluralistic field of discourses on "realist" versus experimental art, Lukács and Benjamin harmonized to disparage Marinetti and futurist aesthetics as fascistic

tools, the tenor of their different arguments rarely veering off key. This tendency and the perception authorizing it have persisted in the equally broad range of contemporary approaches to the phenomenon of modernism, as illustrated by Matei Calinescu (1986) and Geoff Wade (1992), who dismiss Italian futurism as a regressive, aberrant strain of the avant-garde, for its associations with Fascism. The pronouncement offered by Ihab Hassan (1987) also seems to occlude the speculations raised by his suggestive, eloquent portrait of the futurist artist, as he states, "With Marinetti, Futurism veered toward another extreme; with pick and axe, literature became the imaginary sacker of cities. Marinetti pretended to stand on the promontory of the centuries, and declaimed to the air" (17). He immediately adds that "Dadaism and Surrealism have yet to be fully assessed" (17). Oddly enough, the latter two movements, which have received markedly greater attention than futurism, appear open for discussion.

For different positions that show the importance of examining Italian futurism, see *Fascist Modernism* (1993), where Andrew Hewitt works through the model of aestheticization and meticulously maps its historical and ideological developments to locate contiguities between Fascist ideology and Marinetti's practices of art as a site for the production of new modes of living, a concept that might resonate with non-Italian avant-gardists; Peter Nicholls's study on the figuration of gender and technology in futurist aesthetics in "Futurism, Gender, and Theories of Postmodernity" (1987) and his more recent *Modernisms* (1995); and most particularly, the analyses of how women artists negotiated the difficult task of constructing subject positions in futurism conducted by Lucia Re (1989) in "Futurism and Feminism" and Clara Orban (1995) in "Women, Futurism, and Fascism." I also suggest that the provocative interventions enacted by futurists in the culture of daily living to incite revolutions in fashion (1913) and cuisine (1930s) may contradict the conventional dualities between "masculine" modernism and "feminine" mass culture.

14. Other important works among the growing historical and critical research on the space that avant-garde women made for themselves in the futurist movement are Graziella Parati, "The Transparent Woman" (1994); Claudia Salaris, *Le futuriste* (1982); Barbara Spackman, "Fascist Women and the Rhetoric of Virility" (1995); and Lea Vergine, *L'altra metà dell'avanguardia 1910–1940* (1980).

15. Recordings of futurist musical compositions are available on *Dada for Now: A Collection of Futurist and Dada Sound Works* (Liverpool, Ark). I want to thank Bernard Gendron for bringing this recording to my attention. *The Futurist Cookbook,* translated by Suzanne Brill (1989), contains an interesting assortment of writings on the revolution that Marinetti proposed for Italian cuisine, as well as group photographs (including a photo taken after the infamous car accident when Marinetti emerged from the "maternal ditch"), and recipes by avant-garde women and men.

16. The commentary and selections gathered in Salaris (1982) document the range of positions developed by women and men in the futurist movement in debates conducted from 1909 to the early 1940s on woman as an idealized cultural construction, female gender roles, and the functions that avant-garde women envisioned for themselves in the cultural and social revolution.

17. A few illustrative examples include Maria Ginanni's collections of poetry *Montagne trasparenti* (Transparent mountains) and *Il poema dello spazio* (The poem of space), published respectively in 1917 and 1919; Rosa Rosà's important novel *Una donna con tre anime* (A woman with three souls) of 1918; Enif Robert's controversial

Un ventre di donna (A woman's womb), coauthored with Marinetti and published in 1919; Benedetta's experimental novels *Le forze umane* (Human strengths, 1924), *Il viaggio di Gararà* (Gararà's journey, 1931), and *Astra e il sottomarino* (Astra and the submarine, 1935) as well as numerous words-in-freedom, plays, and tactile tables; and Gladia Angeli's provocatively titled epistolary diary *Pagine segrete di una donna* (A woman's secret pages), published in installments between the late thirties and early forties. For the most comprehensive biographic and bibliographic information on women in the Italian historical avant-garde, see Salaris (1982). Lucia Re (1995) carves out new ground in her analysis of the experimental novels *Le forze umane* and *Il viaggio di Gararà* by Benedetta, and *Nascita e morte della massaia* (Birth and death of a housewife, 1939) by Paola Masino.

18. See Clara Orban (1995) for an insightful reading of this scene. My analysis builds on her reading of the birthing metaphor as an erasure of woman, which therefore highlights the transgressive meanings of futurist women's "reappropriation" of the paradigm of social and symbolic rebirth to authorize multiple forms of female generation of self, life, and art.

19. See Salaris (1982, 141–44) for the full text.

20. Portions of the following analysis of Goretti's poem and how her aeropoetics relate to images of the airplane in futurist and Fascist discourses were first presented in my paper "Erector Sets and the Airplane: Aerogenerational Discourses by Women Futurists, 1930–1941," at the Center for Twentieth Century Studies conference on "Women and Aging: Bodies, Cultures, Generations" at the University of Wisconsin-Milwaukee, in 1996.

21. See Keala Jewell's *The Poiesis of History: Experimenting with Genre in Postwar Italy* (1992) for an insightful analysis of postwar debates about neorealist aesthetics and poetry, and the ways that such poets as Pier Paolo Pasolini, Mario Luzi, and Attilio Bertolucci create new meanings precisely by refashioning poetic discourses with traditional modes.

22. The title of this poem and the last three lines are translated by Bassanese (1995, 150). Unless otherwise noted, all translations are my own. See Bassanese's article "Sibilla Aleramo" (1995) for a thorough examination of Aleramo's poetics, and how her images of a mythic feminine self during Fascism competed with those of virility designed in Mussolini's forms of self-representation. For further analysis of Aleramo's forms of self-invention and textuality, see Keala Jewell (1984), "Un furore d'autocreazione."

23. For the original Italian passages, see *Un amore insolito* (1979, 19, 21).

24. The first nine lines of this poem are from Bassanese's translation (1995, 158).

25. My translations of the poems by Pozzi are based on the 1989 Garzanti edition, titled *Parole*, edited by Alessandra Cenni and Onorina Dino. In this edition, Pozzi's poems appear in the form they had before her father edited them, perhaps censoring images and ideas that were not to his own tastes, as Cenni and Dino suggest.

26. Maria Ginanni's piece "Paesaggio interno" (Inner landscape, 1917; in Verdone 1973, 148) exemplifies differences between the models of female subjectivity created by women futurists and the depth model that Pozzi fashions. For example, Ginanni projects dynamic inner life through constantly moving and changing shapes and colors.

27. The English translation of this poem by Nora Wydenbruck (Pozzi 1955, 159) uses "child" instead of "little girl," as indicated by *bambina*.

28. In "La meteora esistenziale e poetica di Antonia Pozzi," Laura Baffoni-Licata (1991, 366–67) performs a reading similar to that of Cenni.

29. The apparent contrasts between Negri's practices in life and literature show the complexities of her position in interwar politics and culture. She clearly treats gender as a problematic category in her prose and poetry works, adopting a critical stance toward socioeconomic conditions and attitudes that oppress women of different classes. She also, however, showed clear sympathies toward Mussolini, and what she perceived as his effective leadership in a project to strengthen Italian national life. Such poems as "L'anello d'acciaio" (The steel ring), which pays tribute to the sacrifice that women made by donating their wedding rings for the war effort (a controversial public demonstration) and "Le foglie" (The leaves), which decries the machine of war, create a site rife with contradictions deserving further scrutiny.

30. As Costa-Zalessow (1992) explains, the passionate voice of sexual abandon created by Negri in several poems published in *Il libro di Mara* appears outmoded today, if not downright melodramatic, yet, like Aleramo's love poems, it constructed a new poetic speaking position at the time. If some of the pieces speak of a slave-like spiritual and erotic dependence on the male beloved, it is also true that in "Quel giorno" (That day) and "Il ricordo" (The memory), we see the active pleasure of female sexuality and the positioning of the female speaker as both the object and subject of erotic desire, which may put into question the common notion that Negri's poems merely serve up rebaked D'Annunzianism.

31. The bibliography of theoretical and critical works on the mother and mother-daughter relations is too extensive to reproduce here. Among the works that are most pertinent for the arguments developed in this study are Alice E. Adams, *Reproducing the Womb* (1994); Jane Gallop, *Thinking through the Body* (1988); Shirley Nelson Garner et al., eds. *The (M)other Tongue* (1985); Marianne Hirsch, *The Mother/Daughter Plot* (1989); Luce Irigaray, *Je, tu, nous* (1993); Milan Women's Bookstore Collective, *Sexual Difference* (1990); Luisa Muraro, *L'ordine simbolico della madre* (1991); and Jane Silverman Van Buren, *The Modernist Madonna* (1989).

32. In "Une chance de vivre" Luce Irigaray critiques the cultural silence on the mother-daughter relation, noting the abundant representations of the mother and son (1987, 203–7).

33. See Lucia Re, "Mythic Revisionism" (1993) for an explication of Muraro's paradigm and how it figures in the theoretical field of Italian feminist thought. Carol Lazzaro-Weis (1993) examines the problems and possibilities articulated in the extensive debates about the symbolic mother and the category of the maternal in Italian feminist theory, politics, and practice.

34. For a pioneering discussion of Fascist theories of woman, see Lucia Re, "Fascist Theories of 'Woman' and the Construction of Gender" (1995).

35. See Teresa de Lauretis, *The Practice of Love* (1994) for a reading of Kristeva's construction of the maternal, which clearly points to the dangers of heterosexism and exclusion posed by working through this category. The forms of lesbian poetic identity formation constructed during Fascism have important implications for my study. The apparent lack of scholarship on this subject, however, has meant forestalling such an analysis in this venue and exemplifies the need to undertake extensive research on the full range of interwar women poets.

Bibliography

Adams, Alice E. 1994. *Reproducing the Womb: Images of Childbirth in Science, Feminist Theory, and Literature.* Ithaca, N.Y., and London: Cornell University Press.

Addis Saba, Marina, ed. 1988. *La corporazione delle donne: Ricerche e studi sui modelli femminili nel ventènnio fascista.* Florence: Vallecchi.

Adorno, T. W. 1973. "Freudian Theory and the Pattern of Fascist Propaganda." In *Sigmund Freud,* ed. Paul Roazen. Englewood Cliffs, N.J.: Prentice-Hall.

———. 1992. *Aesthetics and Politics.* London and New York: Verso.

Aleramo, Sibilla. 1906. *Una donna.* Turin: Sten.

———. 1927. *Amo, dunque sono.* Milan: Mondadori.

———. 1979. *Un amore insolito: Diario 1940–1944.* 2nd ed., ed. Alba Morino. Milan: Feltrinelli.

———. 1980. *A Woman,* trans. Rosalind Delmar. Berkeley and Los Angeles: University of California Press.

———. 1980. *Selva d'amore.* Rome: Newton Compton. Originally published in 1947.

Allen, Beverly. 1986. "Introduction." In *The Defiant Muse: Italian Feminist Poems from the Middle Ages to the Present,* ed. Beverly Allen, Muriel Kittel, and Keala Jane Jewell. New York: Feminist Press.

———. 1992. "Terrorism Tales: Gender and the Fictions of Italian National Identity." *Italica* 69. 2:161–76.

Allen, Beverly, Muriel Kittel, and Keala Jane Jewell, eds. 1986. *The Defiant Muse: Italian Feminist Poems from the Middle Ages to the Present.* New York: Feminist Press.

Alterman, Eric. 1994. "The New Face of Fascism." *Elle* 117 (July): 114–17.

Alvaro, Corrado. 1930. *Gente in Aspromonte.* Milan: Fratelli Treves.

Anderson, Benedict. 1983. *Imagined Communities: Reflections on the Origin and Spread of Nationalism.* London: Verso.

Anguissola, Giana. 1936. *Pensione Flora.* Milan: Mondadori.

Apollonio, Umbro, ed. 1973. *Futurist Manifestos,* trans. Robert Brain et al. New York: Viking Press.

Arslan Veronese, Antonia, ed. 1977. *Dame, droga e galline.* Padua: Cleup.

———. 1987. "Vivere in rosa per vivere in casa: La letteratura femminile italiana fra impegno ed evasione." In *Intorno al rosa,* ed. Centro di Documentazione, Ricerca ed Iniziativa delle Donne. Verona: Essedue Edizioni.

Asor Rosa, Alberto. 1982. *Storia della letteratura italiana.* Vol. 1. Turin: Einaudi.

Astaldi, Maria Luisa. 1935. "La biblioteca." *Giornale d'Italia,* 23 June, 8.

———. 1939. *Nascita e vicende del romanzo italiano.* Milan: Fratelli Treves.

Baffoni-Licata, Laura. 1991. "La meteora esistenziale e poetica di Antonia Pozzi." *Italian Culture* 9:355–69.

Balsamo, Anne. 1996. *Technologies of the Gendered Body: Reading Cyborg Women.* Durham, N.C., and London: Duke University Press.

Bandini Buti, Maria, ed. 1941/1942. *Donne d'Italia: Poetesse e scrittrici.* 2 vols. Rome: Tosi.

Banti, Anna. 1953. "Storia e ragioni del 'romanzo rosa.'" *Paragone* 38:28–34.

Bàrberi Squarotti, Giorgio. 1987. *La forma e la vita: Il romanzo del Novecento.* Milan: Mursia.

Barthes, Roland. 1973. *Le plaisir du texte.* Paris: Éditions du Seuil.

———. 1977. *Image, Music, Text,* trans. Stephen Heath. New York: Hill and Wang.

Barzini, Luigi. 1970. "Italy." *Kenyon Review International Symposium on the Short Story.* 1.4: 95–97.

Bassanese, Fiora. 1995. "Sibilla Aleramo: Writing a Personal Myth." In *Mothers of Invention: Women, Italian Fascism, and Culture,* ed. Robin Pickering-Iazzi. Minneapolis and London: University of Minnesota Press.

Battaglia, Salvatore. 1991. *I facsimile della realtà: Forme e destini del romanzo italiano dal realismo al neorealismo.* Palermo: Sellerio.

Battistini, Andrea. 1986. "L'autobiografia e il superego dei generi letterari." *Annali d'Italianistica* 4:7–29.

Bazin, André. 1971. *What Is Cinema?* Vol. 2, ed. and trans. Hugh Gray. Berkeley and Los Angeles: University of California Press.

Beer, Gillian. 1990. "The Island and the Airplane: The Case of Virginia Woolf." In *Nation and Narration,* ed. Homi K. Bhabha. London and New York: Routledge.

Ben-Ghiat, Ruth. 1990. "The Politics of Realism: *Corrente di Vita Giovanile* and the Youth Culture of the 1930s." *Stanford Italian Review* 8.1–2:139–64.

———. 1991. "Neorealism in Italy, 1930–1950: From Fascism to Resistance." *Romance Languages Annual* 3: 155–59.

Berman, Russell A. 1990. "The Aestheticization of Politics: Walter Benjamin on Fascism and the Avant-Garde." *Stanford Italian Review* 8.1–2:35–52.

Bernari, Carlo. 1934. *Tre operai.* Milan: Rizzoli.

Bhabha, Homi K. 1994. *The Location of Culture.* London and New York: Routledge.

———, ed. 1990. *Nation and Narration.* London and New York: Routledge.

Bianchini, Angela. 1969. *Il romanzo d'appendice.* Turin: ERI.

Bilenchi, Romano. 1972. *Il capofabbrica.* Florence: Vallecchi. Originally published in 1935.

Birnbaum, Lucia Chiavola. 1986. *Liberazione della donna: Feminism in Italy.* Middletown, Conn.: Wesleyan University Press.

Bisi, Camilla. 1916. *Poetesse d'Italia.* Milan: Quintieri.

Blelloch, Paola. 1987. *Quel mondo dei guanti e delle stoffe: . . . Profili di scrittrici italiane del '900.* Verona: Essedue.

Bloom, Lynn Z. 1980. "Heritages: Dimensions of Mother-Daughter Relationships in Women's Autobiographies." In *The Lost Tradition: Mothers and Daughters in Literature*, ed. Cathy N. Davidson and E. M. Broner. New York: Frederick Ungar.

Blum, Cinzia. 1990. "Rhetorical Strategies and Gender in Marinetti's Futurist Manifesto." *Italica* 67. 2:196–211.

———. 1996. *The Other Modernism: F. T. Marinetti's Futurist Fiction of Power.* Berkeley and Los Angeles: University of California Press.

Bocci, Pina. 1933. "Decolaggio." In *Le futuriste: Donne e letteratura d'avanguardia in Italia (1909–1944)*, ed. Claudia Salaris. Milan: Edizioni delle donne.

Bocelli, Arnaldo. 1937. "Scrittori d'oggi: Paola Drigo, *Maria Zef.*" *Nuova Antologia* (October):466–71.

Boine, Giovanni. 1914. *Il peccato e altre cose.* Florence: Libreria della Voce.

Borgese, Giuseppe Antonio. 1923. *Tempo di edificare.* Milan: Fratelli Treves.

Boscagli, Maurizia. 1996. *Eye on the Flesh: Fashions of Masculinity in the Early Twentieth Century.* Boulder, Colo.: Westview Press.

Bottai, Giuseppe. 1992. *La politica delle arti: Scritti 1918–1943.* Rome: Editalia.

Bradbury, Malcom, and James McFarlane, eds. 1991. *Modernism: A Guide to European Literature 1890–1930.* 2nd ed. New York and London: Penguin.

Braidotti, Rosi. 1991. *Patterns of Dissonance: A Study of Women in Contemporary Philosophy,* trans. Elizabeth Guild. New York: Routledge.

Braun, Emily. 1995. "Antonietta Raphaël: Artist, Woman, Foreigner, Jew, Wife, Mother, Muse, and Anti-Fascist." In *Mothers of Invention: Women, Italian Fascism, and Culture,* ed. Robin Pickering-Iazzi. Minneapolis and London: University of Minnesota Press.

Brennan, Timothy. 1990. "The National Longing for Form." In *Nation and Narration,* ed. Homi K. Bhabha. London and New York: Routledge.

Briganti, Paolo. 1986. "La cerchia infuocata: Per una tipologia dell'autobiografia letteraria italiana del Novecento." *Annali d'Italianistica* 4:189–222.

Brill, Suzanne, trans. 1989. *The Futurist Cookbook,* ed. Lesley Chamberlain. San Francisco: Bedford Arts.

Brooks, Peter. 1984. *Reading for the Plot: Design and Intention in Narrative.* New York: Knopf.

Bruno, Giuliana. 1993. *Streetwalking on a Ruined Map: Cultural Theory and the City Films of Elvira Notari.* Princeton, N.J.: Princeton University Press.

Butler, Judith. 1990. *Gender Trouble: Feminism and the Subversion of Identity.* New York and London: Routledge.

———. 1993. *Bodies That Matter: On the Discursive Limits of "Sex."* New York and London: Routledge.

Cadioli, Alberto. 1989. *Tra prosa d'arte e romanzo del Novecento (1920–1960): Appunti di lettura.* Milan: Arcipelago Edizioni.

Caldwell, Leslie. 1986. "Reproducers of the Nation: Women and the Family in Fascist Policy." In *Rethinking Italian Fascism: Capitalism, Populism and Culture,* ed. David Forgacs. London: Lawrence and Wishart.

Calinescu, Matei. 1986. "Modernism and Ideology." In *Modernism: Challenges and Perspectives,* ed. Monique Chefdor, Ricardo Quinones, and Albert Wachtel. Urbana and Chicago: University of Illinois Press.

Calvino, Italo. 1990. "The Dictator's Hats." *Stanford Italian Review* 8.1–2:195–209.

Cannistraro, Philip V. 1975. *La fabbrica del consenso: Fascismo e mass media.* Rome: Laterza.

Cannistraro, Philip V., and Brian Sullivan. 1993. *Il Duce's Other Woman.* New York: William Morrow.

Caplan, Jane. 1979. "Introduction to Female Sexuality in Fascist Ideology." *Feminist Review* 1:59–66.

Cappa Marinetti, Benedetta. 1991. *Astra e il sottomarino: Vita trasognata.* Naples: Editori del Grifo. Originally published in 1935.

Cara, Domenico, ed. 1991. *Le donne della poesia: Oltre il femminile.* Milan: Laboratorio delle Arti.

Cardella, Lara. 1989. *Volevo i pantaloni.* Milan: Mondadori.

Casillo, Robert. 1992. "Fascists of the Final Hour: Pound's Italian Cantos." In *Fascism, Aesthetics, and Culture,* ed. Richard J. Golsan. Hanover, N.H., and London: University Press of New England.

Cavallo, Pietro, and Pasquale Iaccio. 1984. "Ceti medi emergenti e immagine della donna della letteratura rosa degli anni trenta." *Storia contemporanea* 15.6:1149–70.

Cenci, Giovanni, ed. 1991. *Modernismo/Modernismi: Dall'avanguardia storica agli anni trenta e oltre.* Milan: Principato.

Cenni, Alessandra. 1989. "Introduction." In Antonia Pozzi's *Parole,* ed. Alessandra Cenni and Onorina Dino, 7–18. Milan: Garzanti.

Cervigni, Dino S. 1991. "The Modern and the Postmodern: An Introduction." *Annali d'Italianistica* 9:5–31.

Chambers, Iain. 1986. *Popular Culture: The Metropolitan Experience.* New York: Methuen.

Chefdor, Monique, Ricardo Quinones, and Albert Wachtel, eds. 1986. *Modernism: Challenges and Perspectives.* Urbana and Chicago: University of Illinois Press.

Cheles, Luciano. 1991. "Dolce Stil Nero? Images of Women in the Graphic Propaganda of the Italian Neo-Fascist Party." In *Women and Italy: Essays on Gender, Culture and History,* ed. Zygmunt G. Baranski and Shirley W. Vinall. New York: St. Martin's Press.

Cialente, Fausta. 1930. *Natalia.* Rome: Edizioni dei dieci.

Cirlot, J. E. 1971. *A Dictionary of Symbols.* 2nd ed., trans. Jack Sage. New York: Philosophical Library.

Ciuffolini, Alfonso, ed. 1930. *Indagine sulle condizioni di vita dei contadini italiani.* Rome: Confederazione Nazionale dei Sindacati Fascisti dell'agricoltura.

Cixous, Hélène. 1981. "The Laugh of the Medusa." In *New French Feminisms,* ed. Elaine Marks and Isabelle de Courtivron. New York: Random House.

Colomina, Beatriz, ed. 1992. *Sexuality and Space.* New York: Princeton Architectural Press.

Comes, Salvatore. 1970. *Ada Negri da un tempo all'altro.* Milan: Mondadori.

Cominazzini, Leandra Angelucci. 1939. "Foligno." In *Le futuriste: Donne e letteratura d'avanguardia in Italia (1909–1944),* ed. Claudia Salaris. Milan: Edizioni delle Donne.

Conti, Bruna, and Alba Morino, eds. 1981. *Sibilla Aleramo e il suo tempo: Vita raccontata e illustrata.* Milan: Feltrinelli.

Costa-Zalessow, Natalia. 1982. *Scrittrici italiane dal XIII al XX secolo.* Ravenna: Longo.

———. 1992. "Ada Negri." In *Dictionary of Literary Biography*. Vol. 114. *Twentieth Century Italian Poets*. 1st series, ed. Giovanna Wedel De Stasio, Glauco Cambon, and Antonio Illiano. Detroit and London: Bruccoli Clark Layman and Gale Research.

Cowell, Alan. 1994. "The Ghost of Mussolini Keeps Rattling His Chains." *New York Times*, 1 June, A3.

Croce, Benedetto. 1940a. "Grazia Deledda." In *La letteratura della nuova Italia: Saggi critici*. Vol. 6. Bari: Laterza.

———. 1940b. "L'ultima Ada Negri." In *La letteratura della nuova Italia: Saggi critici*. Vol. 6. Bari: Laterza.

———. 1948a. "Ada Negri." In *La letteratura della nuova Italia*. Vol. 2. 5th ed. Bari: Laterza. Originally written in 1906.

———. 1948b. "La contessa Lara-Annie Vivanti." In *La letteratura della nuova Italia*. Vol. 2. Bari: Laterza. Originally written in 1906.

Curti, Daniela. 1987a. "Il linguaggio del racconto rosa: Gli anni 20 ed oggi." In *Lingua letteraria e lingua dei media nell'italiano contemporaneo*. Florence: Felice Le Monnier.

———. 1987b. "Il romanzo rosa. Scrittrici e lettrici: 50 anni di Liala." In *Scrittore e lettore nella società di massa*. Trieste: Edizioni LINT.

Dada for Now: A Collection of Futurist and Dada Sound Works. Liverpool: Ark.

Dalle Vacche, Angela. 1992. *The Body in the Mirror: Shapes of History in Italian Cinema*. Princeton, N.J.: Princeton University Press.

D'Annunzio, Gabriele. 1935. *Cento e cento e cento pagine del libro segreto di Gabriele D'Annunzio tentato di morire*. Milan: Mondadori.

D'Aquino, Niccolò. 1994. "Italy's Political Future." *Europe* 337 (June):4–8.

de Certeau, Michel. 1988. *The Practice of Everyday Life*, trans. Steven Rendall. Berkeley and Los Angeles: University of California Press.

De Céspedes, Alba. 1941. *There's No Turning Back*, trans. Jan Noble. London: Jarrolds.

———. 1949. *Dalla parte di lei*. Milan: Mondadori.

———. 1952. *Quaderno proibito*. Milan: Mondadori.

———. 1972. *Nessuno torna indietro*. Rev. ed. Milan: Mondadori. Originally published in 1938.

Decio Cosenza, Carolina. 1825. *Lettere d'un'italiana*. Naples: R. Marotta e Vanspandoch.

De Felice, Renzo. 1974. *Mussolini il duce*. Vol. 1. *Gli anni del consenso, 1929–1936*. Turin: Einaudi.

———, ed. 1988. *Futurismo, cultura e politica*. Turin: Fondazione Giovanni Agnelli.

De Giorgio, Michela. 1988. "Signore e signorine fra Otto e Novecento: Modelli culturali e comportamenti sociali regolati da uno stato civile." In *Ragnatele di rapporti: Patronage e reti di relazione nella storia delle donne*, ed. Lucia Ferrante, Maura Palazzi, and Gianna Pomata. Turin: Rosenberg and Sellier.

———. 1992. *Le italiane dall'unità a oggi*. Rome-Bari: Laterza.

De Giovanni, Neria. 1987. *L'ora di Lilith: Su Grazia Deledda e la letteratura femminile del secondo Novecento*. Rome: Ellemme.

De Grand, Alexander. 1976. "Women under Italian Fascism." *Historical Journal* 19.4:947–68.

————. 1989. *Italian Fascism: Its Origins and Development.* 2nd ed. Lincoln and London: University of Nebraska Press.

De Grazia, Victoria. 1981. *The Culture of Consent: Mass Organization of Leisure in Fascist Italy.* Cambridge: Cambridge University Press.

————. 1984. "Culture popolari negli anni del fascismo." *Italia contemporanea* 157:63–90.

————. 1992. *How Fascism Ruled Women: Italy 1920–1945.* Berkeley and Los Angeles: University of California Press.

De Grazia, Victoria, et al. 1983. "Alle origini della cultura di massa: Cultura popolare e fascismo in Italia." *Ricerca folklorica* 7:19–25.

de Lauretis, Teresa. 1984a. "Desire in Narrative." In *Alice Doesn't: Feminism, Semiotics, Cinema.* Bloomington: Indiana University Press.

————. 1984b. "Semiotics and Experience." In *Alice Doesn't: Feminism, Semiotics, Cinema.* Bloomington: Indiana University Press.

————. 1987. *Technologies of Gender: Essays on Theory, Film, and Fiction.* Bloomington: Indiana University Press.

————. 1994. *The Practice of Love: Lesbian Sexuality and Perverse Desire.* Bloomington and Indianapolis: Indiana University Press.

Deledda, Grazia. 1903. *Elias Portolu.* Turin: Roux e Viarengo.

————. 1913. *Canne al vento.* Milan: Fratelli Treves.

————. 1920. *La madre.* Milan: Fratelli Treves.

————. 1933. "La Grazia." In *Sole d'estate.* Milan: Fratelli Treves.

————. 1988. *Cosima,* trans. Martha King. New York: Italica. Originally published in Italian in 1937.

Demetrakopoulos, Stephanie A. 1980. "The Metaphysics of Matrilinearism in Women's Autobiography: Studies of Mead's *Blackberry Winter,* Hellman's *Pentimento,* Angelou's *I Know Why the Caged Bird Sings,* and Kingston's *The Woman Warrior.*" In *Women's Autobiography: Essays in Criticism,* ed. Estelle C. Jelinek. Bloomington: Indiana University Press.

Derrida, Jacques. 1980. "The Law of Genre," trans. Avital Ronell. *Glyph* 7:202–32.

Diggins, John F. 1972. *Mussolini and Fascism: The View from America.* Princeton, N.J.: Princeton University Press.

Doane, Mary Ann. 1987. *The Desire to Desire: The Woman's Film of the 1940s.* Bloomington: Indiana University Press.

Douglas, Mary. 1982. *Natural Symbols: Explorations in Cosmology.* Rev. ed. New York: Pantheon.

Drigo, Paola. 1913. *La fortuna.* Milan: Fratelli Treves.

————. 1921. *Col mio infinito.* Ferrara: Taddei.

————. 1932. *La signorina Anna.* Vicenza: Jacchia.

————. 1936. *Fine d'anno.* Milan: Fratelli Treves.

————. 1989. *Maria Zef,* trans. Blossom Steinberg Kirschenbaum. Lincoln and London: University of Nebraska Press. Originally published in Italian in 1936.

DuPlessis, Rachel Blau. 1985. *Writing beyond the Ending: Narrative Strategies of Twentieth Century Women Writers.* Bloomington: Indiana University Press.

————. 1994. "'Corpses of Poesy': Some Modern Poets and Some Gender Ideologies of Lyric." In *Feminist Measures: Soundings in Poetry and Theory,* ed. Lynn Keller and Cristanne Miller. Ann Arbor: University of Michigan Press.

Eco, Umberto. 1995. "Ur-Fascism." *The New York Review of Books,* June 22, 12–15.

Eco, Umberto, Marina Federzoni, Isabella Pezzini, and Maria Pia Pozzato. 1979. *Carolina Invernizio, Matilde Serao, Liala.* Florence: La Nuova Italia.

Esposito, Vittoriano. 1992. *Poesia non-poesia anti-poesia del '900 italiano.* Foggia: Bastogi.

Falcetto, Bruno. 1992. *Storia della narrativa neorealista.* Milan: Mursia.

Falqui, Enrico. 1965. *Nostra "terza pagina."* Rome: Canesi.

———. 1970a. "Poesia e Fascismo." In *Novecento letterario italiano.* Vol. 2. Florence: Vallecchi. Originally published in 1935.

———. 1970b. "Poesia e Resistenza." In *Novecento letterario italiano.* Vol. 2. Florence: Vallecchi.

Fanning, Ursula. 1991. "Angel v. Monster: Serao's Use of the Female Double." In *Women and Italy: Essays on Gender, Culture and History,* ed. Zygmunt G. Baranski and Shirley W. Vinall. New York: St. Martin's Press.

Felski, Rita. 1989. *Beyond Feminist Aesthetics: Feminist Literature and Social Change.* Cambridge, Mass.: Harvard University Press.

———. 1995. *The Gender of Modernity.* Cambridge, Mass.: Harvard University Press.

Fido, Franco. 1986. "At the Origins of Autobiography in the 18th and 19th Centuries: The Topoi of the Self." *Annali d'Italianistica* 4:168–80.

Flora, Francesco. 1945. *Note di servizio.* Milan: Mondadori.

Folli, Anna. 1988. "Lettura di Ada Negri." In *Svelamento. Sibilla Aleramo: Una biografia intellettuale,* ed. Annarita Buttafuoco and Marina Zancan. Milan: Feltrinelli.

Forgacs, David, ed. 1986. *Rethinking Italian Fascism: Capitalism, Populism and Culture.* London: Lawrence and Wishart.

———. 1990. *Italian Culture in the Industrial Era, 1880–1980: Cultural Industries, Politics and the Public.* Manchester: Manchester University Press.

Foucault, Michel. 1972a. *The Archeology of Knowledge and the Discourse on Language,* trans. A. M. Sheridan Smith. New York: Pantheon.

———. 1972b. *Power/Knowledge: Selected Interviews and Other Writings 1972–1977,* ed. Colin Gordon. New York: Pantheon.

———. 1980. *The History of Sexuality.* Vol. 1. An Introduction, trans. Robert Hurley. New York: Vintage.

Frabotta, Biancamaria, ed. 1976. *Donne in poesia: Antologia della poesia femminile in Italia dal dopoguerra a oggi.* Rome: Savelli.

Freud, Sigmund. 1933. "Femininity." In *The Standard Edition of the Complete Psychological Works of Sigmund Freud,* trans. and ed. James Strachey. Vol. 22. London: Hogarth and Institute of Psycho-Analysis, 112–35.

Gallop, Jane. 1988. *Thinking through the Body.* New York: Columbia University Press.

Gallucci, Carole C. 1995. "Alba De Céspedes's *There's No Turning Back:* Challenging the New Woman's Future." In *Mothers of Invention: Women, Italian Fascism, and Culture,* ed. Robin Pickering-Iazzi. Minneapolis and London: University of Minnesota Press.

Garner, Shirley Nelson, Claire Kahane, and Madelon Sprengnether, eds. 1985. *The*

(M)other Tongue: Essays in Feminist Psychoanalytic Interpretation. Ithaca, N.Y., and London: Cornell University Press.

Gentile, Emilio. 1994. "The Conquest of Modernity: From Modernist Nationalism to Fascism." *Modernism/Modernity* 1.3:55–87.

Gentile, Giovanni. 1934. *La donna e il fanciullo.* Florence: Sansoni.

Ghiazza, Silvana. 1991. "La letteratura rosa negli anni venti-quaranta." In *I best seller del ventènnio: Il regime e il libro di massa,* ed. Gigliola de Donato and Vanna Gazzola Stacchini. Rome: Riuniti.

Ghirardo, Diane. 1990. "City and Theater: The Rhetoric of Fascist Architecture." *Stanford Italian Review* 8.1–2:165–93.

Giani Gallino, Tilde. 1986. *La ferita e il re—gli archetipi femminili della cultura maschile.* Milan: Cortini.

Gibbs, Philip. 1934. *European Journey.* New York: Literary Guild.

Gibson, Mary. 1986. *Prostitution and the State in Italy, 1860–1915.* New Brunswick, N.J., and London: Rutgers University Press.

Gilmore, Leigh. 1994. *Autobiographics: A Feminist Theory of Women's Self-Representation.* Ithaca, N.Y., and London: Cornell University Press.

Ginzburg, Natalia. 1989. *Family Sayings,* trans. D. M. Low. New York: Arcade. Originally published in Italian in 1963.

Giocondi, Michele. 1990. *Best seller italiani 1860–1990.* Florence: Paradigma.

Gioia, Dana, and Michael Palma, eds. 1991. *New Italian Poets.* Brownsville, Ore.: Story Line Press.

Golsan, Richard J. , ed. 1992. *Fascism, Aesthetics, and Culture.* Hanover, N.H., and London: University Press of New England.

Goretti, Maria. 1941. *La donna e il futurismo.* Verona: La Scaligera.

Gramsci, Antonio. 1971. *Selections from the Prison Notebooks of Antonio Gramsci,* trans. and ed. Quintin Hoare and Geoffrey Nowell Smith. New York: International Publishers.

———. 1985. *Selections from Cultural Writings,* trans. William Boelhower, ed. David Forgacs and Geoffrey Nowell-Smith. London: Lawrence and Wishart.

Graziosi, Mariolina. 1995. "Gender Struggle and the Social Manipulation and Ideological Use of Gender Identity in the Interwar Years." In *Mothers of Invention: Women, Italian Fascism, and Culture,* ed. Robin Pickering-Iazzi. Minneapolis and London: University of Minnesota Press.

Gregoricchio, Francesca. 1981. *Liala.* Milan: Gammalibri.

Grimaldo Grigsby, Darcy. 1991. "Dilemmas of Visibility: Contemporary Women Artists' Representations of Female Bodies." In *The Female Body: Figures, Styles, Speculations,* ed. Laurence Goldstein. Ann Arbor: University of Michigan Press.

Grosz, Elizabeth. 1992. "Bodies-Cities." In *Sexuality and Space,* ed. Beatriz Colomina. New York: Princeton Architectural Press.

Guadalupi, Gianni, ed. 1994. *Cieli del mondo: Avventure aeronautiche italiane narrate dai protagonisti.* Milan: Anabasi.

Guglielminetti, Amalia. 1909. *Le seduzioni.* Turin: Lattes.

———. 1911. "Aridità sentimentale." *La stampa,* 11 July.

Guglielminetti, Marziano. 1986. "Per un'antologia degli autobiografi del Settecento." *Annali d'Italianistica* 4:140–51.

———. 1987. *Amalia: La rivincita della femmina.* Genoa: Costa and Nolan.

Hall, Stuart. 1973. "Encoding and Decoding in the Television Discourse." In *Stencilled Occasional Papers,* vol. 7. Birmingham, England: Center for Contemporary Cultural Studies.

Haraway, Donna. 1991. *Simians, Cyborgs, and Women: The Reinvention of Nature.* New York and London: Routledge.

Hassan, Ihab. 1987. *The Postmodern Turn: Essays in Postmodern Theory and Culture.* Columbus: Ohio State University Press.

Hay, James. 1987. *Popular Film Culture in Fascist Italy: The Passing of the Rex.* Bloomington: Indiana University Press.

———. 1993. "Invisible Cities/Visible Geographies: Toward a Cultural Geography of Italian Television in the 90s." *Quarterly Review of Film and Video* 14.3:35–47.

Heller, Steven, and Louise Fili, eds. 1993. *Italian Art Deco: Graphic Design between the Wars.* San Francisco: Chronicle Books.

Hewitt, Andrew. 1993. *Fascist Modernism: Aesthetics, Politics, and the Avant-Garde.* Stanford, Calif.: Stanford University Press.

Hirsch, Marianne. 1989. *The Mother/Daughter Plot: Narrative, Psychoanalysis, Feminism.* Bloomington and Indianapolis: Indiana University Press.

Holub, Renate. 1991. "Weak Thought and Strong Ethics: The 'Postmodern' and Feminist Theory in Italy." *Annali d'Italianistica* 9:124–43.

———. 1994. "Between the United States and Italy: Critical Reflections on Diotima's Feminist/Feminine Ethics." In *Feminine Feminists: Cultural Practices in Italy,* ed. Giovanna Miceli Jeffries. Minneapolis and London: University of Minnesota Press.

Huyssen, Andreas. 1986. *After the Great Divide: Modernism, Mass Culture, Postmodernism.* Bloomington and Indianapolis: Indiana University Press.

Intorno al rosa. 1987. Verona: Essedue.

Irigaray, Luce. 1985. *Speculum of the Other Woman,* trans. Gillian C. Gill. Ithaca, N.Y.: Cornell University Press.

———. 1987. "Une chance de vivre." In *Sexes et parentés.* Paris: Minuit.

———. 1993. *Je, tu, nous: Toward a Culture of Difference,* trans. Alison Martin. New York and London: Routledge.

Jahier, Piero. 1919. *Ragazzo.* Rome: Soc. An. Ed. La Voce.

Jameson, Fredric. 1981. *The Political Unconscious: Narrative as a Socially Symbolic Act.* Ithaca, N.Y.: Cornell University Press.

———. 1988. *Ideologies of Theory: Essays 1971–1986.* Vol. 2. Minneapolis: University of Minnesota Press.

Jeuland-Meynaud, Maryse. 1989. "Le identificazioni della donna nella narrativa di Elsa Morante." *Annali D'Italianistica* 7:301–24.

Jewell, Keala. 1984. "Un furore d'autocreazione: Women and Writing in Sibilla Aleramo." *Canadian Journal of Italian Studies* 7:148–62.

———. 1992. *The Poiesis of History: Experimenting with Genre in Postwar Italy.* Ithaca, N.Y. and London: Cornell University Press.

Jones, F. J. 1986. *The Modern Italian Lyric.* Cardiff: University of Wales Press.

Kaplan, Alice Yaeger. 1986. *Reproduction of Banality: Fascism, Literature, and French Intellectual Life.* Minneapolis: University of Minnesota Press.

Kaplan, Cora. 1986. "*The Thorn Birds:* Fiction, Fantasy, Femininity." In *Formations of Fantasy,* ed. Victor Burgin, James Donald, and Cora Kaplan. London and New York: Methuen.

Kinsale, Laura. 1992. "The Androgynous Reader: Point of View in the Romance." In *Dangerous Men and Adventurous Women: Writers on the Appeal of Romance,* ed. Jayne Ann Krentz. Philadelphia: University of Pennsylvania Press.

Kirby, Michael. 1971. *Futurist Performance.* New York: E. P. Dutton.

Krauss, Rosalind E. 1986. *The Originality of the Avant-Garde and Other Modernist Myths.* Cambridge, Mass. and London: MIT Press.

Kristeva, Julia. 1980. *Desire in Language,* trans. and ed. Leon Roudiez, Thomas Gora, and Alice Jardine. New York: Columbia University Press.

Kroha, Lucienne. 1991. "Matilde Serao: An Introduction." In *Women and Italy: Essays on Gender, Culture and History,* ed. Zygmunt G. Baranski and Shirley W. Vinall. New York: St. Martin's Press.

———. 1992. *The Woman Writer in Late-Nineteenth-Century Italy.* Lewiston, N.Y.: Edwin Mellen Press.

Lazzaro-Weis, Carol. 1993. *From Margins to Mainstream: Feminism and Fictional Modes in Italian Women's Writing 1968–1990.* Philadelphia: University of Pennsylvania Press.

Lejeune, Philippe. 1975. *Le pacte autobiographique.* Paris: Éditions du Seuil.

Levi, Carlo. 1945. *Cristo si è fermato ad Eboli.* Turin: Einaudi.

Levi, Primo. 1947. *Se questo è un uomo.* Turin: F. de Silva.

Liala. 1978. *Signorsì.* Milan: Sonzogno. Originally published in 1931.

Lodi, Marinella. 1925. "L'uomo e la morte." *Il giornale d'Italia,* 12 July.

Lombardi, Giancarlo. 1994. "Fuga dallo sguardo-Panotticismo e Fallocrazia in *Quaderno proibito* e *Il rimorso.*" *Igitur* 6.1:103–22.

Lombroso, Cesare, and Guglielmo Ferrero. 1893. *La donna delinquente, la prostituta, e la donna normale.* Turin: Roux.

Lukács, Georg. 1962. *The Meaning of Contemporary Realism,* trans. John Mander and Necke Mander. London: Merlin Press.

———. 1981. "Expressionism: Its Significance and Decline." In *Essays on Realism,* ed. Rodney Livingston, trans. David Fernbach. Cambridge, Mass.: MIT Press. Originally published in 1934.

Luperini, Romano. 1973. *Letteratura e ideologia nel primo Novecento italiano: Saggi e note sulla "Voce" e sui vociani.* Pisa: Pacini.

———. 1981. *Il Novecento.* Vol. 2. Turin: Loescher.

Luperini, Romano, and Eduardo Melfi, eds. 1981. *Neorealismo, neodecadentismo, avanguardie.* Rome-Bari: Laterza.

Lyttelton, Adrian. 1973. *The Seizure of Power: Fascism in Italy 1919–1929.* London: Weidenfeld and Nicolson.

Macciocchi, Maria Antonietta. 1976. *La donna "nera": "Consenso" femminile e fascismo.* Milan: Feltrinelli.

———. 1979. "Female Sexuality in Fascist Ideology." *Feminist Review* 1:67–82.

Mack Smith, Denis. 1983. *Mussolini: A Biography.* New York: Vintage.

Malvano, Laura. 1988. *Fascismo e politica dell'immagine.* Turin: Bollati Boringhieri.

Manzini, Gianna. 1971. *Ritratto in piedi.* Milan: Mondadori.

Marcus, Millicent. 1986. *Italian Film in the Light of Neorealism*. Princeton, N.J.: Princeton University Press.

Mariátegui, Carlos José. 1971. *Seven Interpretative Essays on Peruvian Reality*. Austin: University of Texas Press.

Marinetti, Filippo Tommaso. 1909. *Mafarka le futuriste*. Paris: Sansot.

———. 1973. "The Founding and Manifesto of Futurism." In *Futurist Manifestos*, ed. Umbro Apollonio and trans. Robert Brain et al. New York: Viking Press. Originally published in 1909.

———. 1983a. "Contro il matrimonio." In *Teoria e invenzione futurista*, ed. Luciano de Maria. Milan: Mondadori. Originally published in 1919.

———. 1983b. "L'aeropoema del Golfo della Spezia." In *Teoria e invenzione futurista*, ed. Luciano de Maria. Milan: Mondadori. Originally published in 1935.

Marks, Elaine, and Isabelle de Courtivron, eds. 1980. *New French Feminisms: An Anthology*. Amherst: University of Massachusetts Press.

Marotti, Maria. 1994. "Filial Discourses: Feminism and Femininity in Italian Women's Autobiography." In *Feminine Feminists: Cultural Practices in Italy*, ed. Giovanna Miceli Jeffries. Minneapolis and London: University of Minnesota Press.

Martignoni, Clelia. 1984. "Per una storia dell'autobiografismo metafisico vociano." *Autografo* 1.4:32–47.

Meldini, Piero. 1975. *Sposa e madre esemplare: Ideologia e politica della donna e della famiglia durante il fascismo*. Florence: Guaraldi.

Menapace, Lidia. 1988. "La giornalista, l'atleta, la star: Immagini di donna durante il regime fascista." In *Esperienza storica femminile nell'età moderna e contemporanea*. Vol. 1, ed. Anna Maria Crispino. Rome: Circolo "La Goccia."

Merry, Bruce. 1988. "Ada Negri: Social Injustice and an Early Italian Feminist." *Forum for Modern Language Studies* 24.3:193–205.

———. 1990. *Women in Modern Italian Literature: Four Studies Based on the Work of Grazia Deledda, Alba De Céspedes, Natalia Ginzburg, and Dacia Maraini*. Townsville, Australia: James Cook University of North Queensland.

Milan Women's Bookstore Collective. 1990. *Sexual Difference: A Theory of Social-Symbolic Practice*. Bloomington: Indiana University Press.

Modleski, Tania. 1982. *Loving with a Vengeance: Mass Produced Fantasies for Women*. Hamden, Conn.: Archon.

———. 1986a. "Feminism and the Power of Interpretation: Some Critical Readings." In *Feminist Studies/Critical Studies*, ed. Teresa de Lauretis. Bloomington: Indiana University Press.

———. 1986b. "Introduction." In *Studies in Entertainment: Critical Approaches to Mass Culture*. Bloomington and Indianapolis: Indiana University Press.

Mondello, Elisabetta. 1987. *La nuova italiana: La donna nella stampa e nella cultura del ventennio*. Rome: Riuniti.

Montale, Eugenio. 1948. "Preface." In Antonia Pozzi's *Parole: Diario di Poesia*. Milan: Mondadori.

Morandini, Giuliana. 1980. *La voce che è in lei: Antologia della narrativa femminile italiana tra '800 e '900*. Milan: Bompiani.

Moravia, Alberto. 1929. *Gli indifferenti*. Milan: Alpes.

———. 1941. *La mascherata*. Milan: Bompiani.

————. 1947. *La romana*. Milan: Bompiani.

————. 1951. *Il comformista*. Milan: Bompiani.

————. 1957. *La ciociara*. Milan: Bompiani.

Mosse, George L. 1985. *Nationalism and Sexuality: Middle-Class Morality and Sexual Norms in Modern Europe*. Madison: University of Wisconsin Press.

Muraro, Luisa. 1991. *L'ordine simbolico della madre*. Rome: Editori Riuniti.

Mussell, Kay. 1984. *Fantasy and Reconciliation: Contemporary Formulas of Women's Romance Fiction*. Westport, Conn.: Greenwood Press.

Neera. 1919. *Una giovinezza del secolo XIX*. Milan: Cogliati.

Negri, Ada. 1892. *Fatalità*. Milan: Fratelli Treves.

————. 1910. *Dal profondo*. Milan: Fratelli Treves.

————. 1926. "Risveglio." *Corriere della sera*, 8 August, 3.

————. 1930. *Morning Star*, trans. Anne Day. New York: Macmillan.

————. 1966a. *I canti dell'isola*. In *Tutte le opere di Ada Negri*. Vol. 1. Milan: Mondadori. Originally published in 1925.

————. 1966b. *Il dono*. In *Tutte le opere di Ada Negri*. Vol. 1. Milan: Mondadori. Originally published in 1936.

————. 1966c. *Il libro di Mara*. In *Tutte le opere di Ada Negri*. Vol. 1. Milan: Mondadori. Originally published in 1919.

————. 1966d. *Le solitarie*. In *Tutte le opere di Ada Negri*. Vol 2. Originally published in 1917.

————. 1966e. *Le strade*. In *Tutte le opere di Ada Negri*. Vol 2. Milan: Mondadori. Originally published in 1926.

————. 1966f. *Stella mattutina*. In *Tutte le opere di Ada Negri*. Vol 2. Originally published in 1921.

————. 1993. "Woman with a Little Girl." In *Unspeakable Women*, ed. and trans. Robin Pickering-Iazzi. New York: Feminist Press.

Nerenberg, Ellen. 1991. "'Donna proprio . . . proprio donna': The Social Construction of Femininity in *Nessuno torna indietro*." *Romance Languages Annual* 3:267–73.

————. n.d. "Habeas Corpus. The Gendered Subject in Prison: Reflections on Fascism and Literature in Italy, 1930–1960."

Nicholls, Peter. 1987. "Futurism, Gender, and Theories of Postmodernity." *Textual Practice* 3.2:202–21.

————. 1995. *Modernisms: A Literary Guide*. Berkeley and Los Angeles: University of California Press.

Norindr, Panivong. 1993. "'Errances' and Memories in Marguerite Duras's Colonial Cities." *Differences* 5.3:52–79.

Obici, Giulio, and Giovanni Marchesini. 1898. *Le "amicizie" di collegio: Ricerche sulle prime manifestazioni dell'amore sessuale*. Rome: Dante Alighieri.

Olney, James, ed. 1988. *Studies in Autobiography*. New York: Oxford University Press.

Orban, Clara. 1995. "Women, Futurism, and Fascism." In *Mothers of Invention: Women, Italian Fascism, and Culture*, ed. Robin Pickering-Iazzi. Minneapolis and London: University of Minnesota Press.

Pacifici, Sergio. 1973. *The Modern Italian Novel from Capuana to Tozzi*. Carbondale: Southern Illinois University Press.

Pallotta, Augustus. 1984. "Dacia Maraini: From Alienation to Feminism." *World Literature Today* 58.3:359–62.

Pancrazi, Pietro. 1943. *Scrittori italiani dal Carducci al D'Annunzio.* Bari: Giuseppe Laterza.

Pannunzio, Mario. 1932. "Del romanzo." *Il Saggiatore* 2.11.

Panzini, Alfredo. 1921. *Signorine.* Rome: Mondadori.

Papini, Giovanni. 1913. *Un uomo finito.* Florence: Libreria della Voce.

La paraletteratura. 1977. Naples: Liguori.

Parati, Graziella. 1994. "The Transparent Woman: Reading Femininity within a Futurist Context." In *Feminine Feminists: Cultural Practices in Italy,* ed. Giovanna Miceli Jeffries. Minneapolis and London: University of Minnesota Press.

———. 1996. *Public History, Private Stories: Italian Women's Autobiography.* Minneapolis and London: University of Minnesota Press.

Parsani, Maria Assunta, and Neria De Giovanni. 1984. *Femminile a confronto: Tre realtà della narrativa contemporanea: Alba De Céspedes, Fausta Cialente, Gianna Manzini.* Rome: Lacaita Editore.

Passerini, Luisa. 1987. *Fascism in Popular Memory: The Cultural Experience of the Turin Working Class,* trans. Robert Lumley and Jude Bloomfield. Cambridge: Cambridge University Press.

———. 1989. "Women's Personal Narratives: Myths, Experiences, and Emotions." In *Interpreting Women's Lives: Feminist Theory and Personal Narratives,* ed. Personal Narratives Group. Bloomington: Indiana University Press.

———. 1991. *Mussolini immaginario: Storia di una biografia 1915–1939.* Rome-Bari: Laterza.

Pellizzi, Camillo. 1924. *Problemi e realtà del fascismo.* Florence: Vallecchi.

———. 1925. *Fascismo-aristocrazia.* Milan: Alpes.

———. 1929. *Le lettere italiane del nostro secolo.* Milan: Libreria D'Italia.

Perez de Mendiola, Marina. 1995. "The Pen and the Paintbrush." In *Latin American Women Artists, 1915–1995* (exhibition Catalogue). Milwaukee: Milwaukee Art Museum.

Pertile, Lino. 1986. "Fascism and Literature." In *Rethinking Italian Fascism: Capitalism, Populism and Culture,* ed. David Forgacs. London: Lawrence and Wishart.

Petrignani, Sandra. 1984. *Le signore della scrittura: Interviste.* Milan: Tartaruga.

Petro, Patrice. 1989. *Joyless Streets: Women and Melodramatic Representation in Weimar Germany.* Princeton, N.J.: Princeton University Press.

Petronio, Giuseppe, and Luciana Martinelli. 1975. *Il Novecento letterario in Italia: I contemporanei.* Palermo: Palumbo.

Picchione, John, and Lawrence R. Smith, eds. 1993. *Twentieth-Century Italian Poetry: An Anthology.* Toronto, Buffalo, London: University of Toronto Press.

Pickering-Iazzi, Robin. 1988. "The Poetics of Discovery: Female Storytelling and the *Terza Pagina* in Early Twentieth Century Literature." *Italiana* 1:291–306.

———, ed. and trans. 1993. *Unspeakable Women: Selected Short Stories Written by Italian Women during Fascism.* New York: Feminist Press.

———, ed. 1995. *Mothers of Invention: Women, Italian Fascism, and Culture.* Minneapolis and London: University of Minnesota Press.

Pietravalle, Lina. 1930. *Le catene.* Milan: Mondadori.

Pinkus, Karen. 1995. *Bodily Regimes: Italian Advertising under Fascism*. Minneapolis and London: University of Minnesota Press.

Poliakov, Leon. 1983. *Jews under the Italian Occupation*. New York: Howard Fertig.

Portaccio, Stefania. 1981. "La donna nella stampa popolare cattolica: *Famiglia cristiana 1931–1945*." *Italia contemporanea* 143:45–68.

Possenti, Eligio. 1935. "Volontà costruttiva e realtà nazionale nella letteratura fascista dell'anno XIII." *Corriere della sera*, 27 October, 3.

Pozzato, Maria Pia. 1982. *Il romanzo rosa*. Milan: Espresso Strumenti.

Pozzi, Antonia. 1943. *Parole: Diario di poesia*. 2nd ed. Milan: Mondadori. Originally published in 1939.

———. 1955. *Poems*, trans. Nora Wydenbruck. London: John Calder.

———. 1989. *Parole*, ed. Alessandra Cenni and Onorina Dino. Milan: Garzanti.

Pratolini, Vasco. 1947. *Cronache di poveri amanti*. Florence: Vallecchio.

PrimeTime Live. 1992. "All in the Famiglia," interview with Alessandra Mussolini. April 2. ABC News, transcript no. 239.

Prosperi, Carola. 1911. *La paura di amare*. Turin: Lattes.

———. 1914. *La nemica dei sogni*. Milan: Fratelli Treves.

———. 1915. *L'estranea*. Milan: Fratelli Treves.

Quintavalla, Maria Pia, ed. 1992. *Donne in poesia: Incontri con le poetesse italiane*. Udine: Campanotto.

Radway, Janice A. 1991. *Reading the Romance: Women, Patriarchy, and Popular Literature*. 2nd edition. Chapel Hill and London: University of North Carolina Press.

Ramondino, Fabrizia. 1988. *Althenopis*, trans. Michael Sullivan. Manchester: Carcanet Press. Originally published in 1980.

Rasy, Elisabetta. 1984. *Scrittrici, eroine e ispiratrici nel mondo delle lettere*. Rome: Riuniti.

Ravegnani, Giuseppe. 1930. *Contemporanei: Dal tramonto dell'Ottocento all'alba del Novecento*. Turin: Fratelli Bocca.

Re, Lucia. 1989. "Futurism and Feminism." *Annali d'Italianistica* 7:253–72.

———. 1990. *Calvino and the Age of Neorealism: Fables of Estrangement*. Stanford, Calif.: Stanford University Press.

———. 1993. "Mythic Revisionism: Women Poets and Philosophers in Italy Today." *Quaderni d'italianistica* 14.1:75–109.

———. 1995. "Fascist Theories of 'Woman' and the Construction of Gender." In *Mothers of Invention: Women, Italian Fascism, and Culture*, ed. Robin Pickering-Iazzi. Minneapolis and London: University of Minnesota Press.

Regan, Stephen. 1992. *The Politics of Pleasure: Aesthetics and Cultural Theory*. Buckingham and Philadelphia: Open University Press.

Reich, Jacqueline. 1995. "Reading, Writing, and Rebellion: Collectivity, Specularity, and Sexuality in the Italian Schoolgirl Comedy, 1934–1943." In *Mothers of Invention: Women, Italian Fascism, and Culture*, ed. Robin Pickering-Iazzi. Minneapolis and London: University of Minnesota Press.

Revelli, Nuto. 1985. *L'anello Forte*. Turin: Einaudi.

Rimini, Pia. 1929. "Echi nella notte." *Giornale d'Italia*, 2 June, 3.

Robbins, Bruce, ed. 1990. *Intellectuals: Aesthetics, Politics, and Academics*. Minneapolis and London: University of Minnesota Press.

Romagnoli, Sacrati Orintia. 1828. *Lettere di Giulia Willet*. Rome: Nella Stamperi de Romanis.

Ruinas, Stanis. 1930. *Scrittrici e scribacchine d'oggi*. Rome: Accademia.

Russo, Luigi. 1923. *I Narratori*. Rome: Fondazione Leonardo per la cultura italiana.

Said, Edward W. 1983. *The World, the Text and the Critic*. Cambridge, Mass.: Harvard University Press.

———. 1994. *Culture and Imperialism*. New York: Vintage.

Salaris, Claudia. 1982. *Le futuriste: Donne e letteratura d'avanguardia in Italia (1909/1944)*. Milan: Edizioni delle Donne.

———. 1992. *Artecrazia: L'avanguardia futurista negli anni del fascismo*. Florence: La Nuova Italia.

Scalero, Liliana. 1937. "Le donne che scrivono." *Almanacco della donna italiana*, 211–16.

Schiavo, Alberto, ed. 1981. *Futurismo e fascismo*. Rome: Giovanni Volpe.

Schiesari, Juliana. 1990–91. "Appropriating the Work of Women's Mourning: The Legacy of Renaissance Melancholia." Working Paper no. 2. Center for Twentieth Century Studies, University of Wisconsin-Milwaukee.

Schnapp, Jeffrey. 1990. "Forwarding Address." *Stanford Italian Review* 8.1–2:53–80.

———. 1992. "Epic Demonstrations: Fascist Modernity and the 1932 Exhibition of the Fascist Revolution." In *Fascism, Aesthetics, and Culture*, ed. Richard J. Golsan. Hanover, N.H.: University Press of New England.

Schnapp, Jeffrey, and Barbara Spackman. 1990. "Selections from the Great Debate on Fascism and Culture: *Critica Fascista* 1926–1927" *Stanford Italian Review* 8.1–2:235–72.

Schor, Naomi. 1985. *Breaking the Chain: Women, Theory, and French Realist Fiction*. New York: Columbia University Press.

Schultz, Elizabeth. 1981. "To Be Black and Blue: The Blues Genre in Black American Autobiography." In *The American Autobiography: A Collection of Critical Essays*, ed. Albert E. Stone. Englewood Cliffs, N. J.: Prentice-Hall.

Serao, Matilde. 1901. *Suor Giovanna della croce*. Milan: Fratelli Treves.

———. 1914. *Ella non rispose*. Milan: Fratelli Treves.

Showalter, Elaine. 1983. "Critical Cross-Dressing: Male Feminists and the Woman of the Year." *Raritan* 3.2:130–49.

———. 1990. *Sexual Anarchy: Gender and Culture at the Fin de Siècle*. New York: Viking.

Silverman Van Buren, Jane. 1989. *The Modernist Madonna: Semiotics of the Maternal Metaphor*. Bloomington and Indianapolis: Indiana University Press.

Sismondo, Elisa Zanella. 1935. "Dialogo sulla spiaggia." *Giornale d'Italia*, 18 August, 3.

Smith, Sidonie. 1987. *A Poetics of Women's Autobiography: Marginality and the Fictions of Self-Representation*. Bloomington: Indiana University Press.

Smith, Sidonie, and Julia Watson, eds. 1992. *De/Colonizing the Subject: The Politics of Gender in Women's Autobiography*. Minneapolis: University of Minnesota Press.

Soffici, Ardengo. 1915. *Giornale di bordo*. Florence: Libreria della voce.

Sommer, Doris. 1988. "'Not Just a Personal Story': Women's *Testimonios* and the Plural Self." In *Life/Lines: Theorizing Women's Autobiography*, ed. Bella Brodzki and Celeste Schenck. Ithaca, N.Y.: Cornell University Press.

Sontag, Susan. 1980. "Fascinating Fascism." In *Under the Sign of Saturn*. New York: Giroux. Originally published in 1974.

Sorlin, Pierre. 1991. *European Cinemas, European Societies 1939–1990*. New York and London: Routledge.

Spackman, Barbara. 1990. "The Fascist Rhetoric of Virility." *Stanford Italian Review* 8.1–2:81–101.

———. 1995. "Fascist Women and the Rhetoric of Virility." In *Mothers of Invention: Women, Italian Fascism, and Culture*, ed. Robin Pickering-Iazzi. Minneapolis and London: University of Minnesota Press.

———. 1996. *Fascist Virilities: Rhetoric, Ideology, and Social Fantasy*. Minneapolis and London: University of Minnesota Press.

Stanford Italian Review. 1990. Special issue on "Fascism and Culture," ed. Jeffrey Schnapp and Barbara Spackman. 8.1–2.

Stanton, Domna. 1984. "Autogynography: Is the Subject Different?" *New York Literary Forum: The Female Autograph* 12–13:6–18.

Stara, Arrigo. 1985. "Autobiografia e romanzo." *La rassegna della letteratura italiana* 89.1:128–41.

Sternhell, Zeev. 1986. *Neither Left Nor Right: Fascist Ideology in France*, trans. David Maisel. Berkeley and Los Angeles: University of California Press.

Stille, Alexander. 1993. *Benevolence and Betrayal: Five Italian Jewish Families under Fascism*. New York: Penguin.

Suleiman, Susan Rubin. 1985. "Writing and Motherhood." In *The (M)other Tongue: Essays in Feminist Psychoanalytic Interpretation*, ed. Shirley Nelson Garner, Claire Kahane, and Madelon Sprengnether. Ithaca, N.Y., and London: Cornell University Press.

———. 1990. *Subversive Intent: Gender, Politics, and the Avant-Garde*. Cambridge, Mass., and London: Harvard University Press.

———. ed. 1986. *The Female Body in Western Culture: Contemporary Perspectives*. Cambridge, Mass.: Harvard University Press.

Tannenbaum, Edward R. 1972. *The Fascist Experience: Italian Society and Culture 1922–1945*. New York: Basic Books.

Tartufari, Clarice. 1909. *Il miracolo*. Rome: Romagna.

———. 1911. *Eterne leggi*. Rome: Romagna.

———. 1914. All'uscita del labirinto. Bari: n.p.

———. 1924. *Il gomitolo d'oro*. Milan: Trevisini.

Titta Rosa, G. 1931. "Scrittori e sirene." *La stampa*, 18 August, 18.

Valgimigli, Manara. 1943. *Uomini e scrittori del mio tempo*. Florence: G. C. Sansoni.

Verdone, Mario, ed. 1973. *Prosa e critica futurista*. Milan: Feltrinelli.

Vergine, Lea. 1980. *L'altra metà dell'avanguardia 1910–1940: Pittrici e scultrici nei movimenti delle avanguardie storiche*. Milan: Gabriele Mazzotta Editore.

Viano, Maurizio. 1986. "Ecce Foemina." *Annali d'Italianistica* 4:223–41.

Vitti-Alexander, Maria Rosaria. 1991. "Il passaggio del ponte: L'evoluzione del personaggio femminile di Alba De Céspedes." *Campi immaginabili* 3:103–12.

Vittorini, Elio. 1948. *Il garofano rosso*. Milan: Mondadori.

———. 1973. *Conversation in Sicily*. In *A Vittorini Omnibus*. New York: New Directions.

Voza, Pasquale. 1981. "Il problema del realismo negli anni Trenta: *Il Saggiatore, Il Cantiere.*" *Lavoro critico* 21–22:65–105.

Wade, Geoff. 1992. "Marxism and Modernist Aesthetics: Reading Kafka and Beckett." In *The Politics of Pleasure: Aesthetics and Cultural Theory,* ed. Stephen Regan. Buckingham and Philadelphia: Open University Press.

Whitford, Margaret. 1989. "Rereading Irigaray." In *Between Feminism and Psycho-analysis,* ed. Teresa Brennan. London and New York: Routledge.

Williams, Raymond. 1973. *The Country and the City.* New York: Oxford University Press.

———. 1977. *Marxism and Literature.* Oxford and New York: Oxford University Press.

Wilson, Elizabeth. 1985. *Adorned in Dreams: Fashion and Modernity.* London: Virago Press.

Wilson, Perry. 1993. *The Clockwork Factory: Women and Work in Fascist Italy.* Oxford: Clarenden.

Wood, Sharon. 1995. *Italian Women's Writing 1860–1994.* London and Atlantic Highlands, N. J.: Athlone Press.

Woodmansee, Martha. 1994. *The Author, Art, and the Market: Rereading the History of Aesthetics.* New York: Columbia University Press.

Woodward, Kathleen. 1991. *Aging and Its Discontents: Freud and Other Fictions.* Bloomington and Indianapolis: Indiana University Press.

Woolf, Virginia. 1929. *A Room of One's Own.* New York and London: Harcourt Brace Jovanovich.

Zambon, Patrizia. 1989. "Leggere per scrivere. La formazione autodidattica delle scrittrici tra Otto e Novecento: Neera, Ada Negri, Grazia Deledda, Sibilla Aleramo." *Studi novecenteschi* 16.38:287–324.

Zoppi, Giuseppe, ed. 1939. *Antologia della letteratura italiana ad uso degli stranieri.* Milan: Mondadori.

Zuccotti, Susan. 1987. *The Italians and the Holocaust: Persecution, Rescue, and Survival.* New York: Basic Books.

Index

Robin Pickering-Iazzi is associate professor of Italian at the University of Wisconsin-Milwaukee. She has published articles on nineteenth- and twentieth-century Italian writers and culture, and edited *Unspeakable Women: Selected Short Stories Written by Italian Women during Fascism* and *Mothers of Invention: Women, Italian Fascism, and Culture* (Minnesota, 1995).